The Arbitration Conversation

INSIGHTS AND WISDOM FROM EXPERTS IN THE FIELD

The Arbitration Conversation

INSIGHTS AND WISDOM FROM EXPERTS IN THE FIELD

Amy J. Schmitz

AMERICAN BAR ASSOCIATION
Dispute Resolution Section

Cover design by Sara Wadford/ABA Design

Printed in the United States of America.

28 27 26 25   5 4 3 2

ISBN 978-1-63905-424-4

Discounts are available for books ordered in bulk. Special consideration is given to state bars, CLE programs, and other bar-related organizations. Inquire at Book Publishing, ABA Publishing, American Bar Association, 321 N. Clark Street, Chicago, Illinois 60654–7598.

www.shopABA.org

Immense gratitude and thanks to all those who were interviewed as part of *The Arbitration Conversion*. Thank you also to Lara do Valle Pereira Esteves, Brittany Munn, Favour Oluwafisayo Osa-Oni, and Jennifer Routte for their research assistance. I also thank Colin Rule for his kind forward and collaboration.

For my sisters, who share my love for teaching, learning, and great conversations.

Contents

Foreword

Colin Rule

What does arbitration look like today? It's a simple question, but a surprisingly difficult one to answer.

Arbitration is everywhere these days. It has spread into all levels of disputes, from billion-dollar international cases all the way down to tiny debt collection disputes. There's international arbitration and domestic arbitration, ad hoc and administered arbitration, binding and nonbinding arbitration. In the United States more than 100 million Americans are now subject to mandatory arbitration clauses, either through their employment contracts or through pre-dispute binding consumer agreements. Arbitral institutions release statistics on their own volumes each year, but it is almost impossible to get a wider snapshot of the current state of the field. There's no online map you can consult to see where cases are growing or shrinking, or an updated portal tracking the fairness of arbitration outcomes. And while barrels of (sometimes virtual) ink have been used up fretting about the future of arbitration, how can we know if the field is headed in the right direction if we can't get a clear picture of what it looks like today?

When Amy decided to launch her interview series, *The Arbitration Conversation*, I had no idea where the project would go. Would thought leaders be willing to share their experiences with her? Could we get the top minds in the field to participate? Could she find a narrative through line that would bring everything together, or would it just be a cloud of seemingly unrelated data points?

The challenge with arbitration is that it is private. One major difference with the courts is that arbitral processes are owned by the parties, so there's no obligation to disclose. That privacy can be seen as an advantage by some (but not necessarily all) of the parties to an arbitration, but it can also lead to an air of secrecy. This culture of confidentiality adds to the challenge of getting an accurate picture of what is going on in arbitration. Would that culture hinder people from being honest? Would they be willing to share their experiences in a public conversation? It takes a special kind of interviewer to encourage people to open up about an activity that usually happens behind the veil.

I did know from the start that Amy had the right personality for the project: she is curious, well-researched, disciplined, hospitable, and fundamentally kind. Having known Amy for quite a few years, and having written several articles (and one book) with her, I know she does her homework. I joke that kicking off a project with Amy is kind of like having the best student in biology class assigned to be your lab partner: you know you're going to get an A, but you better be ready to match her pace, because her brain never stops—and she won't slow down if you fall behind.

Certainly, Amy has the cred to lead a global project like this. She has served as an arbitrator, she's represented parties in arbitration, she's taught arbitration, and she's traveled the world to see arbitration in all of its international flavors. Amy has been a thought leader in arbitration since before we first met a dozen years ago: I read her seminal article on "Drive-Thru" arbitration[1] in 2010 and was truly wowed, so I reached out to her to entice her to join the ODR field. She has published at a torrid pace, first focusing on consumer arbitration and later conducting pioneering research on online arbitration (for which she coined the term OArb, now an industry standard).

Now, after more than 115 interviews, the magnitude of Amy's achievement is obvious. Never before has one person collected and synthesized so much up-to-date information about the present and future of arbitration. Amy has engaged with most of the top experts in the field, asking the hard questions and exploring the connections between their work. It is almost impossible to get a clear picture of the global state of arbitration today, but Amy has gotten the closest of anyone. This book is a distillation of her collected insights, wisdom, and best practices. It is a snapshot of the current state of the field, and a guidebook to where the field is going. *The Arbitration Conversation* took a lot of hard work, but those interviews, and this book, are gifts to all of us. Not only will it help us see arbitration's successes and flaws in a clearer light, it will help us open the field to more parties and practitioners, target abuses and abusers, and help arbitration live up to its promise in expanding fast and fair resolutions to all.

Preface

Lemons and Lemonade

As a fan of putting everything into context, this Preface seeks to provide framing and context for the reader. Please note also that this is not a traditional academic book, or even a traditional "how-to" book for the arbitration field. Instead, this book is meant for anyone: arbitrators, students, academics, dispute resolution providers, counsel who deal with arbitration, and anyone else curious about arbitration. It is a unique peek behind the privacy curtain of arbitration, filled with insights gained from interviews of arbitration experts in the field.

A. MY LEMONADE

The story of *The Arbitration Conversation* is an example of making "lemonade out of lemons." It was June 2020, and many professors were scrambling to create course content for classes that would be taught online, with most schools using Zoom. Law professors, in particular, have always been keen on in-person teaching, complete with the Socratic Method. This means that law professors interact with students using questions and answers in a dynamic in-person environment. It is common for professors to walk about the room and interact with students in person. There is an energy from this teaching method that helps engage students and encourages them to "think on their feet." When news of Covid-19 showed an immediate threat to health and safety, schools shut down in an instant and professors had to move their classes online overnight.

Furthermore, travel for presentations and conferences was canceled, along with all social events. Many of us were stuck at home. Arbitrators, lawyers, and professors are all used to frequent travel for the most part and many of us had a "full plate" of travel plans set for spring of 2020. I, personally, had at least eight trips set up for presentations—domestic and international. As a person who enjoys travel, it was quite a jolt to be stuck at home. Moreover, we could not travel to visit family and friends.

At the same time, I have taught arbitration since 2000 and was busy preparing for my arbitration class in 2020/2021. I was personally seeking interesting content and ways to connect students with online teaching. I wanted to make it fun and informative, especially with all the added stresses of the pandemic. I also am a trained arbitrator and have an unending curiosity and interest in learning more about arbitration law and practice. I enjoy learning how arbitrators manage their cases, and considering thorny questions in arbitration law.

I have also been a long-time advocate for using more technology in arbitration as a means for expanding access to remedies, and justice. It has always seemed clear to me that video hearings and text-based processes in smaller cases bring down the cost and complexity of arbitration. This may lower hurdles to obtaining remedies in arbitration, especially in lower-dollar claims where travel and time off of work would make arbitration nonsensical from a rational economic perspective. It is also better for the environment to cut down on unnecessary travel, which is why some dispute resolution professionals have signed a "green pledge" to help cut down on travel in their practice in order to help the environment by cutting down on the emissions from travel. Some research has also shown that text-based processes may help ease biases that come with seeing each other, and harboring assumptions based on appearance, race, and so on.

Nonetheless, the Covid-19 pandemic shutdown moved arbitration processes online in an accelerated fashion for different reasons. The shutdown left disputants and arbitrators with no choice but to move online or wait for an indefinite time to have an in-person hearing. Online arbitration (OArb) went from an outlier to the norm for arbitrating a dispute during the shutdown. I was eager to peek behind the curtain of privacy in arbitration and learn how this transition to technology was going.

With this backdrop, I was talking with my good friend and collaborator Colin Rule, who had recently taken over Mediate.com and Arbitrate.com as the CEO—and we began brainstorming ideas for Arbitrate.com. We were talking about how arbitration was changing in light of the pandemic and how we wanted to further arbitration excellence on many levels. Courts were initially closed starting in March 2020 when the Covid-19 pandemic first hit, but disputes continued to develop and parties sought places for them to be resolved. Meanwhile, arbitration proved to be nimbler than courts per early anecdotal information. We were hearing that arbitration moved more quickly than courts to online fora. This was relatively easy, as most arbitration institutions already had online filing and document storage portals, and the institutions quickly set out ways for arbitrators to move arbitral hearings online using tools like Zoom and Teams. Wouldn't it be interesting to document this move to OArb and investigate firsthand what was working, not working, issues to explore?

Moreover, students want and need to learn about law "in action." Law in the books is often not the same as law in action. Many law classes are doctrinal, asking students to read court cases, legislation, and legal restatements of the law—focusing on doctrinal applications of the law. In reality, however, much of legal practice never reaches any courts and most issues are resolved outside of the courts. This is especially true in arbitration. While I was in practice as an attorney before moving to academia, I learned that most parties simply comply with arbitration awards, and never go to a court in relation to the proceeding. The reality of arbitration is mostly missing from reported cases in a casebook. Nonetheless, students rarely learn about what happens behind the scenes in arbitration. Most arbitration classes focus on case law and legislation around arbitration. Wouldn't it be interesting to shed light on arbitration practice? Arbitration is notoriously private, so the public does not get a chance to observe arbitration or talk to arbitrators about their work.

Meanwhile, I was stuck at home. I, like many, could not do my usual visits to see my parents or enjoy cultural events in person. Furthermore, conferences and get-togethers among professionals and professors were shut down during the pandemic. This was particularly hard for dispute resolution people. As a group, we genuinely like getting together and discussing ideas, and ways to advance the field. I have also been the co-chair of both the Technology in ADR Committee of the American Bar Association Section on Dispute Resolution and the Online Dispute Resolution (ODR) Task Force of the Dispute Resolution Section. All meetings in person were on halt. In short: I missed my friends in dispute resolution! I missed getting an opportunity to meet and talk about ideas. Wouldn't it be interesting to get a chance to see each other and talk about ideas on Zoom?

With everything shut down, it seemed that all we were thinking about were the lemons: canceled events, missing friends and family, financial difficulties, worrying about catching Covid-19 and ending up in the hospital . . . or worse. However, whenever life gives us lemons, we really do have to seek ways to make lemonade.

That brings us back to my conversation with Colin. We joked about starting a webcast about arbitration in order to expand information about the practice of arbitration and expand new voices in arbitration. What would we call it? Arbitration Nation? . . . no, taken. Arbitration Vacation? . . . no, too silly. Arbitration Legislation? . . . no, too narrow. Arbitration Meditation? . . . no, absurd. So, we settled on Arbitration Conversation! I would simply reach out to people I know as leaders in arbitration, and we would tape short interviews. Should not take too much time or be that much work. . . .

Famous last words . . . "not much work." Of course, it ended up being a huge commitment! Each interview took much more time than what is on camera. I would spend time preparing, reading interviewee articles and papers, learning about interviewees, and setting up the interviews. We sometimes had pre-interview meetings as well. Note that I do not have an administrative assistant helping on this. Thank you for Colin Rule, as Colin would add "intro music" to the videos and post them. It was a great deal of work, but it turned out to be a labor of love. I figured that while many of my friends were baking bread during the pandemic, I was interviewing leaders in arbitration. I am so thankful to all those who agreed to be interviewed! The conversations were truly fresh and genuine. I learned a great deal and made new friends—making lemonade.

B. PRACTITIONER LEMONADE

Arbitrators and arbitration institutions were also busy making lemonade out of lemons during the pandemic. In the very first episode of *The Arbitration Conversation*, I interviewed Svetlana Gitman, vice president of the Commercial Division at American Arbitration Association (AAA). We talked about how the AAA transformed their operations in response to the Covid-19 pandemic and the different services and educational options AAA provided for arbitrators looking to transition their practices online.[2] The AAA expanded the education and offerings for Zoom arbitration. OArb became the norm, and the AAA offered to help parties and arbitrators with technical assistance for an additional fee. Arbitrators I spoke with also noted that some court stenographers transitioned into positions as technical assistants to help with Zoom hearings.

Arbitral institutions reported that business increased, as institutions used the moment to remind parties about the advantages of arbitration as a faster, more cost-efficient, and more flexible and personalized process than litigation.[3] Beginning in the spring of 2020, many courts closed their doors to in-person hearings and halted all cases in some circumstances. Many courts focused on devoting any space and socially distanced procedures to criminal cases, pushing civil cases into a line. Courts also were slow to transition hearings to an online medium, like Zoom or Teams, opening the door to increased use of ODR and OArb.[4]

Anecdotally, many courts were limited to telephonic hearings for quite some time. Interviewees in *The Arbitration Conversation* reported how some courts were using the telephone. In contrast, arbitral institutions like the AAA and JAMS were nimbler, and already equipped for online filing and online hearings. The court backlog therefore pushed some parties to arbitration. "Submission agreements"—whereby parties submit existing disputes to arbitration—increased. Of course, all arbitrators were not well equipped at first for OArb, and there are stories of poorly executed online arbitration hearings. Still, some interviewees reported a growth in submission hearings, indicating at least some movement away from the norm of pre-dispute arbitration agreements during the Covid-19 shutdown. This meant more business for arbitrators and arbitral institutions.

As noted throughout the book, various arbitrators shared stories of effectively handling cases during the pandemic shutdown. Even arbitrators who had been apprehensive about online hearings shared stories of ably moving online. Read on for more throughout the book, indicating how arbitrators have made lemonade out of lemons. The bulk of the book focuses on practitioner wisdom and insights—resulting in more practitioner lemonade as we learned from one another throughout conversations.

C. EDUCATOR LEMONADE

Professors also looked for silver linings during the pandemic. Professor Steven Shapiro from the American University, Washington College of Law, spoke on this.[5] Professor Shapiro is the founder and director of the Hospitality & Tourism Law Program, and he is a senior affiliate in the Program on Law & Government, including his work in teaching construction law. We discussed some of the benefits of teaching online. Yes, most professors were lamenting the move to online teaching. There is no question that the energy of teaching and learning in person is a unique and special experience. Nonetheless, there were silver linings to teaching online.

Professor Shapiro discussed teaching in the pandemic and moving classes online quickly. He noted drawbacks, including the lack of nuance and energy when teaching online. The energy of teaching in person is dear to most professors and students in law school programs. However, online teaching adds new dimensions to classes, and forces professors to be creative in our instruction. It also challenged us to "go the extra mile" to inspire student interest and create assessments to understand whether students were learning. It was not enough to provide a lecture, ask a few questions, and hope that students would engage and learn.

For example, adding varied materials helped students learn and created breaks in the monotony. Timing is helpful as well. Videos can be posted in advance, and readings are animated when coupled with explanatory videos or videos that add a practical dimension. Better use of online learning management systems allows for posting PowerPoints to create scaffolding upon which students can take notes and build outlines. These PowerPoints also create a framework for analysis when posted in advance of class. Indeed, the Covid-enforced move to online teaching pushed professors to explore and use their schools' course management systems in new ways.

Creating "clickable" materials and building them into an online learning management system in an intentional manner is not easy. The trick is to be careful not to "spoon feed" course content when posting materials in a digital course management system. The goal is to provide enough information in slides posted in advance of class that (1) students are curious to learn more; (2) students have a roadmap for the class and what they should be aiming to learn; (3) students have a sense of questions they should be exploring while considering assigned materials; and (4) students then have to come to class to "fill in the blanks" and take the materials to the next level.

It is especially tough when classes are all recorded, and students know that they can listen/watch the class later. How do we get students to attend classes live—on Zoom or in person—now that we are back in person? While the Covid-19 pandemic was in full force, we had to be flexible for good reason—as many were ill, and it was unpredictable whether everyone could attend on Zoom. We all had bandwidth and technology breakdowns as well! Let's face it: it was challenging, and we still needed to give each other grace and understanding. Even after classes were back in person, we needed to be flexible, as some students had to continue online attendance for various reasons, and "hybrid teaching" became the new normal.

In some ways, it was easier to make "lemonade" in teaching purely on Zoom, even with classes recorded and materials posted in advance. Breakout rooms and the creation of group exercises helped inspire attendance and participation. In our *Arbitration Conversation*, Professor Shapiro also discussed the use of breakout rooms for teaching arbitration, and how that can facilitate better discussion in some cases.[6] In some ways, students get more of an opportunity to participate on Zoom, as it might be less intimidating than talking in class physically. Also, breakout rooms allow students to discuss posed topics in smaller groups. Professors can easily "pop" into the various breakout rooms to be sure that the conversations are going well, and having students "report out" their conclusions and analysis to the group adds a way to keep the class on course. Breakout rooms can also help students remain engaged when attending a class that is otherwise in person: creating exercises that allow the students in the room to break into physical groups while the online students get a chance to discuss within their own Zoom rooms.

Still, we did learn new tactics for teaching during the Covid-19 lockdown that have endured even after classes resumed in person. For example, we learned that guest speakers do not have to be expensive. For example, arbitration classes greatly benefit from guest speakers with real-world experience, and international guests can be especially exciting for the students. Having guests Zoom into a class from anywhere in the world at no cost adds a great deal to a class. Indeed, *The Arbitration Conversation* became a teaching tool during the pandemic due to its easy access online and easy integration into an online class.

The international angle was particularly interesting for many educators. Ronald Brand, the Chancellor Mark A. Nordenberg University Professor and John E. Murray Faculty Scholar at the University of Pittsburgh School of Law, was also interviewed.[7] Professor Brand was the driving force behind the creation of the University of Pittsburgh's Center for International Legal Education (CILE) and its Master of Laws Program for Foreign Law Graduates. He represented the United States (U.S.) at the Special Commissions and the Diplomatic Sessions of the Hague Conference on Private International Law that produced both the 2005 Convention on Choice of Court Agreements and the 2019 Convention on the Recognition and Enforcement of Judgments in Civil or Commercial Matters. For more than a decade, he has worked with the U.S. Department of Commerce to develop Middle East law school curricula in international commercial law and arbitration, training students and faculty from schools throughout the Middle East and North Africa. In short, he was a perfect person to talk with about international education in the area of arbitration.

In this episode, Professor Brand highlighted the importance of the *Vis Moot International Arbitration* competition. Such arbitration competitions have been a catalyst for legal education throughout the world and making international connections.[8] Even in regions where arbitration was not in the curriculum, Professor Brand has been able to use arbitration competition as a means for creating connections for students throughout the world and introducing students to the field of arbitration.[9] He also explained how he has students share their knowledge and teach each other through these teaching tools.

It should be noted that the *Vis Moot International Arbitration* competition made lemonade out of lemons as an educational vehicle. The competition moved from in person to online, which was quite a production. The purpose of the *Vis Moot* is to foster the study of international commercial law and arbitration and provide practical training to students for international arbitration. This had always been an in-person competition with teams from around the world traveling to Europe for the competition. It has become a prestigious event for law students worldwide. There are two crucial phases in the *Vis Moot* to train advocacy skills: the writing of memoranda for claimant and respondent and the presentation of arguments in oral hearings held before arbitration practitioners and academics.

While the research and writing are important components, most see the oral advocacy piece as particularly important. With the Covid-19 shutdown and continuing health concerns even after vaccines were developed, the *Vis Moot* competition was held online for several years. This did not provide the same networking benefits of in-person competitions, but it opened the door for students to participate even if they lacked the funds for travel. Many schools do not have the funds to send students to the competition, and students generally do not have the independent funds for such travel—especially when it is international. The years of online competition opened the door for some students to participate, although they would not have participated had the competition been in person. While the competition was back in person in 2023, it is hoped that more online opportunities for arbitration competitions open for students.

Another interview that highlighted teaching tools was the interview with Professor Lela Love. Professor Love is a professor of law and the founding director of the Kukin Program for Conflict Resolution at Benjamin N. Cardozo School of Law in New York (NYC). Professor Love also founded Cardozo's Mediation Clinic in 1985—one of the first clinical programs to train law students to serve as mediators. She has served as mediator, arbitrator, and dispute resolution consultant in a wide array of cases. She is the past chair of the American Bar Association Section of Dispute Resolution. Professor Love has won numerous awards and is a very well-known scholar in dispute resolution. It was an absolute honor to have her as a guest in one of my final video interviews.

In *The Arbitration Conversation*, Professor Love discussed teaching dispute resolution, and helping students understand the stark differences between arbitration and mediation. Indeed, some years ago, I did a quantitative and qualitative study that included focus groups, along with interviews, to gather consumers' understandings and assumptions around remedies and dispute resolution. When asked in the focus groups about their understanding of arbitration, consumers generally think it is nonbinding. They often equate it with mediation and may not even see the difference between mediation and arbitration. This is problematic because arbitration has significant implication for consumers' rights and cuts off their ability to bring issues to court. It is therefore important to teach law students the differences between these processes, so that they can better help their clients in the future.

With deep experience as a mediator and teacher, Professor Love had great examples to share. Professor Love shared how she likes to have students do an exercise where they must shift "hats"—first mediate, and next arbitrate (or vice versa) a case based on the same facts. These types of comparative exercises can be very effective. This helps students experience distinctions: mediators help the parties settle their own dispute, whereas arbitrators decide the dispute and render a binding award. Adding another twist, students have to mediate a case first in person and then online—again, helping them see and experience the distinctions.

These conversations reminded me of silver linings for educators. There is no question that it was tough, and perhaps not as "fun" as our usual in-person teaching experience. However, we were challenged to be more creative, and these interviews helped me do that for my arbitration class. Students could learn about all different types of arbitration and hear from the top minds in the field through *The Arbitration Conversation*. They also could laugh at their professor making silly mistakes and "bloopers" in the interviews, seeing that we all make mistakes.

It was great to learn from other educators and hear about new ideas for teaching arbitration and dispute resolution, more generally, including ideas for better-using breakout rooms on Zoom. Using the whiteboard in Zoom can be helpful, and learning management systems allow for broader assignments and "video comments" from students. I also learned about new fact patterns for my "mediation vs. arbitration" assignments. Off camera, many professors also shared ideas for helping students' mental health and for engaging students during the shutdown. For example, using "Zoom coffees" for students to simply "chat and chill" with the professor and each other was a great idea learned through conversations for engaging and helping students during the shutdown. Indeed, the pandemic invited us all to make lemonade out of lemons.

The Arbitration Conversation became "lemonade" in my life, as I had opportunities to talk about arbitration with so many interesting and smart individuals. The conversations also shined a light on the various ways that we all made lemonade out of lemons during the Covid-19 shutdown. The conversations with arbitral institution leaders illuminated how these institutions found ways to help individuals resolve their disputes even when courts were closed, or slow to adapt. Professors shared stories about teaching online and ideas for using digital tools, again highlighting how we found ways to improve our teaching through creativity. Even now, I rewatch interviews and learn new insights that I had not captured during the interview, or first few views. Above all, the interviews provided, and continue to provide, insights, learning, and friendship. Indeed, I am incredibly thankful to all who participated and have provided silver linings.

NOTES

1 Amy J. Schmitz, *"Drive-Thru" Arbitration in the Digital Age: Empowering Consumers through Binding ODR*, 62 Baylor L. Rev. 178 (2010), https://scholarship.law.missouri.edu/facpubs/602/.

2 Svetlana Gitman & Amy Schmitz, *Arbitration Conversation No. 1:* Svetlana Gitman, American Arbitration Association (July 14, 2020), https://arbitrate.com/arbitration-conversation-episode-1-svetlana-gitman-american-arbitration-association/.

3 Svetlana Gitman, *Court Backlogs Make Arbitration an Attractive Option for Resolving Cases*, Corp. Couns. Bus. J. (Oct. 26, 2021), https://ccbjournal.com/articles/court-backlogs-make-arbitration-an-attractive-option-for-resolving-cases.

4 Purdue Global Law School, *Online Dispute Resolution Moves Cases Forward Despite Court Backlog* (Aug. 16, 2021), https://www.purduegloballawschool.edu/blog/news/online-dispute-resolution-moves-cases-forward.

5 Steven Shapiro & Amy Schmitz, *Arbitration Conversation No. 76: Prof. Steven Shapiro, American University Washington College of Law*, YouTube (Mar. 31, 2021), www.youtube.com/watch?v=VX-SBzv_MB8.

6 *Id.*

7 Ronald Brand & Amy Schmitz, *Arbitration Conversation No. 82: Prof. Ronald Brand, University of Pittsburgh School of Law*, YouTube (May 12, 2021), www.youtube.com/watch?v=tfUqdRjRFTI.

8 *Id.*

9 *Id.*

Introduction

Arbitration has long been a staple of dispute resolution, especially for businesses that prefer the privacy, speed, and expert decision-making available in arbitration. Furthermore, companies increasingly include arbitration clauses among the form terms in their boilerplate contracts.[1] This has been the case for a long time in commercial business-to-business contracts. Arbitration makes sense in commercial agreements, especially when there is need for a specialist arbitrator or protection of business secrets. For example, this need for an expert decision-maker has been a harbinger for construction arbitration for decades, and parties to intellectual property disputes benefit from an expert decision-maker as well as arbitration's privacy. Arbitration is also robust for international parties who seek a neutral forum not wed to any jurisdiction, as well as an enforceable award under the New York Convention on the Recognition and Enforcement of Foreign Arbitral Awards (New York Convention).[2]

At the same time, arbitration has become standard in business-to-consumer (B2C) and employment contracts in the U.S.[3] The surge in consumer and employment arbitration has sparked substantial controversy and debate. Skepticism among consumers and employees, who perceive nonnegotiable boilerplate arbitration clauses as inherently biased toward companies, has ignited concerns, often without empirical support.[4] Critics, including commentators and policymakers, have voiced apprehensions that pre-dispute arbitration clauses infringe upon the access to judicial remedies for consumers and employees, and deprive them of informed consent.[5] These critics argue that such clauses disproportionately favor corporate "repeat players" who regularly engage in arbitration and enjoy superior information and power in the process.[6] Moreover, they contend that companies employ these clauses to stifle consumer redress and shield themselves from public scrutiny.[7] This is especially concerning with respect to consumer warranty claims, where a product may be unsafe and public redress is necessary to protect health and safety.[8] Pre-dispute arbitration clauses may cut off access to remedies in small-dollar claims and squelch the efficiencies of aggregated proceedings, litigated in open court, which help spark necessary policy changes.[9] This critique goes as far as to assert that such practices empower companies to essentially craft their own private legal systems.[10]

Nonetheless, there are likewise stories of employees and consumers enjoying arbitration as a better means than court for accessing remedies in certain cases, especially with the advent of virtual hearings that individuals can access from their phones. Nonetheless, regardless of the commentary, arbitration has undergone a transformative evolution in the realm of dispute resolution, significantly reshaping the landscape, particularly in the context of businesses seeking privacy, expediency, and specialized adjudication. Over the years, arbitration has gradually evolved from a discreet alternative to litigation into a mainstream and widely adopted practice. This shift is particularly pronounced as arbitration clauses have become ubiquitous in standard contracts of all kinds.

U.S. courts usually enforce these clauses under the Federal Arbitration Act (FAA)[11] and efficiency-focused arbitration and contract jurisprudence.[12] Proponents of this regime highlight how arbitration clauses can be "fair" and foster satisfying proceedings for companies and individuals. In addition, some arbitration-administering institutions have taken steps toward protecting procedural fairness for consumers and employees who often lack the resources of their corporate opponents. As will be discussed in later parts of the book, most arbitral providers follow due process protocols when administering consumer and employment arbitrations, which include shifting the costs to the company or employer.[13]

Putting aside arguments for or against pre-dispute arbitration clauses, the fact remains that individuals and companies will continue to arbitrate. Arbitration makes sense for a great many types of claims and arbitration continues to be an important tool in the problem-solving toolbox of any attorney, counselor or dispute resolution professional. There is good reason to promote and protect arbitration, especially in contexts that require privacy, expert decision-makers, speed, flexibility, and adaptability. Furthermore, arbitration clauses are enforceable under the FAA and the New York Convention.[14] This is true even if they are included in e-contracts enforceable under the Electronic Signature Act (ESign).[15]

This book will consider lessons learned in talking with arbitrators and arbitration experts in different contexts, including not only consumer, employment, and commercial—but also many additional areas that some readers may not know about. There are many different flavors of arbitration, and the process should be adapted to fit the given context and parties. Indeed, context matters, and this will be a running theme in the book. Consideration of arbitration as a problem-solving tool is another theme this book will discuss through the lens of *The Arbitration Conversation* interviews.

At the same time, "arbitration" as it existed in 1925, when the FAA became law, has changed. Growing use and reliance on the internet have led to the growth of *online* arbitration (what I have termed "OArb" in prior publications).[16] Such OArb includes the use of technology and digital tools to facilitate and execute processes ending in a final determination of a dispute by a neutral third party. For example, such OArb may use asynchronous and/or synchronous communications. It also may involve text-only and/or virtual hearings and mixtures thereof. OArb's use of technology allows parties to upload and submit all supporting documentation to support their claims at times that suit their schedules. Online hearings also save the time, cost, and stress of traveling to and attending in-person processes, which is especially important in a pandemic. Such an OArb system may even provide more accurate and complete redress for consumers, for example, perhaps to an extent greater than that achieved through class actions, which have been criticized for providing insufficient and inequitably distributed relief in some cases.[17]

OArb is just one example of ODR, which more generally encompasses the use of technology to assist in preventing and resolving disputes. Most ODR, however, is not OArb because it involves facilitating communications aimed to spark voluntary settlement.[18] Most ODR is thusly not binding and relies on the parties' later agreement on a resolution. OArb is a distinct subset of ODR because it culminates in a final award rendered by a third-party neutral, usually enforceable in the U.S. under the FAA. This binding nature has caused many to shy away from OArb, even as they have embraced other types of ODR. This is because attorneys and parties often fear a binding award without a chance to present their cases in person, especially where large dollar amounts are at stake or they otherwise fear the consequences of a binding award.

Nonetheless, interest in OArb spiked during the Covid-19 pandemic shutdown.[19] Virtual meeting technology such as Skype, Google Meet, WebEx, and Zoom have made virtual hearings relatively cheap and easy, and individuals have become accustomed to online communications in the lockdown.[20] In larger dollar claims and areas traditionally wed to arbitration, such as labor and construction, in-person arbitration has long been the norm, and there was not great movement toward OArb until Covid-19 forced a wider adoption of virtual hearings.[21] Even at the beginning of the pandemic, most parties were stating an intention to wait to arbitrate until they could do so in person—often due to inexperience with using virtual platforms or long-held beliefs that in-person hearings are always the best method for resolution. Furthermore, parties who benefit from delay presumably benefited from the "Covid excuse" for putting off litigation or arbitration. As the pandemic continued, however, parties grew eager to resolve their disputes, and arbitrators warmed up to virtual arbitration.[22]

Still, OArb is a relatively new phenomenon.[23] The lessons learned in this book are especially acute and important with respect to OArb and technology, because the pandemic shutdown greatly accelerated arbitration's move online. Many of the interviews included discussion of OArb, tips, tricks, dos, and don'ts, which I share in this book. I also have collected OArb protocols that have emerged, and have included an appendix in the book (Appendix A) that includes cites to the protocols, which should be very helpful for arbitrators and counsel in arbitration.

This has been an interesting time for arbitration, as arbitrators have learned how to arbitrate online and have faced new issues around cybersecurity and what to do when parties have differing access to technology. This book will explore this move to OArb from a practical and problem-solving lens. Additionally, the book sheds light on related considerations with the surge of AI and other technological disruption of the law, including arbitration.

Arbitration, like most things in life, changed when the Covid-19 pandemic hit in 2020, and in-person life came to a standstill. Because so many of the interviews took place during the shutdown, this book cannot help but note this dramatic shift. At that time, we all became connected only through our phones and computers. This included schools at every level. Classes went from the usual face-to-face (F2F) frenzy of educational energy to online meetings and online delivery of course materials. Many professors, me included, started thinking about how to engage students in an online class. How do we keep students interested and learning in a pandemic when all classes are on Zoom or Teams? How do we create learning energy in a virtual world, as we are used to working with students in person and engaging with students as we walk a room? This is especially problematic in law school, where we use the Socratic Method, and interactive discourse is essential to learning. How do we do this online? This book also includes lessons learned for teachers and instructors of dispute resolution.

Furthermore, what happens when legal procedures that had always been in person are suddenly online? In the law, litigation and arbitration have focused on somewhat stringent in-person procedures. In fact, arbitration predates litigation in history and was traditionally an important in-person event. There are stories of ancient Egyptian arbitration, vividly noting the drama of the arbitral events used for resolving disputes and rendering decisions on important matters. Arbitrators were often the community elders, trusted for their sage wisdom and long-standing understanding of communal norms. Parties to a dispute would formally present their arguments to the sage arbitrators, following a certain "pomp and circumstance" that was vital to the decision-making process and perceived outcome legitimacy. The process was historically built to be in-person. This book will distill lessons learned for arbitrators now administering hearings online.

It has been a complete joy interviewing arbitrators and arbitration experts for *The Arbitration Conversation*. This is not just because it created "lemonade," as discussed in the Preface. It also has illuminated important lessons learned. This book aims to explore these lessons through the lens of the many interviews. These interviews have created a "time capsule" for perpetuity as well as an important "peek behind the curtain" of arbitration. The interviews during the Covid-19 shutdown provide important insights regarding the quick shift to OArb, including instruction on how technology can bring us closer to one another without travel. We also learned how in-person contact matters for psychological, social, and settlement reasons. The interviews have continued after the shutdown and evolved to shed light on yet more lessons learned for arbitrators, arbitration counsel, students, professors, and anyone else who deals in or with arbitration.[24] I hit 100 episodes on YouTube and have since moved to a podcast without video that is continually growing.[25]

Notably, the videos may be 15–30 minutes, but I generally talked with each person for much longer, sometimes more than an hour. I researched each person before their interview, and read their papers if they had papers they would like me to read. I also met with some of the interviewees before the interviews in order to plan our discussion topics. I am so thankful to each guest, as I learned an absolute ton just talking with all these amazing people! These conversations and interviews with leading arbitrators and arbitration authorities have been a gift. Note that we never received any sort of advertising fees, and the videos and podcasts remain free and open to the public.

This book will hopefully be both informative and entertaining. It will include "lessons learned" and important insights from the public interviews, as well as some of my own commentary and research. I have examined the videos to identify themes that emerged from the discussions over the course of four years. This book is therefore meant for any arbitrator, person seeking to get into arbitration, students learning about arbitration, or counsel representing parties in arbitration. Please note that the lessons and stories I share in the book are only based on the already public interviews as published and open to the public—and share no information from private conversations. This is important from an ethical perspective, as I would never share anything through this book that is not already public. Note also that not all interviews made it into the book due to space limitations and timing of interviews, as I was writing this before some interviews were released.

I also add that originally, I thought about collecting essays from the interviewees and telling stories, much like the mediation *Stories Mediators Tell* book.[26] However, you cannot replicate that wonderful book! I wanted to provide something different. It was enjoyable digesting all I learned, and am learning, to determine lessons learned. I listened to each interview many, many times. My family and friends laughed as I listened and took notes. I looked for takeaways and hoped that would be useful for practitioners, students, and educators. Additional research is woven into the fabric of the chapters where needed, although this book is not meant to replace or replicate more academic books about arbitration.[27] This is a more conversational book. It hopes to share a unique "peek behind the curtain" of arbitration in this way, recounting arbitration conversations.

NOTES

1 "Boilerplate" has taken on its own cultural meaning in today's society. *See* Todd D. Rakoff, *The Law and Sociology of Boilerplate*, *in* BOILERPLATE: THE FOUNDATIONS OF MARKET CONTRACTS 204 (Omri Ben-Shahar ed., 2007).

2 New York Convention on the Recognition and Enforcement of Foreign Arbitral Awards (New York Convention), 9 U.S.C. §§ 201–208; *id.* §§ 301–307 (implementing the Inter-American Convention on International Commercial Arbitration (Panama Convention)).

3 Of the 100 largest U.S. companies (as listed in *Fortune*), many have had arbitration agreements since 2010, including class arbitration waivers. Imre Stephen Szalai, *The Prevalence of Consumer Arbitration Agreements by America's Top Companies*, 52 U.C. DAVIS L. REV. ONLINE 233, 234 (Feb. 2019), https://lawreview.law.ucdavis.edu/online/vol52/52-online-Szalai.pdf. The data shows that 81 of the 100 companies have used arbitration agreements, and 78 of those 81 companies use class waivers. A majority of U.S. households (it could be two-thirds of U.S. households) are covered by consumer arbitration agreements. In 2018, there were at least 826,537,000 consumer arbitration agreements in force, and the actual number is probably higher, considering this only takes a look at some companies. *Id.*

4 *The Enforcement Opportunity: From Mass Arbitration to Mass Organizing, Chapter Three*, 136(6) HARV. L. REV. 1652 (Apr. 9, 2023); *Consumer Protection for Gig Work?, Chapter Two*, 136(6) HARV. L. REV. 1628, 1636–38 (Apr. 9, 2023).

5 Cameron Molis, *Curbing Conception: How to States Can Ease the Strain of Predispute Arbitration to Counter Corporate Abusers*, 24 U. PA. J. L. & SOC. CHANGE 3, 413–15 (2021).

6 *See* Jean Sternlight, *Consumer Arbitration*, *in* ARBITRATION LAW IN AMERICA: A CRITICAL ASSESSMENT 127, 129–40 (2006) (highlighting American law's enforcement of mandatory consumer arbitration under pre-dispute form contracts); Richard Frankel, *Corporate Hostility to Arbitration*, 50 SETON HALL L. REV. 707, 710–11, 731–35, or 742–45 (2020).

7 *See* Amy J. Schmitz, *Untangling the Privacy Paradox in Arbitration*, 54 U. KAN. L. REV. 101, 120–25 (2007) (discussing privacy in arbitration).

8 I have been among those that have critiqued harsh consumer arbitration provisions, and have proposed that the existing dispute resolution template of the Magnuson Moss Warranty Federal Trade Commission Improvement Act (MMWA) should incorporate consumer arbitration reforms to protect consumers' access to warranty remedies and clarify how MMWA claims may be arbitrated fairly. Amy J. Schmitz, *Curing Consumers' Warranty Woes through Regulated Arbitration*, 23 OHIO ST. J. ON DISP. RESOL. 627, 627–32, 661–86 (2008) [hereinafter *Warranty Woes*] (discussing need for procedural protections in consumer arbitration proceedings); Amy J. Schmitz, *Dangers of Deference to Form Arbitration Provisions*, 8 NEV. L.J. 37, 37–55 (2007) [hereinafter *Deference*] (advancing procedural regulation of arbitration in lieu of precluding arbitration).

9 Schmitz, *Warranty Woes*, *supra* note 8, at 640–86.

10 *See* Stephen J. Ware, *Default Rules from Mandatory Rules: Privatizing Law through Arbitration*, 83 MINN. L. REV. 704, 704–12, 754 (1999) (discussing how "arbitration privatizes the creation of law"). *See also* Amy J. Schmitz, *Mobile-Home Mania? Protecting Procedurally Fair Arbitration in a Consumer Microcosm*, 20 OHIO ST. J. ON DISP. RESOL. 291, 313–15, 371 (2005) (discussing how manufacturers' use of form arbitration agreements has privatized dispute resolution in the mobile home industry).

11 Federal Arbitration Act (FAA), 9 U.S.C. §§ 1–16 (covering domestic arbitration), §§ 201–208 (implementing the Convention on the Recognition and Enforcement of Foreign Arbitral Awards (New York Convention)), §§ 301–307 (implementing the Inter-American Convention on International Commercial Arbitration (Panama Convention)). *See also* Green Tree Fin. Corp. v. Randolph, 531 U.S. 79, 91 (2001) (emphasizing the "liberal federal policy favoring arbitration agreements").

12 Jeffrey W. Stempel, *Arbitration, Unconscionability, and Equilibrium: The Return of Unconscionability Analysis as a Counterweight to Arbitration Formalism*, 19 Ohio St. J. on Disp. Resol. 757, 812–13 (2004) (highlighting restrained application of unconscionability in the wake of rising formalism).

13 Theodore J. St. Antoine, *Making Employment Arbitration Fair and Accessible*, 12 Arb. L. Rev. 4–7, 13 (May 1, 2020), https://elibrary.law.psu.edu/cgi/viewcontent.cgi?article=1285&context=arbitrationlawreview. *See also* Robert W. Emerson & Zachary R. Hunt, *Franchises, Consumers, and Employees: Choice and Arbitration*, 13 Wm. & Mary Bus. L. Rev., 487, 502–06 (2022).

14 Federal Arbitration Act (FAA), 9 U.S.C. §§ 1–16 (covering domestic arbitration); *id.* §§ 201–208 (implementing the Convention on the Recognition and Enforcement of Foreign Arbitral Awards (New York Convention)); *id.* §§ 301–307 (implementing the Inter-American Convention on International Commercial Arbitration (Panama Convention)) (2006).

15 Electronic Signatures in Global and National Commerce Act, 15 U.S.C. § 7001 (2006) (making electronic contracts enforceable to the same extent as written contracts; effective October 1, 2000).

16 Amy J. Schmitz, *"Drive-Thru" Arbitration in the Digital Age: Empowering Consumers through Regulated ODR*, 62 Baylor L. Rev. 178, 178–244 (2010) (proposing "OArb" as a distinct type of online dispute resolution).

17 *See generally* Linda S. Mullenix, *Ending Class Actions as We Know Them: Rethinking the American Class Action*, 64 Emory L.J. 399, 399–418 (2014).

18 *See generally* Amy J. Schmitz & Colin Rule, The New Handshake: Online Dispute Resolution and the Future of Consumer Protection (2017); Amy J. Schmitz, *Building on OArb Attributes in Pursuit of Justice*, *in* Arbitration in the Digital Age: The Brave New World of Arbitration 182 (Maud Piers & Christian Aschauer eds., 2018).

19 Melody Alger, *Conducting Arbitrations and Mediations Remotely during the Covid-19 Crisis and Beyond*, 68 R.I.B.J. 15 (May 2020).

20 *Id.*

21 *Id.*

22 Karen Maxwell, *Could Arbitration Support Courts during the COVID-19 Crisis?*, Thomson Reuters: Practical Law Arbitration Blog (May 27, 2020), http://arbitrationblog.practicallaw.com/could-arbitration-support-courts-during-the-covid-19-crisis/.

23 Schmitz, *supra* note 16, at 178–244 (proposing "OArb" as a distinct type of online dispute resolution); Amy J. Schmitz, *Arbitration in the Age of Covid: Examining Arbitration's Move Online*, 22 Cardozo J. Conflict Resol. 245–92 (2021).

24 *See* https://arbitrate.com/the-arbitration-conversation/.

25 The Arbitration Conversation, https://arbitrate.podbean.com/ (last visited Sept. 7, 2023).

26 Eric Galton & Lela P. Love, Stories Mediators Tell (2013).

27 See, for example, Tom Stipanowich & Amy J. Schmitz, Arbitration: Practice, Policy and Law (1st ed. 2022).

Chapter 1
Arbitral Adaptability

The pandemic shed a spotlight on the need to be agile and adaptable as an arbitrator and as parties and counsel in arbitration. At its core, arbitration is a choice-based/contract-based process. Arbitrators that were interviewed talked at length about the adaptability and flexibility of arbitration, with some interviewees noting that parties turned to arbitration over litigation because they could bypass backlogs in courts during the pandemic shutdowns. This chapter may be of particular interest for arbitrators and counsel in arbitration seeking ideas around adaptability in leading their arbitration processes. Courts are not nearly as adaptable as arbitration to change due to the rules of civil procedure and other applicable court rules. Nonetheless, some attorneys and arbitrators fall into routines and blindly adopt court-like procedures instead of intentionally considering how to adapt a process to their cases and parties. This chapter seeks to remind readers of this allowance for adaptability.

Svetlana Gitman—vice president of the American Arbitration Association (AAA) in the AAA's Chicago office[1]—shed light on adaptability. In the first interview of *The Arbitration Conversation*, Gitman discussed how the biggest challenge for institutions at the beginning of the Covid-19 pandemic shutdown was figuring out what to do about in-person hearings when you cannot be in person. This was especially true with large cases already scheduled to be in person, with parties and attorneys who may not have been comfortable or accustomed to virtual hearings. Of course, there were also logistical challenges of moving work online in general.

However, Gitman shared that moving to OArb was relatively easy for the AAA because they already had electronic filing and case management in place, and had started using more virtual hearings before the shutdown. Clients had been asking for more virtual capacities for years, as it saves everyone time and money. Additionally, many law offices, along with the offices of the AAA in Chicago, already used platforms like Zoom. They also had people with experience working remotely, and embraced the adaptability of arbitration to fit the process to the "new normal."

Indeed, the pandemic "jolt" to the system shined a light on adaptability as a strength of arbitration. Courts are often hamstrung by rules, statutorily required procedures, limited resources, and institutional resistance to change. It was hard for many courts to pivot online. At first, most courts simply closed, and others used the telephone for hearings, rather than pivoting to Zoom or another video platform. Even after video hearings began to gain traction, they were often mishandled. We all heard the stories of mishaps like the lawyer showing up for court as a cat on a video platform. Of course, there were arbitration mishaps with technology as well, but the anecdotes were most acute with respect to courts.

Gitman also discussed how the AAA used the moment of the pandemic to enhance its e-filing and technological capacities. The AAA now includes an application, or "app," for AAA rules and clauses to make things easier for all involved. It also held trainings and arbitrators were encouraged to learn best practices for using video platforms and following cybersecurity protocols. On this topic, Chris Poole, chief executive officer of the Judicial Arbitration and Mediation Services (JAMS), another large provider of alternative dispute resolution (ADR) services worldwide, was interviewed. Poole also noted how JAMS adjusted quickly in the pandemic shutdown, and arbitrators rose to the occasion in learning new technologies.[2] Chapter 7 includes further discussion of OArb, and new possibilities for arbitration online.

Notably, however, there was still resistance to OArb at first. In fact, at the start of the Covid-19 pandemic, there was a strong hesitancy toward online hearings in arbitration. Arbitrators were concerned that the security and privacy were insufficient in virtual hearings. Furthermore, some arbitrators worried that credibility could not be examined in virtual hearings. Nonetheless, necessity is the mother of invention, and it pushed arbitrators to be adaptable. Once April and May of 2020 indicated that the pandemic would persist, parties began to shift toward OArb more easily and readily. The adaptability of arbitration shined, as parties realized that they needed closure for their disputes. It also was easier to find workable dates for hearings more quickly—without the need to plan for travel. Moreover, allowing for online hearings became imperative for health and safety in the pandemic. Virtual hearings became a new normal.[3]

Adaptability was not simply something that occurred in commercial arbitration. Labor arbitration also moved online quickly during the Covid-19 pandemic.[4] Professor Rick Bales from Ohio Northern University is an expert in labor arbitration, and he shared an update during the pandemic in our interview. He noted that labor arbitration "came to a screeching halt" at the beginning of the pandemic shutdown. All pending arbitration hearings were put on pause to wait for in-person hearings.

Adaptation became necessary, however, just as it did with commercial arbitration. Once it became apparent that the Covid-19 pandemic would not end quickly, people started to try virtual hearings.[5] Once they tried it, they felt more comfortable with online arbitration hearings and even embraced it. Again, the disputes did not go away, and the process had to adapt for the times.[6] With less legal restrictions on the process, arbitration could rise to the occasion and adapt as long as the parties received a fair process and opportunity to be heard.

In fact, Professor Bales noted that he had not done any online hearings for labor arbitration before the Covid-19 pandemic.[7] However, he had done three online hearings by the time he was interviewed. In subsequent correspondence, Professor Bales recalled that he did his first online arbitration hearing in about June of the pandemic year. Now, his labor arbitrations, mainly in the middle of the country, are about 80 to 90 percent in person. He reports that the online hearings result from need for adaptability, in that parties often prefer the convenience and cost savings of online hearings, especially when the advocates and their witnesses are scattered across the country.

Nonetheless, there may also be regional differences in preferences for in-person versus online hearings. Again, this means that arbitration is adapting to the needs of the parties and their appetites for online hearings. For example, Professor Bales reports that there is still a preference for in-person hearings in the middle of the country, excluding the Chicago area, where he has heard anecdotally that online hearings are somewhat more common. Additionally, using OArb has become more common on the coasts of the U.S., and at least some arbitrators on the coasts will only do online hearings.

Noting the adaptability of arbitration, Professor Bales also explained how adding status conferences to plan for virtual hearings is a tool for problem-solving. This is because these additional meetings lead to more cost-saving settlements. Status conferences allow for more interactions and bring the parties together to agree on virtual or in-person proceedings, creating space to settle. Also, parties who use the flexibility of arbitration to share documents and work together to develop discovery plans tend to move toward productive communications, saving time and money.

That said, gamesmanship can thwart problem-solving. Professor Bales has noted the robust debate over whether an arbitrator can or should order an online hearing over a party's objection, which is discussed later in this book. The short answer became "yes" and there was a baseline assumption for online hearings during the Covid-19 shutdown.[8] However, the issue has returned, albeit in a different context. Professor Bales has observed that arbitrators, parties, and attorneys have mostly learned that OArb can be done fairly, and that judging witness credibility is not a strong argument by itself for an in-person hearing.[9] Still, there is often resistance to online hearings based on "wanting one's proverbial day in (in-person) court." Nonetheless, the reality is that parties sometimes use these arguments for delay, forcing parties to incur travel costs, or otherwise seeking strategic advantage. In this way, arbitrators must remain vigilant in using their power to adapt a process to the problem and the parties—while not allowing gamesmanship to augment costs and time of a process.

Still, flexibility and adaptability of arbitration remained a theme in many of my interviews. Karl Bayer, who is an avid arbitrator,[10] noted how he was apologetic to parties whose proceedings had to continue virtually in the wake of the Covid-19 pandemic. He originally thought that it would be a negative to use virtual hearings. However, he quickly was "converted" after seeing how online hearings could be more adaptable. In many cases, virtual hearings provide an easier and less-expensive experience. Arbitrator Bayer opined that virtual hearings have become a better way to proceed for many parties more generally, in his view.

Arbitrator Bayer opined that Zoom was his preferred platform for online hearings. There has been some movement on this question as Teams and other platforms compete for business. Nonetheless, that adaptability and ease seem to be key reasons that many prefer Zoom. Zoom had some security concerns at the beginning of the pandemic shutdown when everyone literally "zoomed" into Zoom. However, Zoom responded with upgraded security features and is exceptionally easy to use. Of course, this raises important questions about human psychology: the Zoom preference may merely reflect the fact that Zoom was the first to capture the market in the pandemic shutdown, which caused us all to feel comfortable with that platform to the exclusion of newcomers?

Still, Arbitrator Bayer shared additional tips for using Zoom to adapt a process and make online proceedings run smoothly. He emphasized that the number one thing for an attorney representing a party in online arbitration hearings is to learn the platform of the arbitrator. If the arbitrator will use Zoom, then make sure you understand the platform and practice using the platform in advance. It makes everything run more smoothly. Arbitrator Bayer also noted that it is wise for an arbitrator to set up breakout rooms for the parties and their counsel to allow for them to confer privately during the proceedings, if needed. Also, witnesses can be put in breakout rooms during the process, especially if the parties want to ensure confidentiality and privacy around the process. Arbitrators should prevent private chats and have all parties agree to rules around improper coaching of witnesses. Moreover, arbitrators must remind all parties of cybersecurity protocols and work to preserve the privacy of hearings. Again, this shows how adaptable arbitration can be to serve the parties' needs.

This is not to say that adaptability of arbitration points toward OArb in all cases or for all parties. Again, optionality is foundationally important. Processes should be adapted for the problem and parties. Furthermore, not all arbitrators are technologically inclined. In those cases, if the parties desire an online hearing, it makes sense to hire a reasonably priced "technical bailiff" or the like to assist with the process. This is now quite common, and arbitral organizations like the AAA will provide technical assistance for online hearings for an additional fee. The cost is relatively minimal for technical assistance and is far outweighed by the cost savings of online versus in-person arbitration hearings in many cases.[11]

Additionally, it is important to remember that a digital divide continues to exist, especially in rural versus urban areas. Additionally, older individuals who are not comfortable with online processes may prefer in-person hearings. Furthermore, people sometimes need to "vent" in person and may seek an in-person process for its psychological value. For this reason, some arbitrators became adept at adapting in-person processes to make them safer during the height of the Covid-19 pandemic.

Professor and Arbitrator Michael Pitton from the University of Iowa College of Law spoke about ways to adapt in-person arbitrations safely by following the CDC guidelines and SCOTUS protocol during the Covid-19 lockdown.[12] Professor Pitton had handled in-person arbitrations during the pandemic and explained how the adaptability and flexibility of arbitration allowed him to find places with sufficient space, and set forth rules regarding masks and sanitization that would apply in the hearings. It did add more time to plan for safety protocols at the outset, but he felt that it was still easier for the cases involved to go through documents with witnesses in person versus online. Arbitration does not have to happen in a courthouse, making it easier to adjust in-person hearings to provide sufficient distancing. The complications of a public hearing do not apply in arbitration. Accordingly, Professor Pitton found it fairly easy to adjust in-person arbitration to account for health and safety protocols.

Adaptability is also a strength of arbitration when it comes to accessibility for differently abled individuals.[13] Professor David Larson from Mitchell Hamline School of Law uncovered a great deal in this regard. Professor Larson is an expert in accessibility and dispute resolution, so he was a perfect person to interview on this topic. He emphasized how our lives are moving online in a myriad of ways, so it is not a huge surprise that mediation and arbitration would also move online. He warned that the parties must understand the needs of all parties and witnesses before any process or hearing is to occur in order to adapt the process for the people involved. Preparation is essential. Parties and witnesses must have access to a platform. Accordingly, all must try it out before a process occurs to assess whether everyone is comfortable with the technology.

This is relevant not only for people with disabilities but also for people who are not familiar with the platform being used. Age can also play a factor, as digital natives who grew up using technology are often more comfortable with an online process than those who are facing technology later in life. From an accessibility standpoint, it is also important to find out whether things like live transcription of the exchanges or audio description is necessary for any parties involved. As Professor Larson noted: "Prepare so that people can participate."[14] Indeed, if done correctly and with intention, an online process can be more accessible than an in-person process. Moreover, it is often easier and more convenient for those with disabilities to attend a process or hearing from their homes, instead of battling the difficulties of travel.

Still, much needs to be done to improve accessibility of websites, including arbitration websites.[15] There are no clear federal rules about ADA requirements for websites. The Web Content Accessibility Guidelines Working Group (WCAG WG), which is part of the World Wide Web Consortium Web Accessibility Initiative has provided best practices for improving web accessibility.[16] Utah State University also has developed WAVE, which is a free Chrome extension that will check if your website information is disability accessible.[17] It is also helpful to have an individual who is designated as an accessibility coordinator at arbitral institutions. Any dispute resolution provider should test whatever websites and online services that they provide with disabled individuals to get their feedback and see if they are comfortable using the resources. Again, preparation and providing a "dry-run" is especially important where there are individuals who may not be comfortable with online hearings.

In sum, adaptability was a common theme during my interviews through *The Arbitration Conversation*. The rules of civil procedure do not apply in arbitration, and parties are free to design a process to fit their needs. This flexibility and adaptability took on extra meaning during the Covid-19 pandemic shutdown, as we all faced new obstacles and dilemmas. Arbitration beat litigation to the punch in allowing for online and adapted in-person hearings when it was unsafe to proceed in accordance with "usual practices." Furthermore, arbitrators had much more leeway in adjusting spaces and procedures than judges to account for health and safety guidelines. Anecdotally, some litigants even withdrew cases from the courts to proceed with arbitration, knowing that the backlog and hindrances may push their cases out even further, such that they may not reach trial for years. Adaptability of arbitration was and is an essential benefit and lesson learned through *The Arbitration Conversation* time capsule.

NOTES

1 Svetlana Gitman & Amy Schmitz, *Arbitration Conversation No. 1: Svetlana Gitman, American Arbitration Association*, ARBITRATE.COM (July 14, 2020), https://arbitrate.com/arbitration-conversation-episode-1-svetlana-gitman-american-arbitration-association/.

2 Chris Poole & Amy Schmitz, *Arbitration Conversation No. 99: Chris Poole, CEO of JAMS*, YOUTUBE (Nov. 21, 2021), www.youtube.com/watch?v=x8irGjNWqTo.

3 Gitman & Schmitz, *supra* note 1.

4 Rick Bales & Amy Schmitz, *Arbitration Conversation No. 27: Prof. Rick Bales of Ohio Northern School of Law*, Arbitrate.com (Oct. 21, 2020), https://arbitrate.com/arbitration-conversation-no-27-prof-rick-bales-of-ohio-northern-school-of-law/.

5 White & Case, 2021 International Arbitration Survey: Adapting Arbitration to a Changing World, https://arbitration.qmul.ac.uk/media/arbitration/docs/2021-International-Arbitration-Survey-Adapting-arbitration-to-a-changing-world.pdf (last visited Nov. 13, 2023).

6 *Id.*

7 Richard A. Bales, *COVID-Related Labor Arbitration Awards in the United States and Canada: A Survey and Comparative Analysis*, 37(1) Ohio St. J. on Disp. Resol. (2022), https://moritzlaw.osu.edu/sites/default/files/2022-08/9-%20Bales%201-54.pdf.

8 "In less than two months, between March and April 2020, practically all arbitration institutions adapted their rules to the possibility that arbitrators can conduct the entire procedure remotely." Horacio Grigera Naón & Björn Arp, *Virtual Arbitration in Viral Times: The Impact of Covid-19 on the Practice of International Arbitration*, Am. Univ. Washington Coll. of Law, www.wcl.american.edu/impact/initiatives-programs/international/news/virtual-arbitration-in-viral-times-the-impact-of-covid-19-on-the-practice-of-international-commercial-arbitration/#:~:text=In%20less%20than%20two%20months,conduct%20the%20entire%20procedure%20remotely (last visited Aug. 31, 2023).

9 Temitayo Bello & Tolulope Adeosun, *Arbitral Proceedings Configuration and COVID-19 Pandemic; Evaluation of Success and Shortcomings—Europe, USA and Canada* (June 16, 2022), https://papers.ssrn.com/sol3/papers.cfm?abstract_id=4137570.

10 Karl Bayer & Amy Schmitz, *Arbitration Conversation No. 59: Mediator, Arbitrator, and Special Master Karl Bayer*, Arbitrate.com (May 26, 2021), https://arbitrate.com/arbitration-conversation-no-59-mediator-arbitrator-and-special-master-karl-bayer/.

11 *Id.*

12 Michael Pitton & Amy Schmitz, *Arbitration Conversation No. 65: Prof. Michael Pitton of the University of Iowa College of Law*, Arbitrate.com (Sept. 15, 2021), https://arbitrate.com/arbitration-conversation-no-65-prof-michael-pitton-of-the-university-of-iowa-college-of-law/.

13 David Larson & Amy Schmitz, *Arbitration Conversation No. 2: Prof. Dave Larson, Mitchell Hamline School of Law*, Arbitrate.com (June 15, 2020), https://arbitrate.com/arbitration-conversation-episode-2-prof-dave-larson-mitchell-hamline-school-of-law/.

14 *Id.*

15 David Allen Larson, *Digital Accessibility and Disability Accommodations in Online Dispute Resolution: ODR for Everyone*, 34(3) Ohio St. J. on Disp. Resol. (June 24, 2019), https://ssrn.com/abstract=34I08885.

16 Utah State, *Web Accessibility*, https://it.usu.edu/web/accessibility.

17 *Id.*

Chapter 2
Problem-Solving Toolbox

Related to adaptability is problem-solving. As lawyers, we are called to help clients essentially solve their problems. These problems are firstly legal, but they often involve other "problems"—financial, social, psychological, physical, societal, and so on. There are many relational and economic aspects enmeshed with what may first appear as a "legal" issue in the lawyer's office. It is up to an attorney (who also promises to be a sound counselor) to dissect any given situation and collaborate with clients in designing the best plan to help clients with their problems. This includes identifying the best tools for the situation, or problem, and parties. Attorneys and dispute resolution professions must decide and use the best tools in an effective and efficient manner.

Here is where dispute resolution processes such as arbitration and mediation come into play. Dispute resolution processes are all tools in a lawyer's problem-solving toolbox and should be used as such. In dispute resolution literature, we often talk about "fitting the forum to the fuss." This simply refers to our job as lawyers or dispute resolution professionals to examine a situation and find the process that best fits the "fuss"—or problem. This also relates to system design, considering the goals, stakeholders, resources, power dynamics, and cost/benefit analysis in developing a framework for addressing a given "fuss." Furthermore, lawyers and dispute resolution professionals should also consider the "folks"—or the people involved. In other words, they must consider the "fuss" and the "folks" (or this could be the people and the problem).

Arbitration should be viewed in this context. In fact, in quite a few conversations with experts, the need to see arbitration as a tool in a "problem-solving toolbox" was mentioned. This is a shift in the traditional view of arbitration as merely "private litigation" or purely adjudicative within doctrinal frameworks for enforcement. Approaching arbitration as a problem-solving tool changes the framing in ways that can inform practice for the better. This chapter therefore illuminates a problem-solving approach and adds important insights for arbitrators and counsel to consider in helping parties solve their problems. This includes ideas about how they might want to "mix and match" with mediation and arbitration, and other forms of conflict prevention and resolution tools. There are even contexts where one might consider the idea of "problem-solving" coaches. Indeed, technology adds even more flexibility for these tools and allows for greater creativity in creating the proper process for given problems and people.

A. MIXING AND MATCHING

Professor Tom Stipanowich from Pepperdine University Law School[1] is very well known in arbitration, and in the dispute resolution field more generally. Professor Stipanowich is also an expert in "mixing and matching" processes—considering discussions on mixed mode and problem-solving perspectives in dispute resolution.[2] Processes that can be mixed range from negotiation to mediation, to arbitration, and everything in between. "Mixed mode" in this vein means that you move back and forth among lanes when resolving disputes, not limiting the process to one procedure (for example, not limiting the process to strictly mediation or strictly arbitration). In real-world dispute contexts, this is quite common. For example, parties may file an arbitration claim and begin a process but decide midway to end the dispute through a directly negotiated resolution or a mediated settlement, with possibly greater buy-in than they may have for a third-party decision of an arbitrator.[3]

Professor Stipanowich has a long history of research and practice in this area and has written extensively on the topic.[4] In the U.S., prototypes of tiered dispute resolution developed in labor, construction, and mercantile settings. This occurs when parties first try to settle through mediation and arbitrate if the mediation does not end the dispute. This can be a very apt problem-solving tool in some contexts where the parties hope to reach a mutual resolution but fear that they may end up with a stalemate in arbitration. They may provide in their dispute resolution agreement that they will arbitrate any disputes left after a good faith attempt to settle through mediation because they want to avoid litigation. More than three decades ago, provisions for tiered (stepped) dispute resolution with mediation as a preliminary stage began to appear in standard form construction contracts. Today, multitiered dispute resolution processes are frequently found in various kinds of commercial and employment contracts. Furthermore, a group of experienced commercial advocates and arbitrators convened by the International Institute for Conflict Prevention & Resolution (CPR) began advising parties that they should seek amicable resolutions as a precursor to binding determinations. Experts like Professor Stipanowich advocated for a multistep "funneling" mechanism for dispute resolution that accommodates the varied priorities of businesses.[5]

Still, the literature has revealed some hesitancy regarding med-arb (mediation followed by arbitration). Opinion among lawyers and other dispute resolution professionals is far from unanimous regarding contractual stepped dispute resolution provisions, especially when using the same neutral for mediation and arbitration. Practitioners and academics have conflicting perspectives regarding the utility of such arrangements. Critiques of contractual commitments to negotiate or mediate disputes in advance of arbitration or litigation often begin with a sense that you cannot force anyone to agree to agree. There is also fear that parties and counsel will employ these processes in ways that allow for gamesmanship.

Timing is an issue in orchestrating stepped processes. Critics of contractual dispute resolution provisions sometimes contend that the decision to come to the bargaining table or to employ a mediator and the timing of such decisions, hinge on specific circumstances that may not become apparent until disputes arise or thereafter. Additionally, some argue that the optimal moment for informal settlement tends to occur at some point during the adjudicative process, after the parties have garnered sufficient information about the case and their chances in adjudication. Furthermore, there is concern about confidentiality and how honest parties and counsel will be in a stepped process, especially where the same individual will serve as mediator and arbitrator.[6]

In particular, confidentiality concerns arise when an arbitrator plays multiple roles, such as having a neutral serve as the mediator and "switch hats" to serve as the arbitrator in the same case. The concern is that the neutral will learn things in mediation that the parties would not want an arbitrator to know, such as confidential "bottom line" settlement numbers that are often discussed while in caucus with parties in mediation. In contrast, parties would not share such information with an arbitrator. That said, it is unclear that parties fear these confidentiality issues, especially when they trust the neutral selected and benefit from that neutral knowing the case and parties.

Some neutrals report that they feel quite adept at changing roles and appropriately cabining information learned in a mediation when asked to "switch hats" to serve as arbitrator. There are some neutrals who have branded themselves as especially experienced in "switching hats," noting that this can save the parties time and money. It is more efficient for the parties to use the same neutral as the mediator and arbitrator because it saves the time that it would otherwise cost to bring a new neutral "up to speed" for an arbitration after a failed mediation. Moreover, Professor Stipanowich surmised that about 98 percent of the time, the case is resolved in mediation during a stepped process, making it the rare occasion in which a neutral has to move from mediator to arbitrator.[7]

Still, parties may "hold back" in mediation or the conversation may be less productive in a mediation where it is known that the mediator could become the arbitrator. Accordingly, parties may want to hire a new neutral as arbitrator if there is need for a final resolution after a failed mediation.

Furthermore, "mixing and matching" allows for more creativity than simply med-arb. Instead, there are cases where it might make sense to have an arb-med, or even a med-arb-med. For example, parties to a complex commercial dispute may ask a neutral to arbitrate a discrete valuation issue or central legal question, which would then clear the pathway for a successful mediation. This can narrow the issues for the mediation, paving a path for a negotiated settlement in which the parties may have more "buy-in" and process satisfaction.

On the topic of mixed mode dispute resolution, family arbitrator Lisa Hamilton provided insights, as an experienced attorney and dispute resolution professional in British Columbia, Canada.[8] Ms. Hamilton handles family litigation, mediation, arbitration, negotiation, and parenting coordination files. She is particularly adept at problem-solving in family cases. She reported that parts of Canada, including British Columbia, see a large volume of family arbitrations—and Ms. Hamilton handles many of these arbitrations.

Arbitration is a tool that is usually used in conjunction with mediation in family cases in British Columbia. For example, it is quite common for separating partners to use med-arb, with most cases settling through mediation. Still, arbitration can be a good "backstop" that provides an incentive for parties to engage meaningfully in the mediation, knowing that finality will otherwise be provided through arbitration. Notably, the family litigation process in British Columbia requires parties to see various judges during the course of proceedings. This leads families to seek arbitration in order to have one expert neutral throughout the life cycle of their cases. This is perhaps a big reason why arbitration has become such a popular alternative in British Columbia for family cases, although it raises questions for access to justice (A2J) if those who can afford arbitration are opting out of the litigation norm in order to get a superior process with one instead of multiple neutrals.

Ms. Hamilton also discussed the confidentiality concerns around "switching hats." Ms. Hamilton voiced a sentiment similar to other interviews: "switching hats" is less of a problem in reality than it is in theory. She noted that it is always the parties' choice as to whether they want the same neutral to serve in both capacities, and she is always very transparent with parties about the pros and cons of using the same neutral. Additionally, some neutrals are simply uncomfortable serving in both capacities, and will always engage another neutral to serve as mediator or arbitrator—depending on the switch. Indeed, not all neutrals are trained or skilled in both modalities. Nonetheless, using the same neutral often makes sense because the parties presumably chose that individual because of trust and expertise, and it is fairly easy for most skilled neutrals to essentially "forget" any information learned in mediation that could taint the arbitration. Judges do this all the time when they exclude evidence that they already heard.

We also discussed the use of arbitration as a discrete problem-solving tool for narrowing the issues in a mediation. Ms. Hamilton gave the example of property valuations in family cases. Separating partners may wish to arbitrate the valuation of an important asset in order to clear a hurdle to negotiation or mediation. In this way, the process may begin with arbitration and move to mediation after the valuation question is resolved. If mediation still fails to produce a settlement, the parties may end up back in arbitration to finally end the disputes.

These examples show how switching hats can be beneficial for problem-solving in a contextual manner. As Professor Stipanowich has reported in the past, conscientious drafters will want to focus on the basic functionality of the multitiered dispute resolution system, and even consider means for changing lanes from mediation to arbitration, and back again. Wise drafters might ask the parties key questions, including who should be at the table, are there certain discrete issues that could be addressed in arbitration before mediation, should different individuals serve as mediator and arbitrator? The tiered process should offer users a clear and cohesive administrative platform for dispute resolution. The creative urge to develop customized multistep dispute resolution processes must be tempered with care, and terminology should be used consistently at all stages. The problem with lack of crystal clarity is exemplified by *Fluor Enterprises Inc. v. Solutia Inc.*,[9] in which questions regarding the "commencement" of mediation in a contractual provision for tiered dispute resolution resulted in competing motions for summary judgment and judicial parsing of the agreement and incorporated terms. Parties should also ensure that they clearly comply with their planned process, such as formally requesting mediation or taking other required steps per the contract.

With conscientious drafting, mixing and matching demonstrate how arbitration can be a tool in the problem-solving toolbox. Arbitrators and neutrals with a problem-solving perspective may also approach a process with a different frame that may be more productive and helpful for the parties. The following section discusses this further when it comes to planning and helping clients find optimal results.

B. PROBLEM-SOLVING PLANNING

Problem-solving was also a theme in my interview with arbitrator Nick Gowen.[10] Mr. Gowen provided insights on how arbitration fits in a larger problem-solving strategy. He noted how arbitration is unique from litigation because it is a creature of contract, making it more amenable to the parties' needs and goals. For this reason, litigation does not provide the same flexibility as arbitration for problem-solving. Furthermore, arbitration is not tethered to the rules of civil procedure or rules of evidence, so there is a lot less discovery in arbitration—at least when arbitrators are careful in advancing efficiency.

Indeed, some have lamented the "judicialization" of arbitration that occurs when attorneys insist on extensive discovery and essentially import complex procedures into an arbitration process. This can be problematic and does not promote problem-solving. Parties and their attorneys are wise to consider arbitration as a device for limiting the costs and time associated with resolving a dispute. It is important to be intentional and careful in limiting discovery to what is necessary for a full and fair opportunity to be heard in arbitration. Accordingly, this requires attorneys to be disciplined in only asking for the discovery that is essential to the case. Furthermore, attorneys should pick and choose their battles. Again, attorneys trained in the rules of civil procedure must adjust their mindsets for arbitration to focus on problem-solving.

Arbitrator Charles E. Harris II also provided great information and insights regarding contract drafting with respect to arbitration agreements.[11] He astutely noted how arbitration terms are often an afterthought and parties may fail to consider their needs at the time of contracting. For example, parties can prevent problems from becoming disputes by specifying what type of discovery will be permitted in any eventual arbitration. Also, parties should be careful in including "carve-outs" that can cause disputes, and litigation. Again, it is essential to be intentional in contract drafting in order to further problem prevention.

Another common criticism of arbitration is that arbitrators are prone to split claims down the middle, or "split the baby"—instead of ruling on the merits in the same manner as a judge in a court of law. However, the truth is that most arbitrators are thoughtful, intelligent people looking to make the right decision based on the evidence. Nonetheless, parties and their attorneys are prudent to think seriously about mediation and settlement negotiations before the arbitration proceedings get too far into full steam. Once an arbitration hearing begins, it is unlikely that the parties will settle. Usually, once the hearing begins, it will continue until there is an award. This creates risk in that parties and their attorneys should not bank on expecting to win. Attorneys likewise should be careful in expecting to win in a summary proceeding—as arbitrators rarely grant dispositive motions for fear that the award will be overturned for failure to provide a full and fair opportunity to be heard.[12]

Additionally, arbitration may not be the best problem-solving tool in cases where third parties are to be joined. If those parties are not in privity of contract on the arbitration agreement, it is unlikely that they will voluntarily join the proceeding. Arbitrators will not automatically join third parties simply because they are involved in the claim. Again, the rules of civil procedure, including rules regarding joinder, are not applicable to arbitration. Instead, the arbitration contract governs the proceedings. Attorneys with a problem-solving mindset must consider their clients' goals and use the process that best fits those goals—which in some cases may be litigation.

Professor John Lande, in his interview, also talked about problem-solving to decipher the optimal way to get the best result for the client.[13]

We discussed his books *Lawyering with Planned Early Negotiation: How You Can Get Good Results for Clients and Make Money*[14] and *Litigation Interest and Risk Assessment: Help Your Clients Make Good Litigation Decisions*.[15] Sadly, parties and lawyers often make bad decisions when they go to trial. Parties often get a worse result in trial or arbitration than they would have obtained overall through negotiation or mediation. Professor Lande therefore provides a framework for analyzing cases and disputes with a problem-solving mindset. He sets out three key elements that must be analyzed: (1) expected outcome if you go to trial or arbitration hearing, (2) tangible costs, and (3) intangible costs (stress, loss of opportunities and relationships, etc.). This systematic analysis should include an early case assessment with the clients that is open and honest, leading to creation of a plan for addressing the issues at hand. The plan should account for the fact that an outcome in arbitration or trial is very uncertain. This is especially true in arbitration, where precedent does not apply and data is lacking.

Timing is also important when considering arbitration as a tool in one's problem-solving toolbox. Planning must be the first move, which includes a thorough analysis of one's bottom line and walk-away point. Any attorney must do this analysis with their clients, regardless of an attorney's negotiation approach or style. Knowing one's interests is also essential, which should include an assessment of intangible as well as tangible needs, costs, and benefits. Moreover, lawyers are not free in most cases, meaning that any BATNA (best alternative to a negotiated agreement) should take attorney fees into account—looking at likely fees if one went to mediation versus arbitration versus trial. Additionally, parties must consider relationships and intangible costs to relationships when disputes go unresolved for long periods of time.

Parties, in collaboration with attorneys, should think seriously about their opening offers, as well as incremental offers that would be wise in response to counteroffers. Often, the parties begin negotiations with unreasonable demands or low-ball offers—which can set a bad tone for further negotiations. Furthermore, where parties and their attorneys are not able to negotiate on their own, or the gap is too wide, mediators can be helpful in illuminating parties' risks and case assessments. Mediators may help the parties and their lawyers see that they have unrealistic expectations for what would happen if a given case went to trial or an arbitration hearing.[16] Again, mediation is yet another tool in a problem-solving toolbox—one that often eliminates the need for an arbitration hearing. This relates to the preceding "mixing and matching" discussion.

C. DISPUTE SYSTEM DESIGN

All of these tools (negotiation, mediation, arbitration, etc.) should be considered from a dispute system design perspective—which is a framework for considering dispute resolution methods with a problem-solving mindset. The field of dispute system design (DSD) arose in response to the increasing demand on the part of organizations and others for more effective institutional approaches to managing conflict and disputes. In other words, DSD stems from the need for more effective conflict management approaches within organizations and other entities. This holistic approach mirrors the emergence of systems thinking in diverse fields. A system involves sequential steps or processes aimed at achieving specific outcomes. For instance, a fast-food restaurant's order-taking process forms a simple system, while the broader operational architecture involves interlocked systems like food preparation and employee supervision.

In the same vein, the term "design" involves devising the appearance, structure, or operation of something, aligned with its purpose. System design, in various professions, includes functional analysis and looking at how all the various parts and processes work together. Dispute system design similarly considers functional analysis and considers these shared practices.[17] However, the definition of a dispute system and the complexities of DSD have received a great deal of academic attention in recent years. A dispute system encompasses methods or processes for conflict management, including negotiation, mediation, arbitration, and litigation. These processes, along with other conflict-handling approaches, form the components of dispute systems.

Dispute systems vary in complexity, scope, formality, structure, resources, authority, and purpose. They can range from simple complaint boxes for customer feedback to intricate mechanisms like truth and reconciliation commissions. Dispute systems are devised to address specific events, manage existing disputes, or prevent potential conflicts from escalating. For example, parties involved in a construction project may employ a real-time dispute resolution system called a Dispute Review Board (DRB), featuring neutral technical panelists who provide recommendations to prevent and address disputes.

Dispute systems may be plotted along continua of responsive to proactive interventions and from one-time to ongoing solutions. Responsive systems handle existing disputes, whereas proactive systems aim to prevent escalation of conflicts into disputes. Ongoing systems manage specific disputes over an extended period, whereas one-time systems target single events.

In this landscape, arbitration's relevance lies in its role as a dispute resolution method that can be integrated into a broader DSD program. As a more formal process, arbitration offers binding decisions in most cases. When designing a comprehensive dispute system, arbitration can be strategically positioned within the continuum of methods based on the nature of disputes, desired outcomes, and the level of formality required. This positioning ensures that arbitration serves as a vital component in an organization's holistic approach to conflict management.

This was the focus of my *Arbitration Conversation* with Professor Janet Martinez from Stanford Law School.[18] Professor Martinez is co-author of the important text *Dispute System Design: Preventing, Managing, and Resolving Conflict.*[19] With a system design approach, lawyers as problem-solvers take a step back to consider parties' goals, stakeholders with respect to the dispute, and how much control the parties want over the process and the outcome of a dispute.

Accordingly, the focus is not simply on "winning" or "losing"—or even the parties' positions. Instead, parties need to consider their interests, goals, and risk aversion. Furthermore, if the parties want strict control over the outcome, they are wise to negotiate or mediate, but if the parties seek to cede control to a third party, they may want arbitration or litigation. This question of control must also be balanced with appetite for risk. Again, litigation and arbitration come with more risk, and likely higher attorney costs.

That is just a start in terms of DSD considerations. Professor Martinez shed light on other factors to consider in selecting the right process for the case and context:

1. Power. Arbitration occurs via a contract, although it may not be a balanced agreement. Usually, for example, the merchant or employer has more power in consumer or employment agreements, respectively. Parties should consider whether it is possible to help even out the power, for example using an arbitration process that includes due process protocols (such as those protecting consumers).
2. Expertise. Expertise may be needed in some contexts. For example, the parties would be wise to use arbitration for an intellectual property (IP) claim where they will want an IP expert to resolve an IP dispute. A generalist judge in litigation may not fit the parties' goals.
3. Timing. Like Professor Lande, Professor Martinez emphasized that timing is important, as it may be valuable to go upstream and consider intervening with mediation at an early point in the life cycle of a dispute. Often, the parties wait to mediate or negotiate until it is too late, and a dispute has become adversarial.
4. Prevention. Companies also would be wise to train executives in the basics of negotiation and problem-solving. Companies may even employ conflict coaches to help organizations manage conflicts in ways that prevent disputes from becoming claims. All too often, system design is an afterthought. It should be considered within the business strategy of any company in order to cut dispute resolution costs, support company morale, and boost goodwill.

Again, these are just a few considerations for problem-solving from a design perspective, using the framework put forth by Professor Martinez and her co-authors. This should be considered in light of the literature on dispute system design, including the book that Professor Martinez wrote with Professors Lisa Amsler and Stephanie Smith.

Indeed, problem-solving is relevant in arbitration, along with system design more generally. Arbitrators repeated this theme over and over again.[20] Arbitrator Deborah Hylton noted in her *Arbitration Conversation* interview how she uses full-spectrum dispute resolution, including mediation and arbitration, with a party-driven problem-solving framework. Furthermore, the dispute resolution community more generally is a real community, always willing to help each other become better problem-solvers. Within the community, there are people who say, "if you have an issue, call me," which helped greatly during the Covid-19 pandemic, as everyone scrambled to move online. I can attest, as a member of the dispute resolution community, that it is indeed a real community. Over the years, I have developed very strong friendships with others in the various dispute resolution organizations—and even my ability to get so many arbitrators and dispute resolution experts to entertain my interviews as part of *The Arbitration Conversation* is a testament to the dispute resolution community's generous problem-solving community!

NOTES

1 Amy Schmitz & Thomas Stipanowich, *Arbitration Conversation No. 5: Amy Interviews Prof. Tom Stipanowich of the Pepperdine Caruso School of Law*, Arbitrate.com (Aug. 10, 2020), https://arbitrate.com/arbitration-conversation-no-5-amy-interviews-prof-tom-stipanowich-of-the-pepperdine-caruso-school-of-law/.

2 *Id.*

3 *Id.*

4 Thomas J. Stipanowich, *Arbitration, Mediation and Mixed Modes: Seeking Workable Solutions and Common Ground on Med-Arb, Arb-Med and Settlement-Oriented Activities by Arbitrators*, 26 Harv. Negot. L. Rev. 265 (July 26, 2021).

5 *Id.*

6 *Id.*

7 *Id.*

8 Lisa Hamilton & Amy Schmitz, *Arbitration Conversation New Podcast No. 13*: Family Arbitrator Lisa Hamilton (Nov. 21, 2022), https://arbitrate.podbean.com/e/episode-13-family-arbitrator-lisa-hamilton-kc/.

9 Fluor Enterprises Inc. v. Solutia Inc., 147 F. Supp. 2d 648 (S.D. Tex. 2001).

10 Nicholas Gowen & Amy Schmitz, *Arbitration Conversation No. 25: Arbitrator Nicholas Gowen, Partner—Burke, Warren, MacKay & Serritella*, Arbitrate.com (Sept. 30, 2020), https://arbitrate.com/arbitration-conversation-no-25-arbitrator-nicholas-gowen-partner-burke-warren-mackay-serritella/.

11 Charles E. Harris II & Amy Schmitz, *Arbitration Conversation No. 9: Partner, Mayer Brown Charles E. Harris II, Arbitrator and Partner at Mayer Brown in Chicago*, Arbitrate.com (Sept. 7, 2020), https://arbitrate.com/arbitration-conversation-no-9-charles-e-harris-ii-arbitrator-and-partner-at-mayer-brown-in-chicago/.

12 Michael D. Young & Brian Lehman, *Arbitrators Less Prone to Grant Dispositive Motions*, N.Y. L.J. (June 26, 2009), www.jamsadr.com/files/publication/d2148223-c362-4fe1-8545-02f3be68e5da/presentation/

publicationattachment/9f1ad6d7-781f-4e32-9928-00e1ee720a67/young_lehman_nylj_june-2009.pdf; Liz Kramer, *Dispositive Motions in Arbitration? Just Do It*, Arbitration Nation (Aug. 6, 2018), www.arbitrationnation.com/dispositive-motions-arbitration-just/.

13 John Lande & Amy Schmitz, *Arbitration Conversation No. 31: Prof. John Lande, University of Missouri School of Law*, Arbitrate.com (Nov. 11, 2020), https://arbitrate.com/arbitration-conversation-no-31-prof-john-lande-university-of-missouri-school-of-law/.

14 John Lande, Lawyering with Planned Early Negotiation: How You Can Get Good Results for Clients and Make Money (2d ed. 2015).

15 Michaela Keet, Heather Dianne Heavin & John Lande, Litigation Interest and Risk Assessment: Help Your Clients Make Good Litigation Decisions (1st ed. 2020).

16 *Id.*

17 William L. Ury, Jeanne M. Brett & Stephen B. Goldberg, *Designing an Effective Dispute Resolution System*, 4(4) Negotiation J. 413–31 (1988).

18 Janet Martinez & Amy Schmitz, *Arbitration Conversation No. 55: Jan Martinez, Director, Gould ADR Program, Stanford Law School*, Arbitrate.com (Apr. 14, 2021), https://arbitrate.com/arbitration-conversation-no-55-jan-martinez-director-gould-adr-program-stanford-law-school/.

19 Lisa B. Amsler, Janet K. Martinez & Stephanie E. Smith, Dispute System Design: Preventing, Managing, and Resolving Conflict (1st ed. 2020).

20 Deborah Hylton & Amy Schmitz, *Arbitration Conversation No. 56: Deborah Hylton, Fellow of the Chartered Institute of Arbitrators*, Arbitrate.com (Apr. 21, 2021), https://arbitrate.com/video/arbitration-conversation-no-56-deborah-hylton-fellow-of-the-chartered-institute-of-arbitrators/.

Chapter 3

Context Matters Part I

Employment, Consumer, and International Arbitration

Given that arbitration can be an important tool in one's "problem-solving toolbox," it is no surprise that arbitration has many different "faces" and flavors depending on the context. "Fitting the forum to the fuss" (as we say in dispute resolution) requires parties and practitioners to consider arbitration and "problem-solving" in context. This chapter includes some of the lessons learned in talking with employment, labor, and consumer, as well as international arbitrators. Arbitration processes vary depending on context. Indeed, the most successful arbitrators know this, and they become specialized in their areas of expertise. Understanding the industry, context, and culture is essential in arbitration.

It may seem odd to include consumer and employment in the same chapter with international—as they are so vastly different. However, they are grouped together in this chapter to highlight the stark differences. Also, some consumer and employment cases are international, making cultural and legal differences important in what some may see as simpler cases. Consumer cases are increasingly international as consumers purchase goods from around the world, and employment can likewise span borders as individuals work in locations around the globe. The truth is that no one type of case is always simple or always complex. Additionally, it might have made sense to have separate chapters for each context or type of arbitration, but space did not allow. There are an incredible number of niches in arbitration, and this book merely scratches the surface.

The lesson: all arbitration is not the same, all arbitration in one context is not the same, and each case is—different. Arbitrators, parties, and counsel are wise to consider their own context and particular needs and goals as they fashion the right process for their problems and people. Nonetheless, the following highlights some lessons learned from talking with arbitrators and arbitration experts in particular contexts.

A. EMPLOYMENT AND LABOR

Employment and labor arbitration are not the same, although there can be some overlap as some cases may include labor as well as typical employment claims. Labor arbitration primarily involves disputes between labor unions (or unionized employees) and employers. It is often used to resolve grievances arising from the interpretation and application of collective bargaining agreements (CBAs) and other labor-related issues. Some types of arbitration commonly used in labor contexts include grievance arbitration, interest arbitration, and final offer arbitration. Grievance arbitration usually deals with individual or group grievances that arise when there is a dispute over the interpretation or application of the terms of a CBA. The arbitrator's decision is usually binding on both parties.

Interest arbitration is used when labor and management cannot reach an agreement during contract negotiations. In these cases, the arbitrator is appointed to make a final and binding decision on the terms of a labor contract. This often involves things like wages, benefits, working conditions, or other terms of employment. The arbitrator then holds hearings, considers evidence and arguments from both sides, and ultimately issues a binding decision that outlines the terms of the contract.

Final offer arbitration, also known as "last offer arbitration" or "baseball arbitration," is a specific form of interest arbitration where each party submits a final offer, and the arbitrator must choose one of the final offers as the binding resolution. This method is often used as an incentive for both parties to submit reasonable and fair proposals, knowing that an extreme or unreasonable offer is unlikely to be chosen. The specific rules and procedures for these arbitration methods can vary based on the legal jurisdiction and the CBA involved.

Employment arbitration generally involves disputes between individual employees and employers. It often arises from employment contracts that include clauses that require employees to use arbitration rather than litigation to resolve disputes. There are nonetheless various laws involved. Employment arbitration is generally governed by the FAA, whereas labor arbitration is generally governed by the National Labor Relations Act. Courts nonetheless sometimes apply FAA jurisprudence in labor cases, and there are often labor and employment issues in the same case.

Still, a great deal of employment arbitration pertains to arbitration arising out of an employment agreement where the employee is not unionized. For example, we see this with X (formerly Twitter) employees who are seeking to join a class action. These employees face litigation forcing them to pursue their claims through individual arbitrations under their employment agreements. Meanwhile, labor arbitration flows from CBAs, which raises different considerations. Nonetheless, labor and employment may be intertwined, and each situation may have its own nuances. Context matters.

Overall, employment and labor arbitrations have become a norm over the years. This is especially true as the courts condoned arbitration of everything from discrimination to lost wages claims.[1] Professor Richard Frankel from Drexel University spoke in *The Arbitration Conversation* with respect to employment arbitration. Professor Frankel explained the significant issues that arise in employment contexts. He noted how arbitration is quite different from litigation because it is private, and often confidential where the parties include a confidentiality clause in their arbitration agreements. Still, it is important to note that arbitration awards may become public when a party seeks enforcement of an award in court. Nonetheless, concerns about arbitration of sexual harassment claims raised issues in the #MeToo movement as more sexual harassment claims surfaced and were sent to private arbitration that was often cloaked in confidentiality as well.

In fact, concerns regarding arbitration of sexual harassment claims drew bipartisan interest, and, in 2022, Congress passed the Ending Forced Arbitration of Sexual Assault and Sexual Harassment Act (EFASASHA). This act, which passed both the House of Representatives and the Senate in 2022, adds a new chapter to Title 9 of the U.S. Code.[2] The act invalidates any pre-dispute arbitration agreement or pre-dispute class action waiver when an individual or collective group alleges conduct constituting a sexual harassment or sexual assault dispute in a case filed under federal, tribal, or state law.[3] Any issues about applying this chapter to a dispute must be determined by federal law and must be determined by a court.[4] The arbitrator is stripped of authority to determine the validity or enforcement of an arbitration agreement when issues of applicability under this chapter are raised. The rest of the act addresses the technical components of including this new chapter within Title 9 (such as adding the chapter within Title 9's table of contents).[5] The act has been signed into law and is now in force. Still, there are questions about how it will be applied that have yet to play out in the courts.

Similar concerns about privacy and confidentiality also come up with labor arbitration involving police officers who may arbitrate disciplinary claims related to brutality. Of course, criminal claims in these contexts will create transparency with public trials. However, there are some claims that are solely disciplinary actions related to police brutality that will go to generally private and confidential arbitration hearings pursuant to labor agreements. For this reason, some have asked for greater scrutiny with respect to confidentiality and privacy in not only employment but also in labor cases. That said, again, awards may still become public where they are enforced in court.

Professor David Horton from the University of California Davis School of Law spoke with respect to employment arbitration.[6] He highlighted the rise of what he calls "infinite arbitration clauses"—which are very broad arbitration clauses that compel arbitration of any claims arising out of or relating to anything that is connected to or comes out of the contract that contains the arbitration clause. These clauses do not simply cover claims directly from the contract. Instead, they go further to require arbitration of anything with any sort of nexus to the contract. This may include tort as well as statutory claims, including discrimination. Note that EFASASHA does not apply to discrimination claims—only sexual harassment.

Professor Horton explained in his interview that the procedures are different in employment litigation versus arbitration, so forum matters in this context. It is especially important where the employer has all the key information that the employee will need to pursue a discrimination claim, for example. Again, arbitration generally does not allow for the same sort of discovery as litigation. Also, class procedures are generally not available in arbitration, making it cumbersome for employees with similar claims to each pursue their arbitrations separately.

Labor arbitration was also a topic of discussion in several other episodes of *The Arbitration Conversation*. For example, in Episode 27,[7] Professor Rick Bales provided insights into labor arbitration in the age of Covid-19 and how labor arbitration moved online in the wake of the pandemic. Professor Bales also shared insights about labor arbitration more generally. This interview is also discussed in Chapter 1, Arbitral Adaptability, in that Covid-19 pushed labor arbitrators and workers to try online hearings, despite the prior headwinds to change.

Still, there is an aspect to the interview that focuses on labor arbitration that is worth noting here in terms of "context matters." It is important for individuals in the field to understand the culture of labor arbitration, and the foundations of collective bargaining. Furthermore, as noted earlier, although the Supreme Court tends to conflate arbitration under the FAA and arbitration under the National Labor Relations Act, the laws are different because the contexts are different. Additionally, there are often equity and access to justice issues wrapped up with labor cases in which lower-income workers are seeking remedies against a powerful company. Labor arbitrators must be well-versed in labor law and understand the culture as well as the power dynamics. This may mean that the procedure is more casual, and virtual hearings may not be sufficient in some cases where the worker is not comfortable with the technology. Moreover, not everyone has the same access to the internet, let alone quality computers. This must be considered.

Labor arbitration was also the focus of Episode 94 of *The Arbitration Conversation* with Arthur Pearlstein, director of arbitration for the Federal Mediation and Conciliation Service (FMCS).[8] Director Pearlstein explained the work of FMCS in labor arbitration, and its mission to keep industrial peace. As such, FMCS includes mediators as well as around 1,000 private labor arbitrators who are vetted as experts in the labor field. Those selected must be subject matter experts in collective bargaining and labor relations, and have recent experience deciding labor cases. They may also take the FMCS course, and even serve as an apprentice to learn more about the process before serving as neutrals in FMCS cases. These arbitrators selected to be on the FMCS panel must certify, once joining the roster, that they will give up any type of advocacy role in labor cases.

Again, labor arbitration is unique, and parties want labor arbitrators with significant experience and knowledge in labor law and practice. Notably, the most successful arbitrators are not selected because they are prone to decide for one side or the other. Instead, parties look for predictability and reputation in the field. Is it a neutral that the parties have heard of or know? How many cases has this individual arbitrated? Professional background is also important, including prior work in the labor field.

Relatedly, labor arbitrators who have cases get more cases, making it difficult for new arbitrators to break into the field. Parties do not seem to care that much about the arbitrators' daily fees, so offering a lower rate does not seem to attract cases. Arbitration is a service and customers shop for the service, understanding that labor has its own unique context. However, scientific research also shows that newcomer arbitrators with the same background as those who get selected are far behind those who have the "most" work—regardless of qualifications. This means that once an arbitrator gets selected, they keep getting more cases. Newcomers who have not established a reputation suffer on the sidelines. FMCS hopes to help newcomers with apprenticeships and training, but it is a complex problem when parties have the power to make selections.

In sum, labor and employment arbitration are unique contexts—unique from each other and unique from other types of cases, such as commercial disputes. Power dynamics are at play where employees and other workers face employers with greater power. Furthermore, the culture varies—with a greater focus on collective bargaining in the labor context and a loss of access to class actions in typical employment contexts. Above all, it is important for arbitrators in these cases to understand not only the law but also the culture that is integral to the context.

B. CONSUMER

Professor Horton talked about "infinite clauses" not only in the employment context but also in consumer cases. In fact, Professor Horton's idea came from a consumer case, *Wexler v. AT&T Corp.*[9] In this case, Wexler signed up for cell phone service with the mobile service arm of AT&T, and a separate company within AT&T began making unsolicited calls and sending unsolicited text messages to Wexler's cell phone. This led her to sue under the Telephone Consumer Protection Act (TCPA). AT&T sought to compel arbitration of the claim, but the judge in the case refused. AT&T claimed that the clause applied to any claim anyone would bring against it or any of its affiliates forever, even years after the service ended. The judge noted how the clause could be read to cover torts and contract, as well as any other claims for all time. He found that this can be a surprise for consumers, and problematic where the procedures are so different in arbitration verses litigation. This case represents the sort of "infinite clauses" Professor Horton described in *The Arbitration Conversation*.

Professor Horton was not the only guest on *The Arbitration Conversation* to discuss consumer arbitration. Indeed, consumer contexts are different from business-to-business conflicts, especially due to the power differentials and control over the consumer contracts themselves. Consumers generally do not have a choice with respect to arbitration and usually sign contracts without reading them, let alone understanding what arbitration is or how it impacts their rights.[10] This is not to say all consumer arbitration is unfair or "bad" for consumers. Often the arbitration rules at play will require the company to pay most of the costs of arbitration and most arbitrators seek to make fair and equitable decisions. Arbitrators may even help address power dynamics, especially when there are pro se individuals involved.

On the topic of pro se litigants in consumer arbitration, I interviewed Arbitrator Katherine Haennicke in *The Arbitration Conversation*. In particular, we discussed the special issues in managing pro se consumer cases.[11] Despite the "bad reputation" consumer arbitration gets in some cases, there are ways to help make the arbitration process clear and understandable for consumers. Consumer arbitration can be streamlined and simple, and easier to navigate than litigation. It is important for the arbitrator to explain in a preliminary hearing call how the process will work, in plain language. For example, it helps to inform the parties what one needs to prove for a case, and always keep parties apprised of next steps. Arbitration also helps make things easier for pro se litigants by removing detailed pleading requirements and other complexities of the rules of civil procedure.

Still, it can be difficult for arbitrators to strike the balance to remain "neutral" while helping address power and knowledge imbalances where one party is not represented. It is a fine line with pro se litigants—seeking to be helpful without crossing the line to appear biased toward the pro se party. One way to do this is to merely refer pro se litigants to online resources, and not provide specific advice. It can also help to ask open-ended questions with both sides, like "What do you want me to know?" Also, checking in with the parties during the hearing is essential to see whether they have questions.

OArb has also helped to make arbitration cheaper and easier for consumers in many cases. Pro se litigants are finding online hearings easier than in person processes, as they are in the comfort of their homes instead of a formal hearing venue. It also eases the stress of presenting one's case if they are used to using their mobile devices for virtual calls. Some individuals feel quite comfortable sharing information about their cases in a virtual hearing, again in the comfort of their homes instead of a courthouse or stuffy boardroom. Of course, policy questions remain regarding arbitration clauses cutting off access to class relief, and clauses that quiet consumers' voices through confidentiality clauses. Nonetheless, consumer arbitration is not all bad, and there are ways to help make it a better process for consumers, including pro se individuals.

Arbitrator Aric Garza also shared ideas for ensuring a fair arbitration process in consumer cases.[12] He again stressed that arbitrators should be aware of power issues in consumer cases and understand that the consumer may not have any experience with arbitration processes. Arbitrators and case administrators should therefore provide a primer for parties that have never been through arbitration before. Additionally, the rules can be fairly easy to understand. The AAA rules, for example, are quite concise and easier to digest than the federal rules of civil procedure applicable in federal court. The AAA rules also limit the costs for consumers, requiring the business to pay most of the costs of an arbitration process. The pleadings are kept to a minimum, and the arbitrator is usually an expert who will endeavor to advance efficiency and fairness. Again, consumer arbitration is not "all bad," and it can be a better process than litigation in many cases, when handled in an equitable and fair manner.

That is not to diminish policy questions that remain regarding consumer arbitration, especially to the extent that consumer arbitration clauses cut off access to class relief. On the other hand, we live in a new era of consumer arbitration with the rise of mass arbitration filings in some situations. Indeed, through my *Arbitration Conversation* interview with Travis Lenkner, the then managing partner of what was Keller Lenkner LLC (and is now under a new name), I learned a great deal about what happened in the Amazon mass arbitration situation. Mr. Lenkner's firm filed the majority of the 75,000 individual arbitration claims against Amazon, alleging that the company's Alexa-powered Echo devices recorded users without their consent. These mass filings led to Amazon paying millions of dollars in filing fees per its arbitration policies, ultimately leading the company to change its terms of service and allow its customers to file lawsuits in the courts to pursue their claims.[13]

In sum, consumer arbitration can be a fair and equitable process for consumers. It may even be easier and cheaper than litigation in some cases. Nonetheless, arbitration clauses may also operate to effectively cut off access to remedies where consumers must pay high fees and travel to far locations to pursue their rights. Also, arbitration clauses may negatively impact consumer rights, cutting off access to class relief. Still, new issues are arising with the advent of mass arbitration filings, causing some companies to reverse their insistence on arbitration. Furthermore, new bills are introduced yearly to curb employment and consumer arbitration, making this an evolving legal landscape.

C. INTERNATIONAL ARBITRATION

International arbitration is a unique context that is quite different from domestic consumer and employment cases, for example. Even placing international arbitration in a chapter with employment and consumer contexts may give the reader a form of whiplash! However, this grouping is intentional to highlight the importance of context, and the highly different faces of arbitration. In international cases, the law alone can be quite complex where parties are from different countries with different laws and legal systems.[14] For example, Arbitrator and Professor Mohamed Abdel Wahab of the Cairo University Faculty of Law spoke with respect to the Cairo arbitration center. Cairo, Egypt, has a robust arbitration law, which was passed in 1994.[15] Cairo is becoming a center for arbitration, even in comparison with the International Chamber of Commerce (ICC)—known to be a leader for international arbitration institutions. Furthermore, investment treaty arbitration has grown throughout the world, and online capacities have helped elevate arbitration as a more adaptive and effective process than litigation for international cases. Professor Wahab provided interesting insights, noting the growth of arbitration in Cairo in light of these global changes.

Investment treaty arbitration came up with many of the interviews in *The Arbitration Conversation* (discussed later in this chapter). However, a new twist on international arbitration has emerged in the area of trust arbitration.[16] Professor Stacie Strong, a former colleague at the University of Missouri School of Law, who taught at the University of Sydney School of Law at the time of the interview, spoke on this subject. In our *Arbitration Conversation*, we discussed trust arbitration and new laws in New Zealand. Trust arbitration is unique in that it focuses on trust disputes, trusts being instruments that are used to convey or protect property. Trust arbitration usually involves conflicts among beneficiaries and may involve family issues that are best handled in a private process. Trust disputes traditionally have been litigated because courts have had an oversight authority due to the fiduciary responsibilities of trustees. However, arbitration is beneficial in these contexts due to the need for privacy. For this reason, there is growing interest in trust arbitration on the international front.

This interest in trust and family arbitration is also growing in Canada.[17] Arbitration expert Jonathan Eades, senior legal counsel, British Columbia Ministry of the Attorney General, shared insights about a new Canadian arbitration law. As of September 2020, a new law came into focus in British Columbia. Canada is different from the U.S. in that the most important arbitration law is provincial legislation, instead of federal law. The new law creates some additions that will help propel arbitration forward in British Columbia, Canada. For example, the law creates a limited ability to appeal questions of law that arise from the arbitral award. Nonetheless, parties can opt out of this process. Moreover, it seeks harmonization with the New York Convention. Additionally, the law opens the door to arbitration of family and other types of disputes, again respecting the process for its privacy and provision of an expert decision-maker.

Similarly, the interview with Arbitrator Jo Delaney shed light on arbitration in Australia, and issues around how the courts have interpreted arbitration clauses in Australia.[18] There is currently a trend for more arbitration in Australia, particularly with cross-border transactions. This means that there is a growth in the use of arbitration clauses in Australia. Nonetheless, this does not mean that parties automatically go to arbitration when they have an arbitration clause. For example, some parties in construction disputes prefer to just go to court, especially in states where the courts have faster, efficient case management processes. In fact, construction arbitration can sometimes be inefficient and expensive in Australia. Judicialization of arbitration can thwart its efficiency benefits.

The growth of arbitration in Australia has raised new issues around interpretation of arbitration clauses, including questions regarding the level of review to determine when to send cases to arbitration. Additionally, there are still major issues with parties not drafting their arbitration clauses carefully, raising questions that lead to litigation about arbitration. In Australia, there is also growth in the use of multitiered dispute resolution clauses, but these clauses lead to litigation where they are not sufficiently clear to explain how the parties will move through the process. Perhaps a universal lesson for attorneys in all jurisdictions is to draft clear arbitration clauses in order to minimize litigation about arbitration, especially in business and commercial cases.

Context and culture are also important in considering the growth of arbitration in Hong Kong and China.[19] Professor Carrie Shang shared insights about arbitration in the Asia-Pacific region, noting how parties are more interested in arbitration than other means as a primary way to resolve disputes. This is especially true in China with respect to international disputes. Mediation is less popular in China, although interest is growing.

Investment arbitration is particularly robust in China, as China has been funding projects, leading to disputes between investors and the Chinese government. In researching this area, Professor Shang found that there has been a push from the Chinese government to include arbitration clauses in the investment agreements. Nonetheless, questions are now arising as Hong Kong's status shifts from independence to rejoining China. Hong Kong has always been a robust arbitration center, but Professor Shang surmises that it will become an even larger dispute resolution center in years to come.

Investment treaty arbitration has become its own "animal" in the international arbitration world.[20] In *The Arbitration Conversation*, Professor Victoria Sahani discussed what makes investment treaty arbitration different than regular international commercial arbitration. She noted that the ICC has seen an uptick in investment treaty arbitrations, as international investment grows. Furthermore, these arbitrations have a different culture because a state will always be a party, the respondent. Moreover, this type of arbitration is a creature of treaties, and not strictly a matter of contract—like traditional commercial arbitration enforced under the New York Convention.

Investment treaty arbitration is not without controversy. Some have alleged that the more powerful states tend to win and exert influence in these arbitrations. This can be problematic, as this arbitration is final and binding. This has caused some to suggest a need for an appeals body, to create a greater "check" on the system. Some have also advocated for greater use of mediation in these cases. This has gained steam in light of the Singapore Convention—allowing for more international mediation and better use of problem-solving techniques in international cases.

Investment treaty arbitration also has earned a reputation for creating a "club-like" atmosphere, making it very difficult for new and diverse arbitrators to break into the industry.[21] As with other areas of arbitration, arbitrators are selected by the parties, and parties (and their attorneys) tend to repeatedly select the same arbitrators. Attorneys and their clients fear that selecting an unknown or new arbitrator could bring an unexpected result. Attorneys are especially unwilling to take a "risk" in selecting an unknown newcomer to the profession. Accordingly, there is a long way to go to achieve diversity in the investment treaty tribunals.

Arbitration counsel Stephen Anway also shed light on international investment treaty arbitration and calls for reform.[22] Mr. Anway explained that the European Union (EU) has been seeking reform, especially after questions were raised about enforcement of certain bilateral treaty arbitrations due to jurisdictional issues. Even my own simple research backed up our discussion regarding concerns raised in the EU about investment arbitration. This has led to suggestions for the creation of an EU investment treaty court. There is also interest in more transparency for investment treaty arbitration in the EU, and development of international investment protection agreements (IPAs). IPAs have been introduced as means for guaranteeing the protection of investors' assets from one party located in the territory of the other party.

Another conversation on the topic of investment treaty arbitration was with Professor Catharine Titi, a research associate professor (tenured) at the French National Centre for Scientific Research (CNRS), University Paris II Panthéon-Assas, France. She is heavily involved in research related to international investment law and she serves on the editorial board of the Yearbook on International Investment Law & Policy (Columbia/OUP). In *The Arbitration Conversation*, Professor Titi focused on UNCITRAL Working Group 3's work on reforming the investment arbitration system. As noted earlier, investment treaty is unique because these disputes always involve a foreign investor as the claimant and the host state as the respondent. This can create power questions. Accordingly, some years ago, some states started becoming skeptical about investment arbitration. In 2017, UNCITRAL began negotiations to improve the investment arbitration system, including three phases: identifying which topics need to be improved; determining whether reform is desired; and creating an advisory center on investment law. This advisory center would offer advice to developing states when they face an investor state dispute and develop a code of conduct.

Professor Titi noted that countries in Latin America are actively participating in the discussions, even though some states are traditionally seen as preferring regional solutions over international dispute settlement. For example, Ecuador has been very vocal in negotiations, which may be related to the courts in Ecuador finding that its investment treaties were unconstitutional. Professor Titi noted that adaptation is essential to prevent treaties from being terminated and taking away access to international treaty dispute settlement. As already noted, there are also discussions related to reform within the EU, which could compete with the UNCITRAL project in some ways. There is also work to be done on the substantive rules governing investment arbitration.[23]

Professor Andrea Bjorklund also discussed investment arbitration in *The Arbitration Conversation*. Professor Bjorklund is the L. Yves Fortier chair in International Arbitration and International Commercial Law at the McGill University Faculty of Law in Montreal, Quebec, Canada. Professor Bjorklund was named as a representative to UNCITRAL by the International Law Association.[24] She noted that the work has been complex due to the wide array of stakeholders. Multilateral groups are always complex, and reaching consensus is particularly complicated. Some have said that the biggest goal being sought by the UNCITRAL working group was the establishment of a multilateral investment court. This would allow parties to go to the multilateral investment court instead of individual arbitrations. Another proposal would be less ambitious, establishing an appellate body for first instance arbitrations. There could also be the establishment of a two-tiered tribunal with open architecture.

If the investment court is established, it is unclear what mechanism would govern enforcement. The New York Convention and ICSID Convention generally apply when dealing with international arbitration. As mentioned in other interviews, the EU has also been working on its own reforms, including an investment court system similar to the appellate body of the World Trade Organization (WTO), where adjudicators are part-time and awards are considered arbitration awards. Issues remain, such as questions around independence and allowing individuals to serve as both counsel and arbitrator in the system. Again, another consideration is the difficulty of advancing diversity in international dispute settlement. With the small number of justices who would be appointed, there would be high stakes on each individual appointment to ensure that the overall makeup of the court has adequate diversity representation. As noted in Chapter 5, diversity remains an issue in other areas of arbitration as well.

Even within investment treaty arbitration, there are new and interesting niches. Paul Barker spoke about a new niche with respect to renewable energy. Mr. Barker is a barrister with Doughty Street Chambers and a research fellow at Stanford University, focusing his research on the intersection of arbitration and renewable energy.[25] Continuing with the theme of "context matters," this is another example of how context is key even within a subset of international arbitration. We need to consider how the flexibility of arbitration can address climate change issues on an international scale. The renewable energy field is a fascinating mix of technology, innovation, finance, and public policy. The ongoing renewable energy revolution is having a transformative impact on both the global economy and our environment. Moreover, the issues are international in nature and thus arbitration is helpful in this area. Public policy and regulations have been central to the development of renewable energy as a commercially viable business model.

Recognizing how renewable energy is closely linked with climate change policy is important. The 2015 Paris Agreement established targets for decarbonization. The annual investment will cost trillions of dollars per year to meet these targets. There is a huge investment gap, however, so private investment will have to play an important role. Since many projects will be in the developing world, foreign direct investment is going to be an important aspect in promoting renewable energy. Barker is researching how investment treaties can help encourage green investment. This is complex because investment treaties are climate-neutral in that they do not distinguish between high-carbon or low-carbon investments. Climate-related treaty claims have skyrocketed in the last decade, largely due to cuts or cancellations of renewable energy subsidies.

There are many areas of arbitration where climate change and renewables are relevant, such as commercial, investment treaty, and interstate arbitration. One advantage of arbitration is its procedural flexibility and the ability to bring in expert arbitrators with climate-related backgrounds. Investment treaty arbitration is well set up for these types of arbitrations. Claims concerning climate-related processes are going to continue to feature heavily in investment treaty arbitration. Climate change will increasingly become relevant to commercial arbitration disputes, including contracts directly related to the effects of decarbonization. A range of disputes can arise concerning energy supply, power purchase agreements, and IP disputes over licensing of new renewable technologies. For example, a commercial dispute, that on the surface may have nothing to do with climate change, ends up being a dispute over a physical risk of climate change such as a flood or fire.

International investment treaty arbitration is a robust area and there are many reforms being discussed in the EU, UNCITRAL, and worldwide. Furthermore, it includes niche areas that bleed into other areas of international commercial arbitration. Arbitrator Tunde Ogunseitan spoke on topics related to international arbitration, and its added value in complex international matters. He is an arbitrator, mediator, and counsel with extensive practice expertise in the United Kingdom and Nigeria. Ogunseitan provided reflections on the ancient history of arbitration, noting how it is not a Western invention—but something as old as humanity itself.[26] My own research reflects the same. It was also especially interesting to learn how in Ogunseitan's own culture, when there were business and trade disputes, the elders would come out and make a decision. That decision would have to be enforced. Today, the desire for an expert arbitrator who the parties trust to resolve their disputes remains essential. This is why selecting the arbitrator or arbitration panel remains the most important piece in arbitration practice. This is an important "lesson learned" for practitioners to keep in mind. Too often, parties simply select the same arbitrators over and over again, without being mindful of expertise and perhaps considering new arbitrators who may have more acute proficiency in the area. This is especially true in technology disputes.

With respect to international arbitration, Ogunseitan provided insights regarding the cases that he has seen in the United Kingdom and Nigeria—including notes regarding the amount of high-value ad hoc arbitrations that occur around the world. Furthermore, there is a great cost savings in arbitration as compared with litigation—especially in the international context. Context matters, as backed up by ICC data showing how parties save money by arbitrating in international cases. The most substantial cost is the cost of counsel, which is usually lower in arbitration due to time—as arbitration is usually faster than litigation. Whether ad hoc or institutional, arbitration fees can be kept at reasonable levels—but parties should remain vigilant and aware of arbitrator fees. Still, travel can add exponentially to the cost of international arbitration. Parties tend to complain about the cost of the room and paying a private judge, but when you look at those line items compared to the whole cost of the arbitration, travel and other costs add up. This, again, suggests that OArb is worth consideration in international arbitration.

With the theme of considering context, parties and arbitrators are wise to consider a multitiered arbitration system with different dispute resolution mechanisms in the international context. This can save parties money. When certain issues cause delay and need to be resolved quickly, narrowing the issues with mediation or a summary procedure makes sense. Moreover, considering a "conflict coach" or having a problem-solving dispute management system in place may be particularly helpful in cases where the preservation of relationships is key. Traditional arbitration, in many ways, breaks the relationships of the parties and provides an adjudication akin to litigation. If you design a responsive process at the outset, you will save time and help preserve relationships for the parties. If your process is improperly designed and you have not anticipated the types of disputes you may have, you might not serve the parties' goals.

Finally, policy analysts are hard at work with respect to international arbitration. For example, Ludvig Hambraeus, a policy and public affairs executive with the Chartered Institute of Arbitrators (CIArb) in London, UK, was interviewed.[27] CIArb is a leading professional body for arbitration professionals, and they work in drafting policies that may drive aspects of dispute resolution in terms of political and societal impact. Mr. Hambraeus noted how arbitration had to shift and change with Covid-19, and the work of CIArb also had to address new challenges as a thought leader. The pandemic affected all the industries that CIArb works with, so they had to draft new policies due to the pandemic. Again, context matters—and the international context calls for comprehensive ideation around dispute resolution on a global scale.

In sum, international arbitration has many faces and flavors. International arbitration may involve a wide variety of issues and is dependent on the laws of the parties' nations. For example, many countries do not enforce pre-dispute arbitration clauses in consumer contexts. Furthermore, the seat of arbitration under the arbitration contract at issue is quite important when it comes to applicable law and culture. Still, international arbitration is exceedingly important for cross-border disputes because of the New York Convention—making arbitration awards more enforceable than national court judgments in international cases. Investment treaty arbitration is also quite important on international levels, and we are likely to see reforms in coming years. Moreover, arbitrating in a neutral country is often a wise way to accommodate context and culture—avoiding risks of being "hometowned" in one country's courts. Finally, we will likely see growth in climate-related arbitrations—which overlap with so many varied fields and require special expertise.

NOTES

1 Richard Frankel & Amy Schmitz, *Arbitration Conversation No. 8: Prof. Richard Frankel of Drexel University School of Law*, ARBITRATE.COM (Aug. 31, 2020), https://arbitrate.com/arbitration-conversation-no-8-prof-richard-frankel-of-drexel-university-school-of-law/.

2 H.R. 4445, 117th Cong. (2022); *Actions Overview H.R. 4445–117th Congress (2021–2022)*, CONGRESS.GOV, www.congress.gov/bill/117th-congress/house-bill/4445/actions.

3 H.R. 4445, 117th Cong. § 402(a) (2022).

4 *Id.* § 402(b).

5 H.R. 4445, 117th Cong. (2022).

6 David Horton & Amy Schmitz, *Arbitration Conversation No. 10: Prof. David Horton of UC Davis School of Law*, YOUTUBE (June 30, 2020), www.youtube.com/watch?v=SI2f3ubCytc.

7 Rick Bales & Amy Schmitz, *Arbitration Conversation No. 27: Prof. Rick Bales of Ohio Northern School of Law*, ARBITRATE.COM (Oct. 21, 2020), https://arbitrate.com/arbitration-conversation-no-27-prof-rick-bales-of-ohio-northern-school-of-law/.

8 Arthur Pearlstein & Amy Schmitz, *Arbitration Conversation No. 94: Arthur Pearlstein, Director of Arbitration, FMCS*, YOUTUBE (Sept. 28, 2021), www.youtube.com/watch?v=uaqe3CThd48.

9 Wexler v. AT&T Corp., No. 15 CV-0686, 2018 U.S. Dist. LEXIS 20157 (E.D.N.Y. Feb. 5, 2018).

10 Amy J. Schmitz, *Access to Consumer Remedies in the Squeaky Wheel System*, 39 PEPPERDINE L. REV. 279–366 (2012).

11 Katherine Haennicke & Amy Schmitz, *Arbitration Conversation No. 12: Arbitrator Katherine Haennicke from AAA*, ARBITRATE.COM (Sept. 28, 2020), https://arbitrate.com/arbitration-conversation-no-12-arbitrator-katherine-haennicke-from-aaa/.

12 Aric J. Garza & Amy Schmitz, *Arbitration Conversation No. 18: The "Blues Lawyer" Aric Garza on Consumer Arbitration*, ARBITRATE.COM (Aug. 19, 2020), https://arbitrate.com/arbitration-conversation-no-18-the-blues-lawyer-aric-garza-on-consumer-arbitration/.

13 Travis Lenkner & Amy J. Schmitz, *Arbitration Conversation No. 86: Travis Lenkner, Managing Partner of Keller Lenkner LLC, The Attorney Who Took on Amazon*, ARBITRATE.COM (May 30, 2023), https://arbitrate.com/arbitration-conversation-no-86-travis-lenkner-managing-partner-of-keller-lenkner-llc-the-attorney-who-took-on-amazon/.

14 Mohamed S. Abdel Wahab & Amy Schmitz, *Arbitration Conversation No. 6: Amy Interviews Mohamed Abdel Wahab of the Cairo University Faculty of Law*, ARBITRATE.COM (Aug. 17, 2020), https://arbitrate.com/arbitration-conversation-no-6-amy-interviews-mohamed-abdel-wahab-of-the-cairo-university-faculty-of-law/.

15 Egyptian Arbitration Act No. 27 of 1994.

16 Stacie Strong & Amy Schmitz, *Arbitration Conversation No. 13: Prof. S.I. Strong of the University of Sydney*, ARBITRATE.COM (Oct. 5, 2020), https://arbitrate.com/arbitration-conversation-no-13-prof-s-i-strong-of-the-university-of-sydney/.

17 Jonathan Eades & Amy Schmitz, *Arbitration Conversation No. 29: Jonathan Eades, Senior Legal Counsel, BC Attorney General*, ARBITRATE.COM (Aug. 13, 2020), https://arbitrate.com/arbitration-conversation-no-29-jonathan-eades-senior-legal-counsel-bc-attorney-general/.

18 Jo Delaney & Amy Schmitz, *Arbitration Conversation No. 38: Arbitrator Jo Delaney of Baker McKenzie*, ARBITRATE.COM (Dec. 11, 2020), https://arbitrate.com/the-arbitration-conversation-no-38-arbitrator-jo-delaney-of-holman-fenwick-willian/.

19 Carrie Shu Shang & Amy Schmitz, *Arbitration Conversation No. 22: Prof. Carrie Shang of Cal State Polytechnic University, Pomona*, ARBITRATE.COM (Sept. 16, 2020), https://arbitrate.com/arbitration-conversation-no-22-prof-carrie-shang-of-cal-state-polytechnic-university-pomona/.

20 Victoria Sahani & Amy Schmitz, *Arbitration Conversation No. 42: Prof. Victoria Sahani of Arizona State University*, ARBITRATE.COM (Dec. 31, 2020), https://arbitrate.com/arbitration-conversation-42-prof-victoria-sahani-of-arizona-state-university/.

21 Michael Waibel & Amy Schmitz, *Arbitration Conversation No. 49: Michael Waibel, Professor of International Law, University of Vienna*, ARBITRATE.COM (Mar. 3, 2021), https://arbitrate.com/arbitration-conversation-no-49-michael-waibel-professor-of-international-law-university-of-vienna/.

22 Stephen Anway & Amy Schmitz, *Arbitration Conversation No. 69: Stephen Anway, Partner and Co-Chair of IDR at Squire Patton Boggs*, Arbitrate.com (Feb. 2, 2022), https://arbitrate.com/video/arbitration-conversation-no-69-stephen-anway-partner-and-co-chair-of-idr-at-squire-patton-boggs/.

23 Catharine Titi & Amy Schmitz, *Arbitration Conversation No. 20: Prof. Catharine Titi of the University of Paris*, Arbitrate.com (Sept. 2, 2020), https://arbitrate.com/arbitration-conversation-no-20-prof-catharine-titi-of-the-university-of-paris/.

24 Andrea Bjorklund & Amy Schmitz, *Arbitration Conversation No. 43: Prof. Andrea Bjorklund of McGill University Faculty of Law*, Arbitrate.com (Jan. 19, 2021), https://arbitrate.com/arbitration-conversation-no-43-prof-andrea-bjorklund-of-mcgill-university-faculty-of-law/.

25 Paul Barker & Amy Schmitz, *Arbitration Conversation No. 72: Paul Barker, International Arbitrator and Fellow, Stanford Law School*, Arbitrate.com (Mar. 16, 2022), https://arbitrate.com/arbitration-conversation-no-72-paul-barker-international-arbitrator-and-fellow-stanford-law-school/.

26 Tunde Ogunseitan & Amy Schmitz, *Arbitration Conversation No. 93: Arbitrator, Mediator, and Counsel Tunde Ogunseitan*, YouTube (Aug. 17, 2021), www.youtube.com/watch?v=bUuQVVBmcLY&ab_channel=arbitratedotcom.

27 Ludvig Hambraeus & Amy Schmitz, *Arbitration Conversation No. 47: Ludvig Hambraeus of the Chartered Institute of Arbitrators*, Arbitrate.com (Feb. 17, 2021), https://arbitrate.com/arbitration-conversation-no-47-ludvig-hambraeus-of-the-chartered-institute-of-arbitrators/.

Chapter 4
Context Matters Part II
Sports, Intellectual Property, Construction, and More

Context is so important to arbitration and dispute system design that it deserves two chapters—and actually another book. Indeed, there should be a separate chapter for each of these faces and flavors of arbitration, but space does not allow. That will be a project for another day. Nonetheless, the previous chapter considers a few common contexts, but that is just the tip of the iceberg. There are many different areas of arbitration. It is important for arbitrators and legal counsel in arbitration to respect and understand the contours of these different contexts and cultures. An arbitrator who is very skilled in one area or context may not be as skilled in another. An arbitrator or practitioner preparing for an arbitration should be well-versed in that particular type of arbitration, and should not assume competence in one area will translate. All arbitration contexts are not the same. The following examples show the breadth and depth of the various faces of arbitration.

A. INTELLECTUAL PROPERTY (IP)

Intellectual property (IP) disputes are increasingly being resolved through arbitration. Theo Cheng spoke on the topic of IP arbitration, as he runs an alternative dispute resolution firm specializing in commercial, intellectual property, entertainment, technology, and employment disputes. Mr. Cheng discussed the advantages of arbitration over litigation.[1] He explained that arbitration costs less than litigation generally, but especially with IP claims. This is largely due to the flexibility and ability to streamline the process to fit the needs of the parties. This also includes an ability to have an expert decision-maker and targeted discovery.

Additionally, arbitration is private by nature and can be confidential where the parties so provide in their agreement. Confidentiality is especially important with respect to trade secrets and proprietary information, and while protections can be in place in litigation, it is generally easier to keep information confidential in arbitration, although special steps are still necessary where an arbitration award is enforced in court.

Furthermore, having an expert arbitrator deserves emphasis in IP cases. An arbitrator who understands the background technical issues saves the parties the time and money it would otherwise take to educate a generalist judge or jury. Consider the complexities of emerging technologies such as blockchain, and how helpful it is to have a decision-maker who understands the relevant terminology. Also, parties in large and complex IP cases may opt for a panel of three arbitrators, advancing the depth of analysis and understanding that occurs in deliberations among experts. However, in less complex cases, a single arbitrator is a wise choice, in terms of cutting down on costs and time (especially considering the extremely busy schedules of the parties involved).

Speed is another benefit of arbitration that has special significance in IP cases, where advances occur quickly and there is a need to get remedies in place before the IP's improper use is too far gone. For example, although temporary restraining orders in court may be helpful to stop a party from misusing another's IP, getting a quick order is also available under most arbitral institutions' "emergency rules." It is true that the court is needed to put the power of the state behind an order, but arbitral orders usually garner cooperation—as they can quickly be turned into court orders, and parties fear arbitral sanctions. Moreover, getting to a final award quickly can be especially beneficial as time leads to higher damages. Again, arbitration typically results in a faster decision than litigation.

That said, the speed of arbitration is more questionable in large cases with multiple parties and a three-arbitrator panel due to scheduling issues. Nonetheless, it is still faster than litigation in most cases. For international cases, the neutrality of an arbitration forum is an added benefit, thereby eliminating concerns about being "hometowned" in another State's courts. Having a set arbitration location designated in a pre-dispute agreement is also better than facing the forum shopping that occurs in litigation. Moreover, as noted earlier, arbitration awards are more enforceable than foreign judgments in many cases due to the New York Convention, which recognizes the enforcement of arbitration awards throughout the world.

Despite these benefits of arbitration in IP cases, arbitration is not necessarily perfect, and its existing limitations should be addressed. First, injunctions only cover the parties to the arbitration and do not have the backing of the state until entered as a judgment in a court of law. Therefore, preliminary relief in arbitration may not effectively stop the misuse of IP until the award is entered into the court as a judgment. Second, the award can be ineffective for a party looking for a nationwide injunction to stop manufacturing or stop certain conduct in multiple jurisdictions. Lastly, some parties or issues may not be covered by the arbitration, leading to a need for further litigation in court to cover all parties and issues. This harms efficiency as well as the essential need for finality.

Despite these limitations, arbitration can be effective for IP claims. We are seeing a rise in arbitration in the area, and the expertise of arbitrators is of particular importance in many cases. Moreover, speed and cost-savings are attributes of arbitration in this area.

B. SPORTS

Another interview that highlighted the importance of context was conducted with Professor Maureen Weston, who is a professor of law and director of the Entertainment, Media & Sports Dispute Resolution Project at Pepperdine Law School's Straus Institute. Professor Weston is an expert in sports arbitration, including issues around arbitration for the Olympic Games. Professor Weston's passion for sports is not limited to the legal field; she is an avid tennis player and joined the interview for *The Arbitration Conversation* from her tennis club.

Arbitration is the primary method of dispute resolution for professional, international, and Olympic sports.[2] The speed, expertise, and privacy of arbitration are all attributes that help propel it as the norm in professional sports. As one may expect, athletes and teams want to resolve issues quietly and quickly so athletes can quickly return to play. Athletes consent to arbitration by individual contracts, or may be subject to arbitration provisions as part of a collective bargaining contract. Much of sports arbitration relates to labor disputes. At the same time, many athletes have sponsorships and media contracts that include arbitration provisions. Despite the preeminence of arbitration in professional sports, it is currently not used as often in college athletics.

Olympic arbitration is very robust. The Olympic Charter provides for arbitration for all members of the Olympic movement, which covers commercial parties, athletes, and governing bodies. Some Olympic athletes have challenged this provision, but it has been upheld by the Swiss Federal Tribunal. In the U.S., Olympic athletes are covered by the U.S. Amateur Sports Act, which named the AAA as the designated arbitration provider. Under this rubric, complaints are filed with the U.S. Olympic Committee.

After the filing, the final tribunal for all Olympic athletes is the Court of Arbitration for Sport. This can be daunting for many athletes, as the arbitration process can be quite expensive, especially in some sports where individual athletes may lack resources. For example, there are many less-known Olympic sports in which the athletes may not earn any money from endorsements or other revenue flows associated with the more known sports. For this reason, pro bono panels and ombudsmen work with athletes to guide them to the resources they need to participate in an arbitration.

There are some criticisms of the current system of arbitration for Olympians. Power imbalance can be a problem, with athletes who often lack power and may feel that they lack rights or choice in the process.

Additionally, the selection of arbitrators tends to be repetitive, and the ones selected tend to be white men. There is a general lack of diversity among arbitrators. At the same time, there has been some criticism of the privacy of arbitrations, and lack of transparency needed to ensure fairness and neutrality. The European courts recently held that there is a right to public arbitration. In light of these criticisms, the Court of Arbitration for Sport now has public arbitration hearings streamed online.

Another interview that focused on sports arbitration was that with Richard Faulkner, who is a fellow of the Charted Institute of Arbitrators. Arbitrator Faulkner has arbitrated more than 300 cases in a wide range of fields, including sports cases. Faulkner shared insights from serving as an arbitrator for the famous Lance Armstrong arbitration case. Faulkner was one of three arbitrators on a tripartite panel for four arbitrations involving Lance Armstrong.[3] This was an ad hoc, non-administered arbitration that included a very unusual provision in the contract for continuing jurisdiction. This is rare, because usually an arbitrator or arbitration panel is functus officio once an arbitration proceeding is complete. Considering context, the Armstrong case allowed for continuing jurisdiction due to concerns over the actual enforcement and collection of the award.

There had been quite a bit of controversy around the Armstrong case in general. In these arbitrations, Armstrong claimed that SCA Promotions (SCA) had not paid him in a timely manner after winning his sixth Tour de France. SCA defended on the basis that Armstrong had been doping. The panel determined that SCA owed Armstrong the money, but a later American federal grand jury probe revealed new information that sparked SCA to initiate another arbitration using this evidence. The panel reached a 2–1 decision, finding in favor of SCA on the basis that the first arbitration included extraordinarily inaccurate testimony. Although the arbitrators disavowed any reliance on a U.S. Anti-Doping Association report, the panel ordered that Armstrong return the money paid. SCA moved to confirm the award, making it public.

This example of sports arbitration highlights the importance of context. Again, the process was designed for the peculiarities of the case, allowing for continuing jurisdiction, for example. This was very cutting edge at the time. Additionally, the case involved scientific evidence, and witnesses testifying via videoconference. Furthermore, the arbitrators took very strong steps to ensure the security of the evidence and the confidentiality of the transcripts. This was all particularized for this highly watched case.

Nonetheless, parties are often surprised when information in an arbitration becomes public due to related court actions. When a motion is filed in court to vacate or confirm an award, arbitral information is sometimes made public, if not otherwise sealed in some way for cause. Information that parties thought was confidential may be laid out in the arbitration award in federal or state court. At the same time, because there are no rules of evidence in arbitration, all sorts of things may become part of the arbitral record that would never be admitted in court. International issues also come into play, as rules differ in different courts when litigation about arbitration occurs in public courts.

Arbitrator Faulkner also noted how there are now issues around the use of social media that may be especially relevant in sports arbitrations. For example, in a recent Swiss Supreme Court case, *Sun Yang v. AMA*, one of the arbitrators made some very hostile anti-Chinese comments on social media. This raised questions about whether such social media statements provide grounds for removing an arbitrator. A lesson learned in the increasingly digital world is that it is wise to fully research and vet arbitrators before selecting them to serve. It is also wise for arbitrators to share disclosures, even if they are blanket disclosures, with respect to their social media presence. Parties today should search social media as part of gathering as much information as possible before naming an arbitrator.

Arbitrator Faulkner also shared insights with respect to the National Football League (NFL) arbitral process for player discipline. Again, these cases may be high profile and controversial. For example, in the Ezekiel Elliott case, a federal court found that Elliott and the NFL Players' Association were misled in arbitration about the existence of evidence. There were also questions about the impartiality of an arbitrator who was tasked with reviewing the executive director of the NFL's suspension decision, because that same arbitrator was also appointed by the executive director. The judge in the case, therefore, granted a temporary restraining order, halting enforcement of the suspension. A later court reinstated the suspension, but Faulkner surmised that cases like this raise important questions about the independence and impartiality of such NFL arbitral tribunals.

At the same time, contexts differ even within the realm of sports arbitration. There are sports arbitration mechanisms that are quite distinguishable from other sports arbitration spaces. Arbitrator Clifford Hendel, who is the head of Hendel IDR, a Madrid-based law firm where he specializes in international commercial and sports arbitrations, spoke on this topic. In particular, Hendel often serves as an arbitrator for the Basketball Arbitral Tribunal (BAT) in Europe.[4] It was fascinating to learn about this arbitration niche within the realm of sports arbitration, and how Hendel became involved as an American lawyer practicing law in Madrid, Spain. He later became a sports arbitrator with the Court of Arbitration for Sport in Olympic cases, and eventually became involved with the International Basketball Federation (FIBA). He is now very active with FIBA BAT.

BAT, again, provides a very interesting example of how context matters in arbitration. BAT is especially efficient, helping players stay in play. BAT is also different in that it only covers labor disputes in international basketball, making it very specialized. Even so, it is important on a global level because virtually all contractual disputes with professional leagues, except the NBA in the U.S., are potentially subject to BAT's jurisdiction if the parties agree. In fact, BAT has more than 200 cases per year, despite it being fairly new in that it was only developed in 2006.

It is nonetheless unique from Olympic arbitration because there is no acceptance to arbitrate as a condition of participation. BAT arbitrations are also distinguishable because they do not address corporate governance or doping issues. BAT is also different from FIFA's Dispute Resolution Chamber, which is an internal judicial body. FIFA panels include three adjudicators, with one neutral, one representative of labor, and one representative of management. FIFA has 800 to 900 cases per year and a very fast-tracked procedure.

Showing how context matters, BAT arbitrations apply the law of equity. This means that arbitrators do not have to focus on all the various local laws that may apply in each case. Instead, they will consider the contract under the circumstances of the case and have power to modify the contract if one believes that the circumstances are such that the contract should be modified. This furthers goals of efficiency and simplicity, avoiding the burdens of applying the local law of dozens or hundreds of different countries. At the same time, BAT arbitrations have one arbitrator and are generally resolved online, with hearings being rare. Awards are binding under the New York Convention. Due to the efficiency and low cost, BAT has been very successful and is now being used as a model for other sports tribunals.

C. FINRA AND SECURITIES

Another very specialized area of arbitration involves securities cases. Professor Jill I. Gross spoke on this topic. She is the director of the Investor Rights Clinic at Pace University Law School and an expert in securities arbitration and the Financial Industry Regulatory Authority (FINRA).[5] Professor Gross provided great background on FINRA and its arbitration process, including updates on how FINRA arbitration operated during the Covid-19 pandemic. FINRA provides a great example of another situation where context matters.

First and foremost, FINRA arbitration is unique because it is highly regulated by the Securities and Exchange Commission (SEC). Additionally, FINRA has great power in this space because nearly all broker-dealer cases must go to FINRA arbitration under standard required contracts in the securities industry. This means that FINRA includes investor claims, as well as employment disputes. Professor Gross estimated that approximately 55 percent of disputes are those between a customer of a brokerage firm and the brokerage firm or its brokers. The remaining 45 percent are employment disputes, generally between a brokerage firm and an employee.

Like other specialized areas, it seems narrow in concept but can include a very large caseload. Professor Gross estimated that approximately 3,500 cases are filed each year. The process is much more expedient than litigation in that a case generally takes 12–14 months, instead of the years that can engulf a claim in litigation. The process is more regulated than other types of arbitration and has specific rules for not only the basics of the process (such as filing a statement of claim and answer, selecting an arbitrator, etc.) but also discovery, limited motion practice, and hearings. The process tends to be investor friendly in that hearings take place in the residence of the claimant/investor. Hearings may be held before one or three arbitrators, and awards must be paid within 30 days. Nonetheless, the losing party has the ability to file a motion to vacate the award.

As was true in other areas of arbitration, most in-person hearings were postponed in the early days of the pandemic shutdown. However, as parties became impatient with waiting, some processes moved online. Professor Gross noted the tensions during that time: On the one hand, some parties seemed to use the pandemic as means for stalling the hearing (which is in the interest of most respondents); on the other hand, in-person hearings may be preferable for some arbitrators to read credibility and body language. Investors also may lack power and knowledge about the process in comparison to broker-dealers who tend to be repeat players. This causes some to question whether OArb exacerbates power differentials in these cases or is a means for empowering individuals who cannot afford the cost and time involved with travel. Although OArb may actually lower barriers to remedies in some cases, it also may seem daunting to some individuals who lack access or comfort with online hearings.

Another interview that focused on FINRA arbitration was my interview with George Friedman, an expert in securities law and practice. George Friedman is the editor in chief of the Securities Arbitration Alert and had been the FINRA executive vice president and director of arbitration. Friedman shared insights based on his experience at both the AAA and FINRA, and added thoughts related to how the Covid-19 pandemic has impacted operations at FINRA. His experience is deep. He has been an arbitrator, professor, and leader in securities arbitration for many years, and headed a task force to write rules on securities arbitration.

Like Professor Gross, George Friedman also noted the special aspects of FINRA arbitration that flow from FINRA being a self-regulated organization. Again, context matters, and the regulatory scheme of the SEC is an important overlay in FINRA cases. In fact, the SEC responds to complaints and approves rule changes in FINRA arbitration. When FINRA files a rule with the SEC, the rule is published in the federal register and there is a public comment period. This type of public process is not applicable in purely private arbitration such as that under the AAA or JAMS. Additionally, FINRA is able to review each case to look for patterns and amend practices based on that data.

As Professor Gross also noted, FINRA rules are known for being "investor friendly." Still, some investor advocates question this in light of power differentials between investors and brokerage firms, although some aspects of the FINRA rules indicate concern for the investor. For example, investors have power to demand an arbitrator's removal, and FINRA awards are generally public. FINRA also follows up with investors to assist with enforcement. The AAA on the other hand, cannot help with award enforcement other than directing parties to seek enforcement of an award in court.

Resilience and adaptability of arbitration also shine in FINRA arbitrations, as is true in other areas of arbitration. During the beginning of the Covid-19 pandemic, the movement toward OArb was slow. However, as time went on, there was an accelerated movement to OArb, which Friedman expects to continue into the future. In particular, he suspects that many parties will use a hybrid method, having some parts of cases and witness hearings in person and other witnesses online where travel would be difficult or costly. Another consideration is the staff working at arbitration providers who have been exposed to remote work. Organizations like AAA, FINRA, and JAMS will need to reevaluate their office spaces in large cities, now that many personnel and case managers work remotely.

In general, Friedman reported that people by and large are gravitating toward online hearings. There is not much of a generational divide regarding comfort with online hearings now that so many people have become familiar with Teams, Zoom, and the like. In major arbitrations with lots of witnesses, there may be some resistance, but even then, some witnesses are still going to prefer Zoom. With the high cost of travel, parties are questioning whether travel is necessary and worth the cost. Moreover, the delays and difficulties of air travel in modern times have caused many to rethink their flying practices.

In sum, securities arbitration is another important flavor of arbitration. Indeed, a practitioner in general commercial arbitration may not even be qualified to work in the securities industry. Again, it is essential to learn the norms and rules in whatever context one practices. All arbitration is not the same.

D. CONSTRUCTION

Another area where context matters is construction arbitration. Construction is an industry with a long and robust history using arbitration for resolving disputes. Arbitration allows for expert decision-makers, privacy, speed, and flexibility that will assist with solving construction problems. Nonetheless, there are sometimes difficulties related to the multiparty aspect of many construction claims.[6] On this topic, Arbitrator Clifford Shapiro spoke. He is partner at Barnes & Thornburg, LLP, and he is the head of the firm's Construction Law Practice Group. Arbitrator Shapiro provided background on construction arbitration, as well as insights related to multiple-party disputes, estoppel, and the Covid-19 pandemic. The conversation again highlighted how context matters.

Construction is a specialized practice area of law and is uniquely dependent on relationships and efficiently resolving disputes on a project to foster project completion and allow relationships to continue. This is why arbitration has played a role in construction for many years.[7] Construction matters also often involve many parties. For example, when considering the construction of a hospital, there may be the general contractor, the owner, the funders, subcontractors from all the various trades, suppliers, insurers, and more. When there is a construction case with many parties and claims, arbitration can work well. However, there are sometimes questions about whether it is possible to force all parties into one arbitration proceeding because that is only possible where they have all contractually agreed to the same arbitration process. Of course, in litigation, parties can use the rules of civil procedure to join all the relevant parties in one case. Those rules do not apply in arbitration. Again, arbitration is a contractual process.

That said, arbitration provides special attributes in construction, as noted earlier. Accordingly, it often makes sense to provide for the eventuality of a multiparty arbitration at the front end of construction contracts. Construction attorneys know that it is wise to think about this at the time of contracting, and to coordinate a set of contracts so that if there is a dispute, all of the parties can be involved in a single proceeding. For example, it is a good strategy to have all the contracts related to a construction project include "General Conditions" that include the same arbitration provision allowing for a multiparty proceeding. Still, it can be very difficult to have a pre-dispute arbitration clause reach to the far end of the chain, such as all suppliers and subcontractors. Agreements to arbitration should be set pre-dispute, as parties usually will not simply join an arbitration out of the goodness of their hearts. Indeed, it is often in the interest of respondents to refuse to join a proceeding so that they can conveniently blame other respondents in separate proceedings to avoid liability.

Arbitrator Shapiro outlined additional issues that arise in the unique context of construction arbitration. For example, there are cases when a party may be bound to an arbitration clause even if they were not part of the original contract. Estoppel may have important implications in construction cases. For example, a new building owner who was never a party to the original construction contract may find that they are bound to an arbitration provision because they have assumed the obligations of the construction contract, including the arbitration provision. This can be problematic for a new owner who is surprised by the arbitration clause, and then faces proceedings in multiple venues because some claims go to the court system and others go to arbitration.

Furthermore, the speed of each process matters due to the possible application of estoppel. If an issue is tried and decided in arbitration, issue preclusion often applies, and the owner may be bound by that arbitral determination in later litigation. Logistically, arbitration usually moves more quickly than litigation, making this scenario a norm. Still, the application of estoppel may differ in any given case. I had cases in practice that involved lengthy litigation about the application of estoppel because it is a thorny issue in construction due to the multiparty nature of these cases. Questions focus on whether the parties had a full and fair opportunity to arbitrate a given issue, and this can be a problem where different parties have different needs and incentives. Nonetheless, it is important to consider whether estoppel may apply to litigation involving arbitrated claims and issues.

Another consideration in the unique context of construction is the use of stepped processes. Many construction contracts require mediation prior to arbitration in what is often called a stepped process, as discussed in Chapter 2. In this scenario, the mediator can create an informative process, working with the parties to understand their interests and create a process that allows the parties to reach resolution without the need for an adjudicative process. Mediation facilitates settlement and can be helpful in construction cases as means for preserving relationships. Difficulties arise, however, if the mediation does not end the dispute. It is then that parties must decide if they wish to use the same mediator as the arbitrator. Furthermore, construction shows a unique capacity for arbitration to pivot for party needs, allowing for a quick shift to OArb during the Covid-19 pandemic, with hearings moved to Zoom.

E. RAILROAD

Yet another area where context matters is railroad arbitration. Admittedly, I did not know a great deal about railroad arbitration, and my interview with Arbitrator DeAndra Roaché was incredibly informative. Arbitrator Roaché is the founder of Cynergis ADR and is an experienced arbitrator, mediator, and trainer. She shared background on the procedural nuances in railroad arbitration, as compared to labor arbitration in other industries. She also shed light on the need for greater diversity in railroad dispute resolution.[8] She is truly a leader in the field and brings varied experiece to the field.

First, some background: the ADR processes utilized in the railroad industry reflect the rich history of the industry, as it is one of the original labor industries in the U.S.[9] Moreover, the railroad industry joins the airline industry as the key areas governed by the Railway Labor Act. What many do not realize is that railroad and airline cases are different from most other private-sector labor cases, which are governed by the National Labor Relations Act. Under the Railway Labor Act, various sections have different formats for arbitration. For example, section 3 governs minor disputes and designates a specialized process for discipline and grievances, whereas section 6 governs major disputes regarding collective bargaining and the negotiation process of the contract itself. The National Mediation Board (NMB) plays a key role in administering these cases. For example, it certifies appointments of arbitrators to serve as neutrals on labor/management boards in the railroad industry. The NMB also often furnishes panels of arbitrators from which the airline parties select a neutral for airline System Boards of Adjustment. There is a great deal of federal government oversight and federal budget implications.

It is not easy to become an accepted and successful arbitrator in these cases. This is especially true for women and people of color. Although African Americans and Asian Americans built our country's railroad system, it has been a white male-dominated industry, which has extended into related arbitration and dispute resolution in the field. It is difficult for people not involved in the industry to be able to enter the industry due to being viewed as "non-railroaders." Furthermore, few women are seen as true "railroaders." This means that the pipeline is dominated by men. It was nonetheless inspiring to hear from Arbitrator Roaché, who is a leader in the area who hopes that administrators, decision-makers, and parties come to realize that diversity strengthens organizations and fosters better outcomes for the industry and in the ADR profession as a whole. The railroad industry is a vital component of transporation that should include dispute resolution professionals that represent society.

At the same time, railroad arbitration was ahead of the virtual curve when the Covid-19 pandemic hit. The railroad industry already had virtual hearings and technology in place through the NMB and practices of many advocates and arbitrators who were already using video hearings to save on the costs and time of travel. Additionally, the arbitration process in the field lends itself very well to virtual hearings because arbitration usually relies on electronic submissions.

NOTES

1 Theo Cheng & Amy Schmitz, *Arbitration Conversation No. 11: Theo Cheng on Intellectual Property Arbitration*, YouTube (July 15, 2020), www.youtube.com/watch?v=qZS4n1Cd0zA&ab_channel=arbitratedotcom.
2 Maureen Weston & Amy Schmitz, *Arbitration Conversation No. 14: Prof. Maureen Weston from Pepperdine Law School*, YouTube (July 16, 2020), www.youtube.com/watch?v=dVphHaOW_ds&ab_channel=arbitratedotcom.
3 Richard D. Faulkner & Amy Schmitz, *Arbitration Conversation No. 90: Arbitrator Richard D. Faulkner*, YouTube (July 31, 2021), www.youtube.com/watch?v=nKzzxE-o8WY&ab_channel=arbitratedotcom.
4 Clifford F. Hendel & Amy Schmitz, *Arbitration Conversation No. 37: Sports Arbitrator Clifford J. Hendel*, YouTube (Aug. 31, 2020), www.youtube.com/watch?v=43SfAwpxi5o&ab_channel=arbitratedotcom.

5 Jill I. Gross & Amy Schmitz, *Arbitration Conversation No. 21: Prof. Jill I. Gross of Pace Law School*, YouTube (July 29, 2020), www.youtube.com/watch?v=1ZhD06brOjU&ab_channel=arbitratedotcom.

6 Peter Merril & Amy Schmitz, *Arbitration Conversation No. 74: Peter Merrill, CEO of Construction Dispute Resolution Services*, YouTube (Mar. 24, 2021), www.youtube.com/watch?v=4OPeETaltrE.

7 Clifford Shapiro & Amy Schmitz, *Arbitration Conversation No. 26: Arbitrator Clifford Shapiro, Partner at Barnes & Thornburg, Chicago*, YouTube (Aug. 11, 2020), www.youtube.com/watch?v=3wki0Ic8RUU&ab_channel=arbitratedotcom.

8 DeAndra Roaché & Amy Schmitz, *Arbitration Conversation No. 46: Arbitrator, Mediator, and Trainer DeAndra Roaché of Cynergis ADR*, YouTube (Oct. 9, 2020), www.youtube.com/watch?v=5d11emoyGaQ&ab_channel=arbitratedotcom.

9 *Id.*

Chapter 5
Dedication to Diversity

Lack of diversity has been a long-time issue in arbitration. Arbitrators, especially in the more lucrative commercial and international cases, have traditionally been older white men. It can be difficult to be selected as an arbitrator if you are a woman, person of color, or otherwise anything but a white man.[1] This has important implications for fairness, justice, and "being heard" in the arbitral system.

For example, the dynamics of gender diversity can significantly impact arbitration and dispute resolution, just as in other settings. Statistics bear out differences in decision-making between male and female arbitrators and, similarly, judges. Of course, it is impossible and incorrect to make assumptions or generalizations about men or women as decision-makers. Still, there are indications, for example, that having women involved in group decision-making has tangible effects on the dynamics and the quality of decision-making. Again, this is not to say that all women or all men think or decide issues in any given manner, or that all those in one group think or act alike. Instead, it is recognizing that having a diversity of viewpoints can enhance any decision-making process.

Some scholars have argued that, regardless of whether men and women actually "think differently," some international adjudicative panels' constituencies perceive that there are such differences, and that the perceived legitimacy of these panels can be increased through greater gender diversity. Many users of international arbitration services might perceive arbitrators and their awards as more "legitimate" if there were more female arbitrators appointed to their cases.[2] Much greater attention must be paid to the important differences that gender and other aspects of diversity make in decision-making and adjudication. A 2013 survey of experienced U.S. arbitrators sponsored by the College of Commercial Arbitrators (CCA) indicated that only about 15.4 percent of the respondent group were women—a percentage that precisely reflected the percentage of female members in the CCA at the time.[3]

Meanwhile, arbitral organizations have talked about the need to expand diversity among their arbitrators, but change has been difficult because parties still control arbitrator selection for the most part. With this backdrop, several of the interviews in *The Arbitration Conversation* have focused on ideas for expanding diversity in arbitration. For example, some interviewees shared ideas such as random selection, setting up approved panels, and direct appointment to help new and diverse arbitrators get their foot in the door to arbitration. Another interviewee shared ideas for expanding information about arbitrators to promote diversity. This chapter will share insights and ideas that came from these various conversations.

The field of arbitration is much like other practice areas of the law, in that diverse peoples have historically been underrepresented in meaningful positions at higher levels. It is therefore not a surprise that challenges with respect to diversity have been top of mind in arbitration. Arbitration organizations, such as AAA, JAMS, and CPR, have pledged to increase diversity in arbitration by including more arbitrators with diverse characteristics on their rosters and ensuring that rostered diverse arbitrators are selected to serve.[4] One interviewee shared that the AAA itself has gone from 23 percent of its roster being diverse in 2012 to having 27 percent diverse appointments by 2018.[5] At the same time, International Chamber of Commerce (ICC) statistics indicate that the number of women in ICC arbitrations was as little as 7 percent in 2010, but has since risen to 21 percent in 2019.[6]

Still, these numbers only account for the percentages included on the roster of arbitration organizations. This does not mean that women and diverse arbitrators are being selected. Mirèze Philippe, the special counsel of the ICC International Court of Arbitration, said "the needle is moving but there still remains a lot to be done."[7] Other experts in arbitration also note that policies are not enough. Professor Ben Davis, for example, called for substantial action and noted the need to hold institutions with diversity goals accountable in reaching their goals.[8]

Nonetheless, increasing the number of diverse arbitrators on institutional rosters is a start and will hopefully increase selection of diverse arbitrators in real cases. Lack of diversity was highlighted in the publicized case involving the artist Jay-Z, who found himself a party to an arbitration.[9] Jay-Z was in a disagreement involving his clothing line, and subject to an arbitration agreement in the contract at issue. He resisted arbitration, noting that the names presented for possible selection included no black arbitrators.[10] Just as we have seen in courts, it is important to have decision-makers who can empathize and identify with the parties.[11] Professor Ben Davis noted in his interview that he surmises about 1 percent of arbitration practice attorneys in law firms are African American.[12] Indeed, Professor Davis shared stories from his time at the ICC as a black American arbitration leader. Professor Davis also noted that an initial step toward advancing diversity in arbitration is for law firm partners to provide real opportunities for young attorneys of color. This includes opportunities to take on arbitration cases, and to assume leadership roles in arbitration.[13]

In another interview, arbitration leader Mirèze Philippe shared her experiences as a female arbitration leader in top positions with the ICC. She noted, "women were doing the same work as their male counterparts and remained backstage, but never on-stage."[14] She was instrumental in starting Arbitral Women in hopes of raising profiles for women in arbitration. Providing visibility, supporting successes and achievements, and providing spaces where women in arbitration can be supported will help them advance to prominent roles in the future.[15] It nonetheless remains difficult for newcomers to break in and be selected for commercial and international arbitration cases.

The other aspect of promoting diversity in arbitration is analyzing how existing arbitrators are selected. In another interview, Professor Michael Z. Green, Professor of Law and Director of the Workplace Law Program at Texas A&M School of Law, noted how many people focus on the supply problem without diving more deeply into asking whether diverse arbitrators are being selected.[16] Professor Green explained how it goes beyond the fact that some parties and their attorneys may harbor biases. There is also the practicality that attorneys are likely to choose the same arbitrators over and over to justify their choices to their clients. It is risky to choose an arbitrator who is not familiar. This makes it very tough for new arbitrators to break into the industry. Attorneys have a lot of influence in choosing arbitrators for their clients and they tend to lean toward selecting people they know. Professor Green has put forth ideas for increasing diversity in his scholarship.[17]

Arbitration is also unique from the court system. People can blatantly not choose arbitrators because of their gender or race without the same restrictions that exist in the court system. Beyond explicit bias, implicit bias also influences a party's selection of arbitrators.[18] It goes beyond looks. There can be bias based on somebody's English skills or if they are an immigrant as well. Arbitrators are constantly trying to assess credibility in a hearing, and there is fear that an arbitrator will consider what somebody is wearing, size, height, age, if they have good hygiene, and so on, in making a decision about a person's trustworthiness. OArb also may bring in biases due to video "peeking" into people's homes. Zoom puts people in individuals' homes and cars—which opens the door to more perceptions and biases. Guardrails and OArb protocols should be in place to address these issues. This will be discussed in more detail in later chapters.

Still OArb may open the door to arbitration for some. For example, arbitrators and parties who face physical challenges may have more opportunities in OArb because they can avoid the hurdles of travel. Traveling to an arbitration hearing can be very difficult for some individuals with disabilities. Furthermore, an arbitrator in a wheelchair, for example, may feel more empowered and have better command of an online hearing. Screen readers and other accessibility assistance when online may also help arbitrators and parties, as well as attorneys, participate more fully in an arbitration that is online, versus traditional in-person hearings.

Confirmation bias may also be problematic in arbitration. If the arbitration does not end in a party's favor, implicit bias could turn into confirmation bias and prevent the party from working with a diverse arbitrator again. This puts a great deal of pressure on diverse arbitrators. There is fear that if anything goes poorly in an initial arbitration, newcomer arbitrators will never again get a chance to arbitrate.

Interviewees on the topic of diversity generally agreed that these challenges are tough to address, especially given that the parties generally have freedom to select who they want as the arbitrator. Nonetheless, interviews also revealed a variety of suggestions for promoting the selection of diverse arbitrators. Professor Sarah Cole from The Ohio State Moritz College of Law has provided ideas in her article, as well as in her interview in *The Arbitration Conversation*.[19] One suggestion included providing more in-depth background and information about arbitrators. Although this may seem to cut both ways, one interviewee also noted that it would be helpful to include arbitrators' photos.[20] Including a picture brings up potential drawbacks of playing into people's implicit biases based on how someone looks, but providing a photo could have a humanizing influence that encourages some parties to choose an arbitrator that they do not otherwise know. It takes away the fear of the unknown in some cases. Another idea would be to have the providers create lists with 30 to 35 percent diverse arbitrators and then have the parties label each arbitrator on the provider's list either acceptable or not acceptable. It could then be up to the arbitral provider to make the ultimate designation from the acceptable arbitrators.[21]

Another idea for promoting diversity is to essentially set quotas. For example, CPR developed a suggestion of requiring one out of three people on a panel of arbitrators to be a woman or a person of color to increase diversity.[22] This could raise some controversy, but CPR is a private entity and this would open the door for new arbitrators, especially, who may not otherwise get a chance to gain experience. Another suggestion is to have service providers use a selection algorithm that includes a higher percentage of diverse arbitrator candidates in the pool, thereby increasing chances for selection of a diverse arbitrator. Arbitration providers could also increase administrative assignment of diverse arbitrators in cases where parties do not have access to usual listing procedures, and the parties have not otherwise selected an arbitrator or arbitration panel on their own.[23] For example, AAA case administrators already have power to assign arbitrators to consumer cases, subject to challenges by the parties. Perhaps administrators could use randomized selection with greater numbers of diverse arbitrators in other cases as well. This would increase diverse arbitrator exposure, especially in comparison to current practice, which largely leaves the parties free to select the same arbitrators who they have always selected—who are mainly white men.[24]

In sum, there is great need to promote arbitrator diversity and to open doors for new arbitrators. Selecting the same arbitrators repeatedly does not provide opportunity for new individuals to enter the field. This is problematic for arbitration and creates an unhealthy cycle. Indeed, it is important for stakeholders to come together and identify means for change. It is not sufficient to state goals without providing action items. It is hoped that we can work as a community to design spaces where members can gather and share ideas and communicate among themselves. The dispute resolution community is generally a problem-solving community, and it is hoped that we can problem-solve to change the trajectory of arbitration and open the field to new voices.

NOTES

1 Concerns regarding ethnic and gender diversity in dispute resolution have drawn increasing attention in recent years. *See* David H. Burt & Laura A. Kaster, *Why Bringing Diversity to ADR Is a Necessity*, Ass'n of Corp. Couns. (2013), https://appropriatedisputesolutions.com/site/wp-content/uploads/2013/01/Why-Bringing-Diversity-to-ADR-is-a-Necessity.pdf.

2 For related commentary and research, see Susan D. Franck et al., *The Diversity Challenge: Exploring the "Invisible College" of International Arbitration*, 53 Colum. J. Transnat'l L. 429 (2015). *See also*, Joshua Karton & Amy Schmitz, *Arbitration Conversation #35: Prof. Joshua Karton, Queens University Law School*, YouTube (Aug. 31, 2020), https://www.youtube.com/watch?v=iKIHnI3msz8 (discussing research regarding diversity and the importance of social connections and networking in arbitration).

3 Thomas Stipanowich, Reflections on the State and Future of Commercial Arbitration 363–66 (2014).

4 Benjamin Davis & Amy Schmitz, *Arbitration Conversation No. 4: Amy Interviews Prof. Benjamin Davis of University of Toledo College of Law*, Arbitrate.com (July 27, 2020), https://arbitrate.com/arbitration-conversation-no-4-amy-interviews-prof-benjamin-davis-of-university-of-toledo-college-of-law/.

5 *See* Sarah Rudolph Cole & Amy Schmitz, *Arbitration Conversation No. 7: Prof. Sarah Cole of the Moritz College of Law at OSU*, Arbitrate.com (Aug. 24, 2020), https://arbitrate.com/arbitration-conversation-no-7-prof-sarah-cole-of-the-moritz-college-of-law-at-osu/.

6 International Chamber of Commerce, ICC Dispute Resolution 2020 Statistics 4–31 (2021).

7 Mirèze Philippe & Amy Schmitz, *Arbitration Conversation No. 36: Mirèze Philippe Special Counsel ICC International Court of Arbitration*, YouTube (Aug. 31, 2020), https://www.youtube.com/watch?v=6URk_FvjHX0.

8 Davis & Schmitz, *supra* note 4.

9 Cole & Schmitz, *supra* note 5; Stephen Ware & Amy Schmitz, *Arbitration Conversation No. 45: Prof. Stephen Ware, Kansas University School of Law*, Arbitrate.com (Feb. 3, 2021), https://arbitrate.com/arbitration-conversation-no-45-prof-stephen-ware-kansas-university-school-of-law/.

10 *See* Davis & Schmitz, *supra* note 4.

11 Michael Green & Amy Schmitz, *Arbitration Conversation No. 16: Prof. Michael Green of Texas A&M School of Law*, ARBITRATE.COM (Oct. 19, 2020), https://arbitrate.com/arbitration-conversation-no-16-prof-michael-green-of-texas-am-school-of-law/.
12 Davis & Schmitz, *supra* note 4.
13 *Id.*; Cole & Schmitz, *supra* note 5.
14 Philippe & Schmitz, *supra* note 7.
15 *Id.*
16 Green & Schmitz, *supra* note 11.
17 *See, e.g.*, Michael Z. Green, *Arbitrarily Selecting Black Arbitrators*, 88 FORDHAM L. REV. 2255 (2020).
18 Green & Schmitz, *supra* note 11; Ashley Rafael & Amy Schmitz, *Arbitration Conversation No. 71: Ashley Rafael, General Counsel, Midway Moving & Storage Inc.*, YOUTUBE (Mar. 5, 2021), www.youtube.com/watch?v=MZ8OLOxHNPM&ab_channel=arbitratedotcom.
19 Sarah Cole, *Arbitrator Diversity: Can It Be Achieved?*, 98 WASH. L. REV. 985 (2021) (noting that in 2012, AAA reported that 23 percent of its roster was diverse for gender and race).
20 Cole & Schmitz, *supra* note 5.
21 *Id.*
22 *Id.*
23 Green & Schmitz, *supra* note 11.
24 *Id.*

Chapter 6
Moving OArb into the Mainstream

As referenced throughout the book, there has been growth in OArb. OArb is just one example of ODR, which generally encompasses the use of technology to assist in preventing and resolving disputes. Technology has become an important tool in preventing and resolving disputes and deserves special attention in our increasingly digital world. Most ODR platforms, however, are not OArb because ODR involves the facilitation of communications to aid voluntary settlement.[1] In contrast, OArb is a distinct subset of ODR because it culminates in a final award rendered by a third-party neutral, which is usually enforceable under the FAA and New York Convention, as noted earlier. This finality is especially attractive where the parties need an expert to determine key issues of law and fact, and do not want to spend time merely negotiating or mediating the issues.

OArb includes virtual hearings, such as Zoom or Teams arbitration. It also includes a wide variety of other uses of technology and digital tools to facilitate and execute processes ending in a final determination of a dispute by a neutral third party. For example, OArb may use asynchronous and/or synchronous communications for parties to present their cases to third-party arbitrators in an online forum. Communications may be text-only or include virtual hearings, and mixtures thereof. OArb's use of technology also allows parties to upload and submit supporting documentation to support their claims at times that work in their schedules since there is no need to travel to a physical office. Online hearings also save time, cost, and stress of traveling to and attending in-person processes. Such OArb systems may even provide more accurate and complete redress than class actions in some cases.[2] Nonetheless, OArb may not be right for all cases or all people, and questions remain with respect to forcing OArb over a party's objection.

A. GROWTH OF OARB IN THE PANDEMIC

The idea of OArb is not new. E-commerce providers such as eBay have been using OArb for consumer disputes for a long time.[3] Nonetheless, there are now many OArb providers who provide text-only or video hearings.[4]

Moreover, traditional arbitration providers, such as the AAA and others, now provide virtual hearings, especially in the wake of the pandemic. Arbitration providers are now even partnering with ODR providers to have their own text-only and virtual hearing options.

Importantly, *The Arbitration Conversation* started during the Covid-19 pandemic, while OArb simultaneously spiked and became mainstream.[5] Virtual meeting technologies such as Zoom, Skype, Google Meet, WebEx, and Teams have made virtual hearings relatively cheap and easy. These video technologies became a lifeline for many during the pandemic shutdown, as individuals became accustomed to online communications during the lockdown.[6] Even in large-dollar claims, such as international construction deals, Covid-19 prompted parties to arbitrate online.[7] "The increase in the use of virtual hearing rooms appears to be the result of how the practice of arbitration has adapted in response to the COVID-19 pandemic, as users have been forced to explore alternatives to in-person hearings."[8] Arbitrators even began ordering virtual arbitration over a party's objection to ensure health and safety during the pandemic.[9]

Indeed, my interviews in *The Arbitration Conversation* evidence a dramatic expansion of OArb due to Covid-19 shutdowns and health restrictions. Additionally, as the interviews continued and the lockdown continued, interviewees began emphasizing how they believed that OArb and virtual hearings are likely to continue post-pandemic. The institutionalization of OArb also indicates that OArb is here to stay.[10]

OArb is no longer "exotic" or unusual, as it has become among the regular offerings of traditional dispute resolution institutions such as the AAA, the Judicial Arbitration and Mediation Service (JAMS), and the International Institute for Conflict Prevention & Resolution (CPR)—all prominent arbitral institutions that were referenced earlier. For example, the AAA offers a secure portal for parties to file claims, upload and manage their claim-related documents, and view and rank potential arbitrators for selection.[11] Arbitrators for AAA also use the portal to access and manage their cases.[12] In addition, the AAA offers virtual hearing capacity and guidance.[13] This includes Zoom hearings with the AAA as host, as well as direct assistance with the Zoom hearing. AAA also offers online arbitration training, as well as "protocol" documents and tips for using virtual platforms.

Although we could all observe the shift to OArb during the pandemic shutdown, it was especially helpful to also talk with arbitration leaders and experts regarding this shift in *The Arbitration Conversation*. As noted earlier in this book, the very first episode of *The Arbitration Conversation* shed light on how the AAA quickly pivoted to virtual hearings in the wake of the pandemic, building on the capacity that the AAA already had for the use of technology.[14] Accordingly, it is no surprise the AAA saw a massive increase in virtual hearings from March 2020 through May 2022.[15]

JAMS also offers various teleconferencing and videoconferencing options to assist in arbitration,[16] as does CPR.[17] In the wake of the pandemic, CPR also expanded their OArb online training sessions to help neutrals and advocates learn how to use Zoom to arbitrate online effectively.[18] OArb protocols have been issued by arbitral institutions and experts as well. These protocols generally outline best practices for virtual hearings, and Appendix A to this book includes many of the protocols that appeared in the wake of the Covid-19 pandemic. Additionally, CPR released an annotated model procedural order for video arbitration proceedings.[19] Of course, ad hoc arbitrators are also using virtual hearings—especially in the pandemic's wake.

Arbitrators and lawyers may be resistant to change, but the convenience and efficiency of OArb seem to be luring increasing numbers to take advantage of virtual hearing options. Hybrid options have expanded as well. For example, arbitral parties may choose to attend in person, while witnesses may be able to attend virtually. Having the online option may reduce travel time, help with scheduling, and assist with the expenses of a process. Still, there is always resistance to change and there are good reasons why OArb may not be best for some cases.[20]

B. RESISTANCE TO OARB

OArb is not without its critics. While OArb processes may empower some individuals by easing some of the social and power pressures of in-person communications, these processes may not work for all individuals in all cases. People continue to have differential access to technology and the internet.[21] This has become glaringly apparent in the wake of the pandemic, as families without adequate access to the internet struggled to educate their children during school shutdowns in the Covid-19 pandemic.[22] In 2020, Pew Research Center reported that one in five U.S. parents with schoolchildren at home during school shutdowns stated that it is very or somewhat likely their children will not complete their work due to lack of access to a computer or internet.[23] The shutdown taught that universal access to the internet is important.[24]

It is also important to note that there is differential access to technology based on income and background. In the U.S., Pew Research Center reported in 2019 that income remains an issue when it comes to internet access, as 99 percent of U.S. adults making more than $75,000 used the internet, in contrast with 86 percent of adults making less than $30,000 in 2019. Additionally, how one accesses the internet is essential when it comes to OArb, as those with high-speed Wi-Fi on a computer are generally better able to present their cases because they can more easily upload documents and engage with the proceedings. This is important considering that Pew reported, as of February 2021, that only 77 percent of U.S. adults used home broadband.[25] Indeed, mobile-friendly processes are essential and policymakers should work to expand internet access—especially for rural and vulnerable groups.[26] Furthermore, newcomers to OArb often need access to technical "helpers" to assist with the technology required for OArb. Individuals also should have access to free Wi-Fi and "kiosks" with help available for any ODR connected with the court.[27]

Even where individuals have access to the internet, that does not mean that they are comfortable with technology. For example, older individuals who did not grow up using technology may suffer a disadvantage in OArb. As another example, those who are comfortable with and knowledgeable about using Zoom have an advantage in Zoom hearings, as they may be more savvy regarding lighting and placement of a camera. They also know how to manipulate documents in a proceeding and work with breakout rooms, where necessary. Furthermore, an individual arbitrating from a quiet office will usually have an advantage over those stuck in a coffee shop or house full of children. Of course, this all becomes especially important when an arbitrator is assessing witnesses online to reach a final and binding decision. The stakes may not seem as high when parties and neutrals use virtual technologies for facilitating communications in a mediation, for example.

Some also may resist OArb due to the loss of face-to-face interactions and hallway conversations that can sometimes lead to settlements.[28] One interviewee in *The Arbitration Conversation* candidly stated after the online interview that this arbitrator strongly prefers in-person proceedings and did not intend to continue with OArb after the pandemic subsided. The reason was the loss of in-person interactions that may be more likely to help settlement. Even more recently, I have heard this sentiment among some arbitrators who prefer in-person hearings and have returned to in-person now that we are in a safer place with respect to the pandemic. Some researchers also have emphasized the importance of psychology and in-person interactions as a counterbalance to pro-ODR assumptions.[29] Arguably, Zoom breakout rooms and intermittent phone discussions during a proceeding may foster settlement, but in-person interactions continue to hold great importance.

Several arbitrators and advocates also have legitimate concerns about the use of remote technology for viewing and hearing evidence. For example, how can an arbitrator on Zoom or Teams be sure that a witness is not being coached off camera? Although witnesses may be clandestinely "coached" during in-person proceedings through secret notes, the online environment allows for a greater ability to coach witnesses. That said, there are precautions that arbitrators can take to prevent improper coaching in OArb. For example, arbitrators should ask witnesses to pan the room to show that there is no one else in the room. They also should disable "chat" functions within conferencing software (such as Zoom) and require witnesses to be sworn in, promising to tell the truth and refrain from improper communications. Attorneys should also understand that they violate ethical rules if they secretly "guide" witnesses in their answers. See also the index of OArb protocols added as Appendix A to this book—as many have established tips and tricks for ethical and efficient OArb hearings.

In sum, OArb expanded exponentially during the Covid-19 pandemic. However, that does not mean it is right for all people or all cases. In-person arbitration should remain an option, and arbitrators should take special care to ensure all parties in OArb feel comfortable with the process and have the full ability to present their cases. In some cases, this may even mean that the arbitrator should call for a continuance amid a virtual hearing to allow for completion through in-person hearings to be sure all parties have a full and fair opportunity to present their cases. Nonetheless, it is also important to remember that people are generally resistant to change, especially when it requires that they learn new things—and this tends to be an issue with OArb. Arbitrators should learn how to ethically and efficiently handle OArb hearings and provide this option to parties, who often benefit from this capacity.

C. WHAT IF A PARTY OBJECTS?

There is no question that OArb is here to stay, and many parties will prefer OArb due to the cost and time savings. Also, arbitrators and advocates have become accustomed to the convenience of virtual hearings. Most of those interviewed confirmed that they had become accustomed to the time, cost, and "stress" savings of avoiding travel and in-person hearings, even despite the drawbacks in some instances (as noted earlier). At the same time, arbitral rules confirm the availability of OArb, and the law around the FAA and digital contracts continue to call for the enforcement of digital arbitration agreements. Furthermore, arbitrators generally have quite a bit of discretion in determining the process and manner for arbitral hearings, provided that it is within the bounds of the applicable arbitral rules and the parties' agreements. Still, there are limitations on this discretion, and fairness must remain paramount.

The FAA provides for the enforcement of arbitration agreements according to their terms. The law certainly does not address virtual arbitration, as the idea would have been inconceivable at the act's passage in 1925! Virtual hearings would have seemed like a science fiction novel. Nonetheless, most have endorsed the enforcement of electronically created agreements and electronically submitted awards, so why not enforce OArb?[30] This is fortified by the E-Sign Act, which "prohibits any interpretation of the FAA's 'written provision' requirement that would preclude giving legal effect to an agreement solely on the basis that it was in electronic form."[31]

Consent remains central to the enforcement of arbitration agreements. Accordingly, how do we know that the parties have consented to OArb where the contract merely calls for "arbitration" and says nothing about the virtual option? The FAA only calls for the enforcement of consensual and valid arbitration clauses.[32] Does blanket assent to "arbitration" include an agreement to online hearings? What if a party objects to online hearings? The National Arbitration Academy (NAA) was one of the first organizations to issue an opinion on ordering online hearings over a party's objection early during the Covid-19 pandemic.[33] On April 1, 2020, the NAA issued Advisory Opinion No. 26, allowing an arbitrator to require parties to participate in virtual hearings without mutual consent in certain extraordinary circumstances.[34] There was concern that respondents would object to online hearings as a tactic to postpone arbitration. Respondents generally benefit from delay. Out of concern for efficiency and addressing this gamesmanship, the NAA found that it may be proper for an arbitrator to order virtual hearings over a party's objection where the "hearing has been postponed previously, an opposition party is non-responsive or declines to provide a reasonable explanation, and/or the case involves continuing liability or time-sensitive matters."[35]

Fairness matters. The NAA advisory opinion stresses that an arbitrator ordering online hearings should be confident that all the parties involved are familiar and comfortable with the video platform to be used.[36] Furthermore, the arbitrator may only order online arbitration where the parties will have "a fair and reasonable opportunity to present their case and will allow the hearing to move forward on the dates previously scheduled."[37] Other arbitral institutions have issued similar guidance, and a wise arbitrator should seriously consider these questions to ensure they do not exceed their authority in ordering online hearings. Exceeding authority is a chief reason that arbitral awards are overturned.

Some courts have also faced arguments related to ordering virtual hearings under the FAA or similar laws. For example, related issues were raised in *Legaspy v. Financial Industry Regulatory Authority, Inc.*[38] In this case, Legaspy asked to stop FINRA from holding a virtual arbitration hearing, but the district court refused Legaspy's request. The parties had signed an agreement saying the hearing would be held at a time and place designated by the director of FINRA, and it would be conducted per FINRA's Code of Arbitration Procedure. The arbitration was scheduled for August 17, 2020, in Florida, but because of Covid-19, FINRA told the parties on June 23, 2020, that the hearing would be either rescheduled or held online through Zoom or telephone conference. Legaspy argued that the online proceedings would be overly burdensome, especially because the other parties would need an interpreter and the cost would exceed his insurance coverage. The court disagreed, concluding that the FINRA rules gave the arbitrators discretion to hold virtual hearings, and Legaspy did not provide sufficient evidence that he could not present an effective defense over Zoom—even if Zoom may be "clunkier than in-person hearings."[39]

As the court noted in *Sullivan v. Feldman*:[40]

> [C]ourts have recognized that "appearing" in a particular location is easier with modern technology. For example, some courts have held that technology allows arbitration decisions to be made in a place other than where the arbitrators are physically located or the final decision is signed."[41] This highlights the courts 'deference to arbitrators' choice of venue, including an online forum.

That does not mean that the arguments against virtual hearings will always fail. In some cases, ordering online hearings could be unreasonable where a party lacks access to or facility with the internet and other required technology. For example, an arbitration agreement's forum selection clause can be unconscionable where the place and manner are unduly burdensome or oppressive for a party.[42] There also are cases where a party has physical limitations that make online participation burdensome. An individual also may lack the required know-how to participate in an online hearing. These are all considerations for an arbitrator to consider. True, arbitrators have quite a bit of discretion in setting the place and manner for arbitration hearings—but fundamental fairness must be respected. Accordingly, it would be unreasonable to force a party to arbitrate online where the party lacked access to and/or comfort with the required technologies. Optionality remains important for fairness and process satisfaction.

D. SUMMARIZING THE EVOLUTION

In sum, as technologies expand, so too does OArb. Its benefits became apparent with the Covid-19 pandemic. When properly designed, OArb may allow individuals to resolve disputes quickly and cheaply, without the cost or hassle of travel or time away from work. That is not to say OArb is perfect or suited to every case or every individual. A digital divide persists, and we must all consider the ethical parameters of ODR as well as the need to protect and expand A2J.[43] The next chapters will dive further into lessons learned in discussing various aspects of OArb as well as practical aspects of arbitration more generally. At the end of the day, technology is not all good or all bad—it is how one uses it. In arbitration, it should be considered along with all other tools with a practical and problem-solving mindset.

NOTES

1 *See generally* Amy J. Schmitz & Colin Rule, *The New Handshake: Online Dispute Resolution and the Future of Consumer Protection* (A.B.A. 2017); *see also* Amy J. Schmitz, *Building on OArb Attributes in Pursuit of Justice*, *in* Arbitration in the Digital Age: The Brave New World of Arbitration 182 (Maud Piers & Christian Aschauer eds., 2018).

2 *See generally* Linda S. Mullenix, *Ending Class Actions as We Know Them: Rethinking the American Class Action*, 64 Emory L.J. 39 (2014).
3 Amy J. Schmitz, *"Drive-Thru" Arbitration in the Digital Age: Empowering Consumers through Regulated ODR*, 62 Baylor L. Rev. 178–244 (2010).
4 Amy J. Schmitz & Janet Martinez, *ODR Providers Operating in the U.S.*, *in* ODR in the United States, Online Dispute Resolution: Theory and Practice: A Treatise on Technology and Dispute Resolution (Mohamed S. Abdel Wahab, Ethan Katsh & Daniel Rainey eds., 2020), chart is freely available at https://ssrn.com/abstract=3599511.
5 Melody Alger, *Conducting Arbitrations and Mediations Remotely during the Covid-19 Crisis and Beyond*, 68 R.I.B.J. 15 (May 2020).
6 *See Use of Technology: The Virtual Reality*, *in* 2021 International Arbitration Survey: Adapting Arbitration to a Changing World, White & Case LLP (May 6, 2021), www.whitecase.com/publications/insight/2021-international-arbitration-survey/technology-virtual-reality.
7 *Id.*; Andrey Panov, *Post-COVID-19 World and the Duty to Conduct Arbitrations Efficiently and Expeditiously*, Thomson Reuters (Aug. 13, 2020), http://arbitrationblog.practicallaw.com/post-covid-19-world-and-the-duty-to-conduct-arbitrations-efficiently-and-expeditiously/; Mark Shope, *The International Arbitral Institution Response to COVID-19 and Opportunities for Online Dispute Resolution*, 13(1) Contemp. Asia Arb. J. 67, 77 (May 2020).
8 2021 International Arbitration Survey, *supra* note 6. "When discussing virtual hearings, two key takeaways emerged from interviews. First, there appears to be a growing expectation that virtual hearings will become the default option in the future for procedural hearings and conferences." *Id.*
9 Karen Maxwell, *Could Arbitration Support Courts during the COVID-19 Crisis?*, Thomson Reuters (May 27, 2020), http://arbitrationblog.practicallaw.com/could-arbitration-support-courts-during-the-covid-19-crisis/.
10 Alger, *supra* note 5.
11 *AAA-ICDR Technology Services*, Am. Arb. Ass'n, www.adr.org/TechnologyServices/aaa-icdr-software-and-online-tools (last visited Nov. 13, 2023).
12 *Id.*
13 Svetlana Gitman & Amy Schmitz, *Arbitration Conversation No. 1: Svetlana Gitman, American Arbitration Association*, Arbitrate.com (July 14, 2020), https://arbitrate.com/arbitration-conversation-episode-1-svetlana-gitman-american-arbitration-association/; *AAA-ICDR Virtual Hearing Guide for Arbitrators and Parties*, Am. Arb. Ass'n (2021), https://go.adr.org/rs/294-SFS-516/images/AAA268_AAA%20Virtual%20Hearing%20Guide%20for%20Arbitrators%20and%20Parties.pdf.
14 Gitman & Schmitz, *supra* note 13.
15 *AAA-ICDR Virtual Events*, Am. Arb. Ass'n, https://go.adr.org/virtual-hearing-statistics (last visited Nov. 13, 2023). Of 19,911 events, 11,372 cases had a virtual event (time range: March 1, 2020–May 16, 2022).
16 *Setting the Industry Standard: Virtual Mediation and Arbitration*, JAMS, www.jamsadr.com/online (last visited Nov. 13, 2023).
17 International Institute for Conflict Prevention & Resolution, www.cpradr.org/dispute-resolution-services/services-offered/arbitration (last visited Nov. 13, 2023).
18 *ADR in the Time of COVID-19: How Neutrals & Advocates Can Use Zoom for Mediations & Arbitrations*, Int'l Inst. for Conflict Prevention & Resol. (Mar. 30, 2020), https://www.cpradr.org/news/adr-in-the-time-of-covid-19-how-neutrals-and-advocates-can-use-zoom-for-mediations--arbitrations.

19 CPR's Annotated Model Procedural Order for Remote Video Arbitration Proceedings, CPR Dispute Resolution, https://static.cpradr.org/docs/4.21%20FINAL%20Annotated%20Model%20Procedural%20Order%20for%20Remote%20Video%20Arbitration%20Proceedings.pdf (last visited Nov. 13, 2023).
20 Amy J. Schmitz, *Arbitration in the Age of Covid: Examining Arbitration's Move Online*, 22 Cardozo J. Conflict Resol. 245–92 (2021).
21 Thom File, *Computer and Internet Use in the United States*, U.S. Census Bureau (May 2013), https://www.census.gov/library/publications/2013/demo/p20-569.html.
22 Suzanne Woolley, Nikitha Sattiraju & Scott Moritz, *U.S. Schools Trying to Teach Online Highlight a Digital Divide*, Bloomberg (Mar. 26, 2020, 7:00 AM), www.bloomberg.com/news/articles/2020-03-26/covid-19-school-closures-reveal-disparity-in-access-to-internet (noting that NYC has an estimated 300,000 students without access to electronics).
23 Emily A. Vogels, Andrew Perrin, Lee Rainie & Monica Anderson, *53% of Americans Say the Internet Has Been Essential during the COVID-19 Outbreak*, Pew Rsch. Ctr. (Apr. 30, 2020), www.pewresearch.org/internet/2020/04/30/53-of-americans-say-the-internet-has-been-essential-during-the-covid-19-outbreak/.
24 Dana Goldstein, *The Class Divide: Remote Learning at 2 Schools, Private and Public*, N.Y. Times (June 5, 2020), www.nytimes.com/2020/05/09/us/coronavirus-public-private-school.html.
25 *See* Vogels et al., *supra* note 23.
26 *See, e.g.*, Rebecca R. Ruiz, *F.C.C. Chief Seeks Broadband Plan to Aid the Poor*, N.Y. Times (May 28, 2015), www.nytimes.com/2015/05/28/business/fcc-chief-seeks-broadband-plan-to-aid-the-poor.html (discussing plans to expand access to the internet for the poor).
27 Amy J. Schmitz, *Expanding Access to Remedies through E-Court Initiatives*, 67 Buffalo L. Rev. 101, 110–60 (2019).
28 Adam Samuel, *Now Plaguing Dispute Resolution Processes: Proceeding in ADR without the Handshakes*, 38 Alternatives to High Cost Litig. 71 (2020).
29 Jean R. Sternlight, *Pouring a Little Psychological Cold Water on Online Dispute Resolution*, 2020 J. Disp. Resol. 1, 1–30 (2020).
30 Caleb Gerbitz, *Are Pre-Dispute Agreements to Arbitrate Online Enforceable?*, 7 Arb. Brief (Jan. 25, 2020), https://ssrn.com/abstract=3561674.
31 Campbell v. Gen. Dynamics Gov't Sys. Corp., 407 F.3d 546, 547–79 (1st Cir. 2005).
32 *See* Theroff v. Dollar Tree Stores, Inc., 591 S.W.3d 432 (Mo. Sup. Ct. 2020) (en banc). In this case, the court held that a party did not consent to arbitration where a former Dollar Tree employee who was legally blind was never provided with a reasonable means to read and understand a form arbitration provision included in hiring paperwork. *Id.*
33 *Formal Advisory Opinion No. 26: Video Hearings*, Comm. on Pro. Resp. & Grievances, Nat'l Acad. of Arbitrators (Apr. 1, 2020), https://naarb.org/wp-content/uploads/2020/04/CPRG-Opinion-Summaries-4.13.2020.pdf.
34 *Id.*
35 *Id.*
36 P. Jean Baker, *During the Pandemic, Virtual Arbitration Offers a Promising Alternative—Provided You Know What You Are Doing*, 74(4) Disp. Resol. J. 157, 157–64 (2020).
37 *Id.*
38 Legaspy v. Fin. Indus. Regul. Auth., Inc., N.D. Ill. 2020 WL 4696818 (2020).

39 *Id.* at 4.
40 Sullivan v. Feldman, CV H-20–2236, 2020 WL 7129879 (S.D. Tex. Dec. 4, 2020).
41 *See, e.g.*, Moyett v. Lugo-Sanchez, 321 F. Supp. 3d 263, 267 (D.P.R. 2018) ("Despite the physical distance between the arbitrators, who may physically be in Georgia, and the FINRA litigants, who are in Puerto Rico, the arbitrators 'sit' in Puerto Rico with the aid of videoconferencing technology."); NGC Network Asia, LLC v. PAC Pac. Grp. Int'l, Inc., No. 09-CV-8684, 2010 WL 3701351, at *3 (S.D.N.Y. Sept. 20, 2010) ("[A]n arbitration award is 'made' in the district where the hearing is held, not the place from which the award was written or mailed." (citation omitted)). *Id.* at *9.
42 Nagrampa v. MailCoups, Inc., 469 F.3d 1257 (9th Cir. 2006).
43 Rebecca L. Sandefur, *The Fulcrum Point of Equal Access to Justice: Legal and Nonlegal Institutions of Remedy*, 42 Loy. L.A. L. Rev. 950–54 (2009).

Chapter 7

Practice Makes Perfect

Another theme that emerged from many of the conversations was the need for parties and arbitrators to "practice" and test technology before launching into video hearings. Technology aside, the interviews highlighted how any individual involved in arbitration needs to consider practicalities, gain experience, and learn from others with practice experience. As with anything, preparation and practice are essential. Upon reflection, *The Arbitration Conversation* interviews also highlighted the importance of exercises like this—these many interviews with experts—because these interviews help illuminate practical aspects of arbitration proceedings. These interviews help one "look under the hood" and learn about the arbitration process so that they can better prepare for their next arbitration. Arbitration is private, and usually confidential where the parties so provide. This means that there is relatively little information about arbitration practice outside of more formal textbooks—which largely focus on law instead of practice. These interviews therefore open a unique window into arbitration practice.

A. DISCUSSING PRACTICE WITH LONG-TIME ARBITRATORS

In the ninth episode of the audio podcasts, legendary arbitrator John Allen Chalk spoke.[1] The conversation illuminated the importance of practice and learning from those who have arbitrated for many years. Arbitrator Chalk discussed his experience arbitrating for more than 30 years, conducting more than 700 arbitrations during that time. Arbitrator Chalk practiced law in various capacities and first served as a mediator before a colleague convinced him to try arbitration. He enjoyed the experience, and the rest is history.

Focusing on lessons learned, Arbitrator Chalk first emphasized the necessity for discipline and preparation in arbitration. All too often, there is a tendency for free-flowing discussion in arbitration hearings, following no schedule or delineated plan. Some arbitrators fail to organize the discussion and provide direction on the flow of the hearings. It is important to have a clear schedule and organization for the evidentiary hearings. Arbitrators can provide a great service by applying disciplined restraint and providing the parties with a suggested schedule for the presentation of evidence and indicating the key questions upon which evidence is needed. Other arbitrators have noted the same, and I have seen the importance of organization in streamlining the process.

As an offshoot of this observation, Arbitrator Chalk emphasized that "less is better"—making it essential that arbitrators thoughtfully write succinct orders and awards. Unfortunately, some arbitrators use long templates and spend too much time in writing overly lengthy awards—needlessly adding to the cost for the parties when the arbitrators are charging by the hour. Indeed, I clerked for a judge that told me to make all my legal memos and draft opinions "half as long and twice as good"—which has turned out to be one of the best lessons I could have learned as a new attorney. Moreover, it is essential that arbitrators are timely in providing awards and orders of any kind. Timeliness is essential, and arbitrators owe the parties expediency.

Arbitrator Chalk also emphasized the importance of practice and preparation, noting that arbitrators must treat any process as serious. Arbitrator Chalk noted that there is a myth that the process belongs only to the parties. It is up to the arbitrator to seriously manage the process and pay attention to deadlines. Furthermore, arbitrators need to spend time upfront learning the issues and reading the case docket materials. There is an incentive for arbitrators to wait to study materials, especially in cases in which the arbitrator is paid a low flat fee for each case. In these cases, the arbitrator is uncertain whether the case will be settled up until the date of the hearings, creating incentive to wait in reading case materials. Still, it is essential for arbitrators to remain vigilant in their preparation and realize that this is their civil and ethical duty. Indeed, it is an honor to serve as an arbitrator, and the best arbitrators are cognizant of this fact and continually remain prepared! It is wise for an arbitrator to donate time rather than charge for time spent getting up to speed, and the donation of time on flat fee cases can be helpful in gaining experience and expertise.

Additional insights and lessons learned emerged from Chalk's many years of practice. Arbitrator Chalk also noted the importance of certainty in making decisions and writing opinions that leave no doubts or issues left unanswered. Arbitrators should not merely ruminate, especially during a hearing. Moreover, they should listen more than they speak. "Don't enjoy the sound of your own voice" is generally good advice, and even more important when serving as an arbitrator. Having a great deal of experience can backfire and turn into a negative when arbitrators waste parties' time pontificating or sharing war stories. Instead, it is wise to listen actively, take notes, and deeply consider the evidence presented. Furthermore, arbitrators must remain true to the parties' agreement. This resonates with the consensual underpinnings of arbitration!

Many years of arbitral practice also revealed important lessons learned in speaking with Arbitrator Bill McGrath regarding motions practice and tips related to a successful arbitration practice.[2] There are various types of motions in arbitration, not all that different than in a courtroom. There are motions regarding discovery (for example, motions to compel the production of documents), dispositive motions, motions for preliminary relief, and even motions related to joinder and whether proper parties are in front of the tribunal. In fact, there is criticism that arbitration has become too much like litigation due to all the motions that often become part of an arbitral process.

Accordingly, it is wise for arbitrators to have a practical view and discourage motions when possible. First, parties should meet and confer before filing motions and seek permission from the arbitrator before having leave to file a motion. Arbitrators have a legitimate power to deny leave to file a motion where it appears that the motion lacks merit and a party is seeking to delay the process or otherwise game the system. Nonetheless, arbitrators must be careful in providing parties with a full and fair opportunity to be heard. There is a continual tension: arbitrators seek to promote efficiency, but they must ensure a full a fair opportunity to be heard regardless of the time involved. Furthermore, arbitrators are unlikely to grant dispositive motions unless it is a very clear case under legal rules that apply without question.

From practice and experience, attorneys in arbitration should learn to be careful in filing dispositive motions. An attorney is wise not to file a dispositive motion unless they have a very strong showing that their client has a substantial likelihood of winning the motion. Unfortunately, the urge remains for attorneys to file dispositive motions due to education and experience enmeshed in a litigator mindset. Additionally, representatives should carefully consider the costs and benefits of filing any motions. It is generally not worth the costs and time to file a dispositive motion when there are factual issues in dispute that warrant further consideration in an evidentiary proceeding. The bar is perhaps higher in obtaining a summary award in arbitration versus litigation. Arbitrators fear that the award will be overturned for failure to provide a full opportunity to present one's case if they grant a motion for summary disposition. Indeed, summary dispositions are quite rare in arbitration.

Representatives in arbitration must also be careful to not waste time and money with motions regarding evidentiary issues. It is again wise for attorneys to consider the cost/benefit analysis of a motion even when considering evidentiary motions. What is the likelihood of success? How important is the motion to the case? Why do you need this motion? What is the cost in terms of billable hours and arbitrator hours with respect to the motion? Any profession "banking" on inefficiency must change, and attorney ethical duties require that attorneys not augment bills to their clients. In other words, the legal profession should not "bank"—or increase its profits—by ignoring ways to be more efficient in order to lower billable hours.

B. EMPHASIZING PRACTICE WHEN LEARNING NEW TECHNOLOGIES

Practice is also essential when thinking about the use of technology. It is wise to have "practice" sessions, such as testing the actual computer or phone, microphone, and setup for virtual hearings. Also, setting up an in-person arbitration room is important for traditional hearings, although this is often overlooked or ignored. Some of the arbitrators discussed the need for hiring a technical assistant to help run OArb hearings if one is not very tech savvy. Furthermore, quite a few arbitrators noted how they improved in their use of new technologies after a few virtual hearings—again highlighting the need for practice.

Arbitrator Julie Hopkins spoke regarding her paper titled "Virtual Practice Makes Virtually Perfect—Practical Considerations for Virtual Hearings Identified through Simulations with Experienced Counsel and Arbitrators."[3] Arbitrator Hopkins delved into the key points discussed in the episode, highlighting the importance of building one's profile as an arbitrator, the significance of technological proficiency in Zoom hearings, and the challenges surrounding oaths and affirmations in virtual proceedings.

Arbitrator Hopkins noted that building a successful career as an arbitrator requires a strong profile. While this can be challenging for women, it is essential to bring something unique to the table that sets you apart from others. By developing specific expertise or a distinctive perspective, arbitrators can effectively market themselves to potential clients and peers. Additionally, to excel as an arbitrator, individuals must invest time in acquiring the necessary skills and knowledge. This involves participating in arbitration training programs, seeking speaking and publishing opportunities, and actively engaging with arbitral organizations. These activities enhance an arbitrator's practical experience, credibility, reputation, and professional network.

Arbitrator Hopkins also provided information on practice for Zoom or other virtual hearings. The success of a virtual hearing heavily relies on the knowledge and skills of all involved parties. Conducting pre-hearing technical "dry run" meetings is crucial as it allows participants to familiarize themselves with the platform, resolve technical issues in advance, and establish a smooth workflow. Implementing this practice as a requirement can effectively address potential problems that may arise during the hearing.

Interestingly, many do not think about their internet speed for OArb. Since the quality of a virtual hearing depends on the participants' internet connection, it is imperative for everyone involved to conduct speed tests beforehand. Participants can mitigate disruptions and minimize audio and video lag by ensuring stable and reliable internet connectivity. This practice is particularly vital for individuals using older computers or attending from less secure locations. To optimize efficiency and convenience during virtual hearings, participants should consider using two screens—one for videoconferencing and another for accessing relevant documents. This setup allows for seamless navigation between video feeds and reference materials, promoting better focus and organization throughout the proceedings. Of course, this raises questions about accessibility as noted earlier, as not everyone can afford the optimal setup.

Everyone is also worried about the veracity of individuals online. Once again, practice is essential. In virtual hearings, it is common for arbitrators, attorneys, and witnesses to be located in different physical spaces. This poses a challenge when determining the appropriate method for administering oaths and affirmations. To ensure consistency and adherence to legal requirements, it is crucial to establish the correct oath or affirmation process before the hearing commences. This helps prevent confusion or disputes regarding the validity of statements made during the proceedings. Parties involved should strive to agree on this matter before the hearing, promoting a smooth and fair arbitration process. Moreover, practice and a dry-run remain foundational.

C. PRACTICE MATTERS, IN PERSON AND ONLINE!

Above all, it is important to consider practice, and learn from those that go before us. This is true for the day-to-day practice. This includes questions around best practices for managing arbitration hearings and dealing with motions, as well as for dealing with technology. Everyone is encouraged to learn from others and be curious about learning. Practice matters and talking with those who have experience is priceless! This is a central lesson learned from *The Arbitration Conversation*.

NOTES

1 John Allen Chalk & Amy Schmitz, *Arbitration Conversation No. 9: Arbitrator John Allen Chalk*, PodBean (Sept. 8, 2022), https://arbitrate.podbean.com/e/episode-9-arbitrator-john-allen-chalk/.

2 Bill McGrath & Amy Schmitz, *Arbitration Conversation No. 17: Arbitrator Bill McGrath of Davis McGrath in Chicago*, Arbitrate.Com (Oct. 26, 2020), https://arbitrate.com/arbitration-conversation-no-17-arbitrator-bill-mcgrath-of-davis-mcgrath-in-chicago/.

3 Julie Hopkins & Amy Schmitz, *Arbitration Conversation No. 57: Independent Arbitrator Julie G. Hopkins from Calgary, Canada*, Arbitrate.Com (Apr. 28, 2021, https://arbitrate.com/arbitration-conversation-no-57-independent-arbitrator-julie-g-hopkins-from-calgary-canada/.

Chapter 8
Eyes on SCOTUS and Congress

The U.S. Supreme Court (SCOTUS) has been very influential in driving the expansion of arbitration and adding significant judicial gloss to the FAA. Furthermore, there have been quite a few important arbitration cases in the Court since the inception of *The Arbitration Conversation*. It is no surprise that some of the interviews focused on SCOTUS arbitration cases. The Court has been active in further shaping FAA jurisprudence in the past three years, and there were an additional five new cases decided in 2022 alone. The related interviews provide important insights and takeaways regarding the trajectory of arbitration law under the current U.S. Supreme Court. In addition to interviews through *The Arbitration Conversation*, we also convened a panel of experts to discuss the 2022 SCOTUS arbitration cases. Furthermore, the interviews shed light on proposed and adopted congressional action.

A. SCOTUS

This part A chronicles these discussions and sets the interviews in the larger context of SCOTUS's interest in arbitration. The "lessons learned" here include the need for arbitrators and counsel to stay up on legal developments. Some arbitrators who have been around for a long time may have an urge to become complacent about the law, but that is dangerous. The cases discussed in the interviews and 2022 online symposium suggest that it has not been easy to predict arbitration case outcomes in recent times, and complacency is unwise. This chapter is included as a warning for practitioners, neutrals, students, and academics to remain updated on the changes in arbitration law.

In the first episodes of *The Arbitration Conversation*, Professor and Arbitrator Bob Bailey spoke regarding an important SCOTUS case examining the "transportation worker" exception under the FAA.[1] The case in question is *New Prime v. Oliveira*, in which the Court unanimously held that the FAA section 1 exception for transportation workers includes all "workers," comprising both employees and independent contractors. Specifically,

FAA section 1 states, "nothing herein contained shall apply to contracts of employment of seamen, railroad employees, or any other class of workers engaged in foreign or interstate commerce." Justice Gorsuch, writing for the Court, first found that the decision of whether this section 1 exclusion applies in a given FAA case belongs to a court of law and not an arbitrator. The Court also clarified that section 1 excludes all transportation workers, including independent contractors, from its coverage. It is important to consider that this case was narrow because it was decided on its limited facts dealing with truck drivers who clearly work in the transportation industry.

Nonetheless, this case signaled some important "lessons learned" regarding the leanings of the changing SCOTUS. The opinion exemplifies the increasingly textualist approach of the Supreme Court, even when it comes to arbitration. For many years, commentators' analysis lacked focus on the nuances of SCOTUS's holdings regarding arbitration. It was a general expectation that the holdings would be pro-enforcement and pro-business when it came to arbitration. This changed with the *New Prime* case, by signaling that holdings will not necessarily be pro-enforcement and pro-business going forward. Instead, the Court focused on the language of the FAA in finding that there was a hierarchy in its sections, so a court must first determine whether the section 1 exclusion applies before it could order arbitration per sections 2 through 4. When questioning the meaning of "worker" in 1925, when the FAA was passed, the Court refused to consider the nuances of "employee" versus "independent contractor" per more modern law. Instead, it concluded that the definition included independent contractors because that would have been the understanding when the FAA was enacted in 1925.

Although not a SCOTUS example, Canada has also wrestled with arbitration clauses in the contracts of independent contractors. And the interview on *Uber Technologies v. Heller* in Canada relates to the questions under discussion in this chapter.[2] Anthony Daimsis focused on this *Uber* case in Canada.[3] In this case, Uber drivers joined together to bring a class action against Uber seeking damages for various violations of employment law in Canada. The key issues focused on the enforcement of arbitration clauses in the Uber driver contracts. The Canadian Supreme Court held that the arbitration clause was unconscionable and therefore unenforceable. This added another layer to these transportation worker agreements under Canadian law. This case clarified unconscionability law in Canada, focusing on two prongs: (1) proof of inequality in the position of parties at the negotiation stage and (2) proof of an improvident bargain (e.g., bad deal). In totality, the Canadian Court questioned whether this appears to be abusive—was it an attempt to preclude remedies? From a comparative view, this is an interesting case because the transportation worker exception would have been a point of inquiry if this were in the U.S. Moreover, the *New Prime* case left many unanswered questions for Uber and Lyft drivers, and the Canada example may be important in considering the "transportation worker" exemption in tandem with unconscionability law in the U.S.

In interviewing Professor Chris Drahozal, he provided insights on another SCOTUS arbitration case.[4] The case was *Henry Schein, Inc. v. Archer and White Sales, Inc.*[5] This was a case that was heard by SCOTUS twice. In round I, the Court held that even if an arbitration claim is "wholly groundless," the arbitrator, not the court, must decide whether the parties must arbitrate where the agreement includes a delegation clause. In round II of the *Henry Schein* case, the Court focused on carve-outs from arbitration clauses, which are provisions within arbitration agreements that specify that certain types of disputes are not arbitrable.

In this case, there was a carve-out for injunctive relief, which is relatively common, because parties seek to preserve the power to go directly to a court when seeking to stop potentially damaging action, such as misusing intellectual property. The question for the Court was whether an arbitrator or court should decide whether a carve-out applies. This becomes more complicated when the parties have agreed that the AAA rules apply, because the rules include a delegation provision that gives arbitrators the power to rule on their own jurisdiction.

The U.S. Court of Appeals for the Fifth Circuit had held that courts should decide whether a carve-out applies, even where there is a delegation clause through the application of the AAA rules. SCOTUS punted the question in *Henry Schein, Inc. v. Archer and White Sales, Inc.*,[6] dismissing certiorari as improvidently granted. Cert was dismissed and the case proceeded to court, not arbitration. An important lesson learned was the importance of clear contract drafting. The lengthy and expensive litigation over these issues harmed the efficiency of arbitration. This could have been prevented with clear contract drafting that designated that the court must decide on the carve-out application, which would make sense in that the parties usually want to be able to proceed directly to court when they include such a provision. The ambiguity caused litigation because the AAA rules conflicted with the spirit of the carve-out in *Henry Schein, Inc.*

Related to *The Arbitration Conversation*, we convened a special symposium related to the SCOTUS arbitration cases in 2022.[7] The following cases were discussed:

1. ***Badgerow v. Walters, No. 20-1143.*** On March 31, where SCOTUS found in an 8–1 decision that the "*look through*" doctrine does not apply to applications to confirm or vacate arbitration awards under sections 9 and 10 of the FAA. This means that award challenges must rely on diversity jurisdiction to get into federal court.
2. ***Morgan v. Sundance Inc., No. 21-328.*** On May 23, SCOTUS ruled unanimously that there is no "*prejudice requirement*" under the FAA for a court to find a waiver of arbitration rights. This holding

stops courts from creating additional hurdles to finding a waiver of the right to arbitrate.

3. ***Southwest Airlines Co. v. Saxon, No. 21–309.*** On June 6, 2022, in another unanimous ruling, SCOTUS held that the FAA section 1 exemption of "*workers engaged in foreign or interstate commerce*" includes classes of workers who are part of the flow or stream of interstate commerce and that there is no requirement under the FAA that these workers to cross state lines in reality.
4. ***ZF Automotive US, Inc. v. Luxshare, Ltd., No. 21–401.*** On June 13, 2022, SCOTUS decided unanimously that 28 U.S.C. § 1782(a), which allows litigants in foreign disputes to rely on American courts to obtain discovery in aid of "*a foreign or international tribunal,*" applies only to foreign courts and tribunals that have governmental authority and that it does not extend to private tribunals. Accordingly, this provision cannot be used to order discovery for evidence to be used in private commercial arbitral tribunals/panels.
5. ***Viking River Cruises, Inc. v. Moriana, No. 20–1573.*** On June 15, 2022, SCOTUS found in an 8–1 decision that California's Private Attorney General Act (PAGA) was in part preempted by the FAA, to the extent that the PAGA allowed employees to evade bilateral pre-dispute arbitration agreements.

Overall, these cases raise new "lessons learned" for the direction of recent SCOTUS arbitration cases. The Court is not merely taking a "pro-arbitration" stance. Each opinion looks directly at the text of the FAA and narrows its holdings to the facts before them. For example, *Morgan*'s holding focuses on the fact that courts were arguably adding hurdles to proving waiver without any textual basis. This could be seen as supporting the "little guy" by making waiver arguments easier to prove for individuals seeking to avoid arbitration, which may seem contrary to the "pro-business" assumption that had developed. The opinion reminds everyone of the importance of the FAA text.

Additionally, *Badgerow* creates a mismatch of sorts by precluding the "look through" jurisdiction for "front end" cases when it comes to "back end" cases. In other words, a party will be able to bring a case to enforce an arbitration agreement at the front end in federal court where the underlying dispute involves a federal question. With *Badgerow*, that same allowance to "look through" the petition to the underlying claim is not permitted for seeking federal jurisdiction in challenging an arbitration award at the "back end." This seems to conflict with prior statements regarding the "strong federal policy" enforcing arbitration.

Southwest Airlines again shows a focus on the text of the FAA in looking at whether a worker is "engaged in foreign or interstate commerce," but left the door open to further lawsuits involving gig workers such a Uber and

Lyft drivers who are at the fringes of being "engaged in foreign or interstate commerce." The Court invited a case-by-case approach and did not clarify *New Prime*. The baggage handlers at issue in *Southwest Airlines* were directly working in the stream of interstate transportation, but the circumstances might be different for an Uber driver who merely picks people up at the airport. Does it matter if the driver crosses state lines on occasion? Does it matter if a driver transports goods versus people? The Court's tendency has left many questions for further litigation, and the Canadian case noted earlier is relevant to the discussion.

The *ZF Automotive* case focused on the language of 28 U.S.C. § 1782(a) in deciding whether the statute can be used for discovery in arbitration. It was a very textual holding in deciding what is meant by "tribunal." The Court chose a narrow reading of the words of the statute and did not adopt a functional analysis of the arbitration process's needs. Arguably, the purpose and functional analysis of 28 U.S.C. § 1782(a) would support allowing the use of the statute to assist discovery in international arbitration, especially because that is how most international cases are decided. This would benefit the process considering that discovery is often necessary in these cases, including discovery from third parties. The holding leaves many questions for practitioners in international arbitration, and perhaps opens up need for clarification of the rules through other measures.

Viking River continues to emphasize the narrow focus of recent SCOTUS arbitration decisions. In this case, the Court glosses over issues related to the private attorney general function of PAGA and does not address its prior decision in *EEOC v. Waffle House, Inc.*[8] The *Waffle House, Inc.* decision held that an arbitration agreement between an employer and an employee does not bar the EEOC from pursuing victim-specific judicial relief, such as back pay, reinstatement, and damages, in an ADA enforcement action. Instead, the *Viking River* Court focused only on the *Viking River* instance and held that the FAA preempted PAGA to the extent that the state law interfered with a bilateral arbitration clause in California employment agreements.

In the wake of *Viking River*, many questions are percolating in the courts. Some courts have read *Viking River* to allow for distinctions between class arbitration and PAGA representative claims such that representative claims remain free to proceed in the wake of an arbitration clause. For example, the court in *Diaz v. Macy's West Stores, Inc.*,[9] compelled arbitration of individual and representative employment claims under PAGA, stating:

> [T]he Court in Viking River clearly distinguished class and PAGA actions. It explained that "[b]ecause PAGA actions do not adjudicate the individual claims of multiple absent third parties, they do not represent the problems of notice, due process, and adequacy of representation that render class arbitration inconsistent with arbitration's traditionally

> individualized form."[10] And the Court clarified that "we [have not] suggested that single-agent, single-principal representative suits are inconsistent [with] the norm of bilateral arbitration as our precedents conceive of it. Instead, we have held that the changes brought about by the shift from bilateral arbitration to class-action arbitration are too fundamental to be imposed on parties without their consent."[11]

With this distinction, the *Diaz* court found that PAGA representative claims are not the same as a class arbitration, and therefore the arbitration clause at issue allowed for the arbitration of representative claims. Think of it practically, as members of a class who receive a notice and fail to opt out are foreclosed from bringing their own lawsuits. That is not true with PAGA representative claims. The workers act as "private attorneys general" and can pursue civil penalties as if they were a state agency, but they are not foreclosing the rights of class members.

Given the Court's lead in narrowly deciding arbitration cases, it is not surprising that lower courts are using a meticulous focus on the arbitration clauses in these cases. On the other hand, in the *Johnson v. Lowe's Home Centers* case in the Eastern District of California, the contract specifically precluded PAGA representative claims and stated that arbitration must be on an individual basis.[12] The *Diaz* contract language was not sufficiently specific concerning PAGA claims and seemed to allow arbitration of representative and individual PAGA claims under the court's analysis, again showing the importance of clear contract drafting.

As expected, other cases[13] disagree on these issues and *Viking River* did not clarify issues such as dismissal for lack of standing.[14] In fact, the California Supreme Court has weighed in on the standing issue. In *Adolph v. Uber Technologies, Inc.*, the Supreme Court of California held that "where a plaintiff has filed a PAGA action comprised of individual and non-individual claims, an order compelling arbitration of individual claims does not strip the plaintiff of standing to litigate non-individual claims in court."[15] In the case, Adolph, an Uber driver, brought individual and class claims against Uber for relief under PAGA. Adolph claimed that Uber misclassified him and other drivers as independent contractors rather than employees.[16] The court found that an employee compelled to arbitrate individual claims regarding Labor Code violations still maintains PAGA standing for claims "arising out of events involving other employees."[17] The court thus rejected the U.S. Supreme Court's interpretation of PAGA in *Viking River*.[18] The court reasoned that the text of the PAGA statute provides that workers have standing to litigate claims on behalf of their fellow employees, and that "[s]tanding under PAGA is not affected by enforcement of an agreement to adjudicate a plaintiff's individual claim in another forum."[19] The court concluded that plaintiffs filing PAGA actions with both individual and non-individual claims do not lose standing to litigate non-individual claims when the individual claims are ordered to arbitration.[20]

In an episode of the new podcast format of *The Arbitration Conversation*, attorney John Lewis, who is an arbitrator and has represented parties in cases regarding arbitration issues, explored *Morgan v. Sundance, Inc.* before it was decided.[21] We discussed the oral arguments in the case, including the Court's concern about dual processes when there is a question of waiver. Still, the Court seemed to indicate a need for uniformity and to expedite dispute resolution. Accordingly, it makes sense that the Court ultimately refused to allow for many different waiver requirements that are not in the text of the FAA. This also points to SCOTUS's focus on the text of the FAA.

B. CONGRESS

The U.S. Supreme Court is not the only body in Washington D.C. interested in arbitration. Federal legislators are continually considering limits on pre-dispute arbitration clauses in employment and consumer cases. In the 100th episode of *Arbitration Conversation*, Congressman Robert C. Scott of Virginia spoke on a proposed law to limit employment arbitration.[22] We discussed the proposed Restoring Justice for Workers Act and its effects on pre- and post-dispute arbitration. Congressman Scott was a sponsor of this bill, which would prohibit the enforcement of pre-dispute arbitration clauses in employment contexts. In the interview, we discussed power differentials in employment arbitration as well as repeat-player advantages for employers who are continually involved in arbitration proceedings versus employees who may only have one arbitration in their lifetime. Most employment arbitration clauses include class action waivers that take away an employee's right to join a class action. There also are questions around the privacy of arbitration, and nondisclosure agreements that may stop an employee from speaking out about topics such as discrimination.

This is just one of the many examples of bills that have been introduced with respect to employment and consumer arbitration. Surely, there are many other bills in committee at the time of this book's publication. The important "lesson learned" for any arbitration student, scholar, or practitioner is that one must always remain apprised of legal changes in the field of arbitration.

Indeed, the FAA was amended for the first time since the 1980s with Public Law No. 117–90, Ending Forced Arbitration of Sexual Assault and Sexual Harassment Act (EFASASHA).[23] This law invalidates arbitration agreements that preclude a party from filing a lawsuit in court involving sexual assault or sexual harassment, at the election of the party alleging such conduct. The law, passed by both the House of Representatives and the Senate on February 10, 2022, adds a new chapter to Title 9 of the U.S. Code.[24] The implementation of this bill was a revolutionary step, considering that most bills dealing with arbitration die in committee.

Furthermore, the act requires that any issues about applying this chapter to a dispute must be determined by a court under federal law. This breaks from jurisprudential trends enforcing delegation clauses that give arbitrators the power to determine their own jurisdictions. Questions about the bill's application remain, calling on us to be vigilant in following legal changes.

In *The Arbitration Conversation* podcast, George Friedman spoke for a second time as the only person to be interviewed twice to date, this time on EFASASHA and the open questions it leaves.[25] Arbitration providers will have to align their rules with the act and decide how to handle cases that include sexual harassment claims. It will be especially complicated where a case involves sexual harassment along with other employment claims. Multiple proceedings could go forward in one case. For example, an employment case might include sexual harassment claims that go to court, while the remaining claims go to arbitration. Which proceeding will go first? Will issue preclusion apply? Many issues will have to be addressed.

In sum, SCOTUS will continue to take arbitration cases, and this jurisprudence will continue to shape the law and practice of arbitration. And there may be further legislation in arbitration. The cases discussed here are just the tip of the iceberg, and no book in print will be perfectly up to date when it comes to evolving jurisprudence regarding arbitration. The lesson learned for any arbitrator, arbitration scholar, student, or counsel representing parties in arbitration: never rely on old memory about the latest Supreme Court cases regarding arbitration. Arbitration is not a "sleepy" area of law. Also, never assume that legislation will not pass—EFASASHA is a case in point. This is certainly a continuing conversation!

NOTES

1 Robert Bailey & Amy Schmitz, *Arbitration Conversation No. 3: Amy Interviews Prof. Bob Bailey of Mizzou Law*, ARBITRATE.COM (July 20, 2020), https://arbitrate.com/arbitration-conversation-no-3-amy-interviews-prof-bob-bailey-of-mizzou-law/.

2 Uber Technologies Inc. v. Heller, 2020 SCC 16, 447 D.L.R. 4th 179 (Can.).

3 Anthony Daimsis & Amy Schmitz, *Arbitration Conversation No. 19: Amy Interviews Prof. Anthony Daimsis*, YOUTUBE (July 25, 2020), www.youtube.com/watch?v=UPdZTS-5YOk&t=33s.

4 Chris Drahozal & Amy Schmitz, *Arbitration Conversation No. 15: Prof. Chris Drahozal of KU Law*, ARBITRATE.COM (Oct. 14, 2020), https://arbitrate.com/arbitration-conversation-15-prof-chris-drahozal-of-ku-law/.

5 Henry Schein Inc. v. Archer & White Sales, Inc., 141 S. Ct. 656 (2021).

6 Henry Schein, Inc. v. Archer & White Sales, Inc., 592 U.S. ___ (2021); Ronald Mann, Justices dismiss arbitrability dispute, SCOTUSblog (Jan. 25, 2021, 5:25 PM), https://www.scotusblog.com/2021/01/justices-dismiss-arbitrability-dispute/

7 Imre Szalai, Sarah Cole, Angela Downes, Amy Schmitz & Colin Rule, *SCOTUS Arbitration Review—A Panel Discussion*, ARBITRATE.COM (Aug. 9, 2022), www.youtube.com/watch?v=AvKBRAsYiu4.

8 EEOC v. Waffle House, Inc., 534 U.S. 279 (2002).

9 Diaz v. Macy's West Stores, Inc., No. CV 19–00303 PSG (MAAx), 2022 BL 421655, 2022 U.S. Dist. LEXIS 212825 (C.D. Cal. Nov. 23, 2022).
10 *See Viking River*, 142 S. Ct. at 1921 (citation omitted); *see also* Hamilton v. Wal-Mart Stores, Inc., 39 F.4th 575, 583–84 (9th Cir. 2022).
11 *Viking River*, 142 S. Ct. at 1922 (citation omitted).
12 Johnson v. Lowe's Home Ctrs. LLC, 630 F. Supp. 3d 1352, 1357 (E.D. Cal. Sept. 21, 2022).
13 Adolph v. Uber Technologies, Inc., 532 P.3d 682 (Cal. 2023); Wing v. Chico Healthcare & Wellness Centre, 534 P.3d 923 (Cal. 2023); Sanchez v. MC Painting, No. S274780, 2022 Cal. LEXIS 4694 (Cal. 2022).
14 California Courts, The Judicial Branch of California, *Appellate Courts Case Information*, https://appellatecases.courtinfo.ca.gov/search/case/dockets.cfm?dist=0&doc_id=2383459&doc_no=S274671&request_token=NiIwLSEmPkw4WyApSCItVENIMFA0UDxTJCNeXz1TICAgCg%3D%3D#_blank (last visited Nov. 13, 2023).
15 Adolph v. Uber Techs., Inc., 532 P.3d 682, 692 (Cal. 2023).
16 *Id.* at 686.
17 *Id.* at 689.
18 *Id.* ("Because '[t]he highest court of each State . . . remains "the final arbiter of what is state law,"' we are not bound by the high court's interpretation of California law.").
19 *Id.* at 691.
20 *Id.* at 696.
21 John Lewis & Amy Schmitz, *Arbitration Conversation Podcast No. 3: Waiver of a Right to Arbitrate?*, PodBean (Apr. 5, 2022), https://arbitrate.podbean.com/e/episode-3-waiver-of-a-right-to-arbitrate/.
22 Robert C. Scott & Amy Schmitz, *Arbitration Conversation No. 100: Congressman Robert C. "Bobby" Scott of Virginia*, YouTube (Nov. 16, 2021), www.youtube.com/watch?v=udUZLubf3Gw.
23 Ending Forced Arbitration of Sexual Assault and Sexual Harassment Act of 2021, CONGRESS.GOV, www.congress.gov/bill/117th-congress/house-bill/4445 (last visited Nov. 13, 2023).
24 Actions Overview H.R. 4445, 117th Congress (2021–22), CONGRESS.GOV (Feb. 11, 2022), www.congress.gov/bill/117th-congress/house-bill/4445/actions.
25 George Friedman & Amy Schmitz, *The Arbitration Conversation No. 4: Examining the Ending Forced Arbitration of Sexual Assault and Sexual Harassment Act of 2021 (EFASASHA)* (Apr. 5, 2022), https://arbitrate.com/the-arbitration-conversation-podcast-2/.

Chapter 9
Costly Judicialization

Quite a few of the interviews emphasized the importance of promoting efficiency in arbitration and fighting the urge to judicialize the process, as Arbitrator Chalk noted. The concept of the "judicialization" of arbitration has garnered substantial attention within legal scholarship and Professor Stipanowich has noted the intrusion of judicial procedures into arbitration processes.[1] For example, extensive discovery and motion practice in arbitration have been cited as examples of this judicialization, adding time and cost to the process. This chapter discusses some of the thoughts and insights from arbitrators and arbitration experts that I interviewed on this topic, noting the push and pull of judicialization.

A. JUDICIALIZATION IN CONTEXT

Interviews raised questions regarding the classic battle between fairness and efficiency—parties may need some discovery to prove their cases, but that can add a great deal to the cost and time of a process. Counsel and arbitrators are wise to curtail such costly procedures, and to use the flexibility of arbitration to their advantage, for example, by promoting consensual document exchange and denying depositions unless they are vital for a case. Still, some cases require more discovery and motion practice. For example, at least one interview focused on new procedures for consolidated and multiparty arbitrations, which usually require more procedures. Furthermore, interviewees noted the importance of drafting sound arbitration contracts and using preliminary hearings to set the boundaries and expectations at the start of any arbitration process. There has been a convergence between arbitration and traditional litigation, potentially impacting the distinctive features that have traditionally set arbitration apart.

Here are some examples of how judicialization has manifested in arbitration:

- Evidentiary procedures: One facet of judicialization involves the adoption of more formal evidentiary procedures and discovery, akin to those seen in court proceedings. This might include more extensive document exchange, depositions, and even interrogatories. While these procedures can enhance the thoroughness of fact-finding, they may also prolong the arbitration process and increase costs, potentially diluting the speed and efficiency that arbitration is known for.

- Expert witnesses: Arbitration often involves reports and testimony of expert witnesses who provide opinions on complex technical or scientific matters. This practice is reminiscent of court proceedings and can enhance the technical rigor of arbitration decisions. However, it can also introduce elements of adversarial litigation and procedural complexity. Additionally, experts tend to add significantly to the cost of arbitration.
- Pre-hearing conferences: Most arbitration proceedings include at least one pre-hearing conference, a practice borrowed from litigation, where arbitrators and parties discuss procedural matters and evidence, and plot out a preliminary order. This can lead to better case management, but it may also contribute to delays and added costs, especially where there are difficulties with scheduling due to multiple attorneys and arbitrators.
- Interim measures and emergency relief: Judicialization may include requests for interim measures or emergency relief in arbitration, akin to court-ordered injunctions or temporary restraining orders. This is similar to a court's ability to provide injunctive relief, although parties may have to get the order enforced in court where compliance is questionable.
- Appellate mechanisms: The introduction of appellate mechanisms or review procedures for arbitral awards can also be seen as a form of judicialization. This would allow parties to challenge awards on the merits, akin to an appeal in a court system, using an additional arbitration appeals panel. While this can enhance the fairness of arbitration, it might also add to costs and prolong the process.
- Detailed written decisions: Arbitrators are increasingly being asked to provide more extensive written decisions, including detailed legal reasoning, similar to court judgments. While this promotes transparency and accountability, it may also contribute to longer proceedings and increased costs.

These examples illustrate how arbitration has been influenced by judicial procedures, potentially altering its characteristics and advantages. The following explores ideas around containing judicialization with an aim toward balancing fairness and efficiency.

B. CONTRACTUAL PLANNING

When designing an arbitration process and writing it into the contract, it is important to consider the inherent urge for lawyers to judicialize arbitration. Professor Hiro Aragaki provided interesting insights on this topic.[2] Too often, commentators jump to the process without considering the contract and the importance of taking time at the outset to contractually design an efficient and fair process. The contractual foundation of arbitration separates it from litigation. Pre-dispute arbitration clauses in larger agreements have become the norm, and contract negotiations usually include little attention to the arbitration provision contained therein. Instead, negotiators focus on the other "guts" of a contract, such as price, product (if applicable), time, and so on. Then, when a dispute erupts, the attorneys are often eager to judicialize the process. Arbitration has therefore been criticized for becoming more and more like litigation, often adding to the cost and time in arbitration, as noted earlier.

Autonomy and consent are foundational components in arbitration. The FAA was from the beginning aimed at honoring parties' contracts. Considering the context of the FAA's passage, it is especially important to highlight how parties should contractually craft a process to fit their case. Even though parties, in the negotiating stage, are hopeful for the best-case scenario and don't think disputes will arise, they should take the time to examine the arbitration provision and address certain questions: Does the arbitration clause include arbitration rules that fit the context? Are there specific procedures that will be needed, and others that would be wasteful in the event of a dispute? Do the parties want to specifically allow for OArb to cut costs and time associated with travel?

It may also be wise to negotiate arbitration terms post-dispute so that the parties can assess their needs for the process and agree on procedures that are appropriate for the case and context. In some cases, discovery is not essential, and it may not make sense to allow extended discovery where it will unnecessarily add cost and time to a process. As discovery should not be disproportionate to the needs of the dispute, arbitrators should press parties to see whether the requested discovery is necessary. However, in some cases, justice may require document production and depositions. One such scenario is when the information is in the more powerful player's hands and there is no other way for one to prove their case.

Rather than spend unnecessary time on motions for discovery, it is best where parties have negotiated and agree on a scheduling order, including a discovery plan. Ideally, parties will agree to a consensual exchange of documents, but in some cases, these are questions for an arbitrator to determine. Here is where the arbitrator should be efficient in answering requests and encouraging parties to reach an agreement on discovery and other process issues. In some high-conflict situations, it may even be necessary to consider sanctions where one party is impeding the process.

In sum, parties generally do not negotiate and plan for their arbitrations thoughtfully. Counsel in arbitration proceedings often move right into an adversarial mode and allow judicialization to creep in as they seek unnecessary discovery and bring motions related thereto. Nonetheless, arbitrators are wise to make clear a desire for the parties to reach a post-dispute agreement on the particularities of the process. This can sometimes help address the judicialization creep, especially when the arbitrator makes clear the added costs of judicialization and the possibility of sanctions for impeding a fair and efficient process.

C. PRE-HEARING CONFERENCES AND PROCEDURES

From a problem-solving perspective, pre-hearing conferences are essential to organize a process.[3] Arbitrator Edna Sussman provided wonderful insights on what it means to be a proactive arbitrator who uses whatever tools are at their disposal with the goal of helping parties reach the best resolution for their needs. One of these tools is mediation, important even in international arbitration. Ever since the Singapore Convention opened possibilities for mediation in international dispute resolution, arbitrators should be especially mindful of opportunities to help the parties reach a settlement. Mediation is not simply a tool in domestic dispute resolution.

It is also important to consider psychology when seeking to promote fairness and address inefficiencies of the judicialization of arbitration. In some cases, it might be important to have the safeguards of a courthouse, and more elaborate procedures. However, that is not true in most cases where it is a fight about money and the parties are likely to waste a great deal of time and money in the run-up to a settlement on the courthouse stairs. It is essential to consider the party goals.

Proactive arbitrators can also create settlement and planning opportunities by walking the parties through the process. Preliminary hearings are tremendously important in staving off judicialization, as an arbitrator helps parties narrow down their needs in terms of discovery and motion practice. These meetings also help the parties see what they will need to prove in the evidentiary hearing, sometimes illuminating risks to discuss with the clients. through preliminary hearings, parties also get a sense of an arbitration schedule and gain awareness regarding the time commitment. Clients often underestimate the time that they and their attorneys will spend in an arbitration process. Arbitrator Sussman also brought up excellent ideas like offering options that the parties may not have thought about, one option being a final offer arbitration.

Under a psychological approach, it is important to be aware of human biases in any process, and for arbitrators to consider the psychological shifts that happen during preliminary discussions and throughout the arbitration. For example, confirmation bias occurs when people seek ways to confirm their initial inclinations. It is important for arbitrators to be careful in considering all evidence and not making assumptions that confirm their biases. Still, an arbitrator must be discerning in seeking ways to narrow the hearings through sufficient preliminary discussions. This may even include dispositive motions on certain issues where there is no legitimate question of law or fact for later determination. Conversations that narrow a case early in the process can be helpful in promoting a fair settlement.

It is also essential to help parties feel that they have been heard. In some circumstances, this means that an arbitrator should hold mini-hearings. These additional meetings, earlier in the process, can help parties feel heard. Additionally, arbitrators are wise to make space for parties to talk among themselves during these hearing times. When meetings are in person, this may mean that there are coffee breaks. In OArb, the arbitrator should allow for breakout rooms on a virtual platform for parties to have informal conversations during breaks.

Another tool worth considering that is similar to "mini-hearings" and ideas above that also aim to narrow issues for resolution is the use of "early neutral evaluation" (ENE).[4] ENE allows for an early evaluative opinion on an element of a dispute before bringing it to court, or it could be part of a court proceeding. Professor Erin Archerd provided insights on this ENE process, which is called "case evaluation" in Michigan, where Professor Archerd teaches. In Michigan, three-person panels in civil cases may provide value for a case before it goes to trial. It is similar to a nonbinding arbitration, or even an evaluative mediation. Although many lawyers and judges have adopted general mediation to encourage settlement, it may be wise to use ENE as a more effective tool in cases where factual questions need to be answered to move toward a settlement. In some cases, all the "facilitation" in the world will not be effective until parties have a sense of how a decision-maker would answer key factual and legal questions.

D. ACCESS TO JUSTICE

There has been increasing interest in addressing issues around access to justice (A2J) in arbitration.[5] I had the opportunity to discuss related issues with Professor Leonardo Valladares Pacheco de Oliveira, lecturer in law at Royal Holloway, University of London. Professor Oliveira worked on comparative analysis of arbitration during his studies and surveyed differential views of arbitration. He noted how arbitrability is an essential question with respect to A2J. U.S. law and European law are very different on the topic of arbitrability. For example, consumer and employment disputes are generally not arbitrable in Europe, while they are arbitrable in the U.S.

Professor Oliveira suggests that this "all or nothing" dichotomy may not be the best for A2J. Instead, it is wise to strike a balance. Some employees and consumers may benefit from avoiding public access and time associated with judicial procedures. Arbitration may provide efficiencies and privacy that serve all parties involved in an employment or consumer case, as noted earlier.

On the other hand, there may be power differentials that suggest the need for analysis of not simply "whether" to arbitrate, but "how" to arbitrate. In some cases, this may suggest the need to use technology to lower the barriers to entry in arbitration. It is essential to make sure arbitrators are procedurally ready for OArb. Efficiency and fairness are two vital elements of a contract, as well as arbitration. And as a resource, unconscionability can be a safety net for policing the fairness of arbitration.

I also spoke on this topic with Stephen Kane, founder and CEO of FairClaims.com, a full-service ODR platform and provider designed to promote efficient, fair, and cost-effective dispute resolution. FairClaims works with sharing economy & B2B marketplaces, insurance companies, and others to resolve disputes quickly and effectively.[6] Mr. Kane was candid in discussing the risks associated with starting an ODR company. Mr. Kane initially did not see how ODR would be practical. It was a foreign idea! Nonetheless, after he got into legal practice, he saw how lawyers don't always want to be more efficient. In fact, not every lawyer likes ODR.

Still, the quest continues to expand access to remedies, and justice. In the "real world," many individuals who are wronged, go without remedies. It is the needle in the haystack, the "squeaky wheel," that takes the time and money to pursue a remedy in small claims cases. Litigation is so expensive that oftentimes the legal fees wipe out anything you may receive in a judgment. Accordingly, it is important to fight judicialization and remain creative in crafting arbitration processes that expand A2J, without adding to the cost of obtaining redress. As lawyers, we need to learn and digest the fact that the practice of law is very different from the theory of law that we focus on in law school.

Mr. Kane shared his experience in creating FairClaims—talking to people, learning about the area, creating a website, and starting arbitration online. He focused on learning what people want, and what people are looking for in an ODR platform. User-focused design is pivotal in dispute resolution. I often say that we all need to consider the three Rs: Research, Revise, Repeat. We should research to learn what users need in a process and how the process design is performed from all angles, revise the process in light of this research, and repeat this research and revision until we get it right. System design is not a "one and done." It is our duty to continually evolve and revise processes to find the best means for expanding A2J.

At the time of the interview, FairClaims was focused on claims of $25,000 and below, although they were looking into expansion. The platform was focused on a system that allowed live hearings or text-based arbitration. FairClaims notably focused on telephone hearings but was considering video for higher dollar claims. Interestingly, they found that many users did not like video, as they worry about having enough bandwidth and getting on screen. We must consider what users want out of an arbitration process. Again, the process should fit the problem and the people.

My interview with attorney Travis Lenkner also addressed A2J issues in arbitration.[7] Mr. Lenkner was the managing partner of what was Keller Lenkner LLC. —which is mentioned earlier. Mr. Lenkner had experience as a litigator at an AmLaw 25 law firm, a legal entrepreneur and investment manager, in-house counsel at a Fortune 50 company, and a law clerk at the U.S. Supreme Court. This was a fascinating discussion that shows how arbitration can help consumers. The Keller Lenkner firm represented thousands of consumers and employees in arbitration where there would otherwise be a class action but for the arbitration clauses in these contracts.

For example, as noted earlier, the Keller Lenkner firm represented more than 75,000 consumers who had been recorded by Amazon's Alexa without their consent, a violation of privacy laws in many states. The Amazon contract had required arbitration under the AAA Consumer Arbitration Rules, in which Amazon assumed most of the costs of each of the many arbitrations. This can work to the advantage of consumers due to speed and low cost, and the Kelly Lenkner firm took advantage of this. It became a "be careful what you wish for" story, as Amazon was unpleasantly surprised by the cost and time involved in defending suits in all the separate arbitrations. After this deluge of arbitration claims, Amazon moved back to a traditional litigation model rather than arbitration.

Individual arbitration still moved forward for Amazon consumers who already demanded arbitration under AAA per the terms of their contracts. There are now new ways for firms to represent many individuals in arbitration. Arbitral institutions like the AAA also have created special processes for mass arbitration claims, and the saga continues for many companies that face many, many individual arbitrations that involve the same issues. Additionally, the AAA has been proactive in requiring application of its consumer and employment rules to promote fairness and A2J. Still, most companies tend to prefer arbitration to class actions, and controversies remain regarding the enforcement of arbitration clauses in consumer and employment contexts. Nonetheless, trimming judicialization and promoting simple arbitration and mediation processes for consumers and employees can be a benefit, and provide individuals with remedies that they may not otherwise obtain if forced to litigate on their own, especially where no class action is available.

E. STRIKING A BALANCE

There are many lessons learned concerning the judicialization of arbitration from a contract, process, and A2J perspective. Arbitration was never intended to be the same as litigation. The arbitration process at its core is a creature of contract, and parties should take advantage of this attribute to design a process that best fits their needs. Wise counsel will take time to negotiate and conclude arbitration agreements that provide the best mechanism for resolving the specifics of their dispute, pre- or post-contract.

Attorneys are much too quick to cling to adversarial and complex procedures out of habit, and law school training that is overly focused on litigation. We all need to be more creative and courageous in crafting arbitration procedures that break from litigation norms.

The flexibility of arbitration allows for procedures that expand A2J by lowering barriers to entry. These barriers include the shackles of civil procedure rules that apply in court—and judicialization. For example, streamlining simple and user-centric procedures can make processes easier for individuals with no legal background. Allowing an individual to join a video call and explain their story may be perfect for some individuals who would never want to face the formalities and costs of going to court. Furthermore, parties and arbitrators should consider the balance of fairness and efficiency in using preliminary hearings to craft a process, and consider ideas like mediation, mini-hearings, and ENE to help make for a more efficient and fair process.

NOTES

1 Thomas J. Stipanowich, *Arbitration: The "New Litigation"* 2010(1) Univ. Ill. L. Rev. (Jan. 24, 2010), https://papers.ssrn.com/sol3/papers.cfm?abstract_id=1297526.
2 Hiro Aragaki & Amy Schmitz, *Arbitration Conversation No. 84: Hiro Aragaki, Professor of Law at Loyola Law School*, YouTube (June 22, 2021), www.youtube.com/watch?v=o0GiKmRTVtQ.
3 Edna Sussman & Amy Schmitz, *Arbitration Conversation No. 78: Arbitrator Edna Sussman, of SussmanADR.com*, YouTube (Apr. 9, 2021), www.youtube.com/watch?v=1_0NanqeFPg.
4 Erin Archerd & Amy Schmitz, *Arbitration Conversation No. 81: Erin Archerd, Assoc. Prof. of Law, Univ. of Detroit Mercy School of Law*, YouTube (May 12, 2021), www.youtube.com/watch?v=sZK9X3F7jiY.
5 Leonardo Oliveira & Amy Schmitz, *Arbitration Conversation No. 87: Prof. Leonardo Oliveira, Lecturer, Royal Holloway, Univ. of London*, YouTube (July 20, 2021), www.youtube.com/watch?v=rbjffQ04okM.
6 Stephen Kane & Amy Schmitz, *Arbitration Conversation No. 67: Stephen Kane, Founder, and CEO of FairClaims.com*, Arbitrate.com (Dec. 21, 2021), https://arbitrate.com/arbitration-conversation-no-67-stephen-kane-founder-and-ceo-of-fairclaims-com/.
7 Travis Lenkner & Amy Schmitz, *Arbitration Conversation No. 86: Travis Lenkner, Managing Partner of Keller Lenkner LLC.*, YouTube (June 22, 2021), www.youtube.com/watch?v=yjXRiJX-ano.

Chapter 10
OArb > Zoom

Earlier chapters discussed OArb and OArb's move into the mainstream, especially during the Covid-19 shutdowns. Many ODR and OArb developers have created comprehensive ODR/OArb platforms that do not simply use Zoom for video hearings. There has been a tendency to equate ODR with Zoom or Teams mediation and arbitration. There are many providers and platforms for OArb, such as FairClaims, eJudicate, CREK, ODR.com, and others. This chapter will talk about some of these platforms and what they provide, adding insights learned by interviewing the leaders and developers of these platforms.

Recent years have seen new technologies disrupting many established industries and institutions. A wide variety of breakthrough technologies, many highlighted in yearly reviews in the *MIT Technology Review*, "blow our minds" every year and seem like something straight out of a science fiction novel.[1] The Covid-19 pandemic meanwhile has inspired additional software developers to enter the ODR market. Of course, this trend began years earlier and many commentators regarding the legal profession have asked what was taking so long for lawyers to embrace the benefits of technology.[2] I am included in this group, long suggesting that ADR professionals and courts should consider the benefits of online processes, especially as ODR and OArb can be reimagined to expand A2J.[3]

ODR's and OArb's efficiency, accessibility, and ease open new avenues to remedies. Across many dispute domains, online processes allow individuals to resolve disputes more quickly, cheaply, and hopefully fairly, using technology as simple as a cell phone, without the costs or hassles of travel or time away from work.[4] Accordingly, ODR has gained significant traction in the U.S. Professor Janet Martinez and I analyzed that growth in 2021 while writing a chapter in *Online Dispute Resolution: Theory and Practice: A Treatise on Technology and Dispute Resolution*.[5] At the time, we canvased ODR providers in the U.S. and found that commercial, small claims, and family disputes were the most common case types for ODR. Most of the ODR processes we reviewed used technology for mediation and case management systems. The information was captured in Appendix A to our chapter: "Summary of

Select U.S. ODR Providers," based on the larger chart we compiled.[6] At the time, we saw that OArb was a much smaller slice of the ODR pie than online mediation and negotiation. It seems that the OArb slice is growing, however, and my interviews illuminated some of that growth, including platforms that go beyond Zoom arbitration.

A. CREK

Chittu Nagarajan, who is the founder and CEO of CREKODR.com, and a long-time collaborator with Colin Rule at eBay and Modria, spoke with me in *The Arbitration Conversation*.[7] She has a background in law, and found that ODR was well-suited for e-commerce disputes. At the same time, she was surprised that India was known as a technology hub but did not use technology for resolving disputes when she first started in the ODR field. In 2003, she started ODR India, allowing for technologically driven negotiation and mediation. She built the system with feedback from Colin Rule, who suggested that she try using it for eBay India disputes. In 2007, Rule was working with eBay and PayPal and asked Nagarajan to join him, where they created an online community court.

This eBay community court selected jurors from their online community, and the disputes would be put to these online jurors. This was a type of crowdsourced arbitration. There were certain criteria to select the jurors, and they came from a pool of both sellers and buyers on eBay India. After three years with community courts at eBay and PayPal, Rule and Nagarajan decided they wanted to take their technology beyond e-commerce. They were very concerned with A2J and started Modria in 2011.

Modria was one of the first ODR companies to be venture-backed and have the support of a tech startup, in the vein of other Silicon Valley startups. The system was a modular ODR platform used for family disputes, property assessments, tax appeals, e-commerce, and a variety of other disputes. Rule and Nagarajan sold it to Tyler Technologies in 2017, and now Tyler is using the Modria system in many U.S. and worldwide courts.

In 2019, Nagarajan started CREK ODR. Her vision was always to have ODR available to all at a reasonable cost, in order to expand A2J and access to remedies. ODR technology can be expensive, but excessive cost defeats the purpose of ODR. Accessibility is essential. Any mediator, small ODR organization, or enterprise customer who wants end-to-end ODR should be able to use CREK's design. Furthermore, CREK has a new partnership with Mediate.com and is being rolled out in conjunction with ODR.com. Similar to Modria, the new ODR.com system based on CREK is a modular system to be used by a variety of industries and clients.

There has been a high demand for arbitration, and CREK is customized for a variety of languages and processes—including both mediation and arbitration. Within CREK, it permits documents-only as well as full scale arbitration, including video hearings. The platform was built to support arbitration end-to-end, for a variety of use cases. It also supports a single arbitrator deciding cases, as well as tripartite tribunals and even automated resolutions. Automated decisions could be based on data fed into the system, always remaining mindful of ethical standards. Nagarajan also noted how young individuals in India and elsewhere are very interested in OArb and bring in an exciting perspective, including greater facility and trust in technology. Indeed, CREK and any ODR providers are wise to listen to the needs of the next generation of digital natives.

B. SMARTSETTLE

Another interesting platform for ODR and OArb is Smartsettle. On this topic, Graham Ross, who is a UK lawyer and accredited mediator with more than 30 years of experience in technology and the law, shared thoughts. Graham Ross is a leading UK expert in the field of ODR and co-founded the UK's first ODR service, a blind bidding service called WeCanSettle, in 2000. Mr. Ross has been the head of International Marketing at Smartsettle Resolutions, Inc., and founder and president of TheMediationRoom.com.

When Ross first qualified as a lawyer, he became interested in Prestel, a program that displayed text on the TV, and began thinking about how technology could assist lawyers.[8] Fast forward to 2000, Ross and another lawyer started the very first blind bidding system. These blind bidding systems help parties move toward their zone of potential agreement and reach fair settlements with lower legal costs. Blind bidding also avoids the time lag and the problem of parties having to sit on offers and counteroffers.

There are multiple variations on blind bidding, and it can assist in negotiation, mediation, and/or arbitration. You can make open offers and make hidden offers that the other party does not see. You tell the computer your bottom and top lines in terms of settlement, and this enables you to make more active, dynamic negotiations. If at any stage the hidden bids meet or overlap, the system will announce a settlement, such that the algorithm is essentially ending the disputes. Assisting enforcement, the parties can agree to be bound by this settlement per a settlement contract. Additionally, the parties could agree that the arbitrator should enter an award based on this process. Such blind bidding can speed up the process toward settlement and may be right for certain parties and disputes, depending on party needs.

Blind bidding systems can be particularly beneficial for organizations handling large volumes of disputes, such as insurance companies. Furthermore, the speed can be useful due to the time-value of money. It is far better for all the parties to find a fair settlement soon after a liability arises and avoid the eventual drift into court that often occurs with traditional negotiation among busy lawyers who fail to stay on top of communications. It especially makes sense for an insurer to use this system and gain traction by providing a more attractive offer early, in the hope that the dispute can be settled without the legal costs of arbitration or litigation. Additionally, it is good for the consumer or insured to get the money sooner, rather than later, when they likely have bills to pay (related to whatever liability is at issue).

Smartsettle One adds a type of "e-nudging" to the process by rewarding those that make generous moves in negotiation. Smartsettle is trying to encourage people to make bids speedily and justly, to reach an agreement. This is a nuanced process, in which certain rules determine whether or not there is an agreement. Let us suppose one party is willing to pay $10,000 and the claimant is happy to accept $8,000. There is a range where any figure between $8,000 and $10,000 is acceptable. The machine works out which party made more attempts to settle, gave a little bit more, or charged a little bit less. This happens via an algorithm that decides which party had to make the smaller last move from his secret bid to get into that zone between $8,000 and $10,000 that is acceptable to both. The algorithm does not reward parties that seem to be holding back or playing games. The process is akin to an arbitration, using transparent algorithms.

This is not a pure "bot" arbitration. The parties need to agree to the use of the algorithms and the blind-bidding process. Furthermore, if the final bids do not meet and there is no overlap, then the system invites parties to consider moving further toward agreement. Furthermore, if there is no agreement even after such nudging, both parties have the option of bringing in another process called the expert neutral decider (END). With this process, human beings are brought in to assist. A panel of three looks at the documents and information submitted by the parties, and the panel provides what they believe to be a fair settlement. In the end, the bid closest to the middle one becomes the settlement amount. This is a mix of an early neutral evaluation and algorithmic-nudged arbitration. It provides optionality, as different parties have different needs. This is not merely Zoom or Teams arbitration.

C. EJUDICATE

Another OArb platform that has been percolating and growing is ejudicate.com, an online arbitration service provider based in Los Angeles, California (learn more at http://ejudicate.com). Richard Ormond and Jake Stango, the founders of ejudicate.com, spoke about their company. This is a platform very similar to JAMS and AAA, but it uses a unique technology that was patent pending at the time of the interview.[9] The difference is that instead of being a traditional platform, everything is cloud-based and done entirely asynchronously. It starts as a document-only arbitration process, with e-judges assigned to efficiently and cheaply resolve the dispute based on the documents. That said, an e-judge has the discretion to ask for a live hearing, which can be telephonic or video.

The A2J problem was an impetus for the creation of the platform. It is common knowledge that most individuals merely "give up" and cannot pursue their claims because of the high costs of litigation. The cost to arbitrate could be more than the amount in dispute and therefore these efficiencies create far greater economies of scale, providing A2J for everybody. Ormond had been a litigator for 22 years and saw this firsthand. It can be very frustrating to see clients "win" a case and still have no remedy to show for it after paying litigation costs.

It is not simply about costs. New OArb platforms like ejudicate aim to be user-friendly and user-centric. The key is to provide A2J for all types of people, whether or not they have money. There is a barrier to entry for anyone seeking remedies, hurdles to hiring a lawyer or paying for an arbitrator and other difficulties in getting your day in court. User testing and user-centric design are critical, and even the language used on a platform needs to be clear, without the obscurities of legalese. Accordingly, in crafting the process, the ejudicate developers used real-time user testing and conducted user interviews. In the interviews, the developers stated that they still were conducting testing daily and had a new partnership with Brief.[10]

At the time of the interview, the ejudicate customer base was business-to-business, so they focused their initial launch on simple monetary claims.[11] The platform allows for multiple individuals to participate. The language used is easily understood by anyone, with or without a law degree. The platform also includes a glossary accessible on the website, because often relevant legal terminology is hard to understand. Wisely, they hired outside users to test the system, something that is important for anyone creating an ODR or OArb system. When flaws are found, developers can quickly remedy the situation, due to the flexibility of OArb systems versus traditional in-person litigation.

Another unique aspect of this OArb system is how it recruits arbitrators or e-judges. As described in the interview, ejudicate's system is quite flexible. The founders compared it to "Uber for lawyers." Essentially, e-judges should have at least ten years of expertise in a particular field, no professional discipline against them, and have the availability to handle these cases on a flexible basis. This is convenient for lawyers who work from home or work part-time. They can log in, see what cases fit their qualifications, and, once they clear conflicts, they are ready to take the case. By having the platform assign the judges, it becomes much more efficient and possibly lessens the concern for bias and repeat-player advantages that come with giving the parties or a sole case administrator all the power in arbitrator selection. For monetary claims or declaratory relief claims, what is most important is the judge's background and experience.

The process is straightforward. As noted earlier, most cases are handled on the documents. At least, this was true at the time of the interview. At the time, hearings were rarely requested, but available via Zoom or telephone in most cases. Most clients were on a subscription model that was credit-based, although there was capacity for "one-off" customers.

D. FAIRCLAIMS

Another OArb platform is FairClaims, which is also discussed in Chapter 9 as it relates to judicialization and the need for more streamlined arbitration. In *The Arbitration Conversation*, Stephen Kane, founder and CEO of FairClaims.com, explained the FairClaims platform and process.[12] FairClaims generally handles cases that would otherwise go to small claims court. This includes disagreements over loan repayments, past due invoices, car repairs, and other issues around $10,000 to $25,000 and under. The process is an OArb process, fully online arbitration.

According to the website, there is a hearing after the parties upload the evidence:

> The hearing will be a 30-minute phone call. Your Arbitrator will first ask both sides to tell their side of the story. Then the Arbitrator will ask specific questions to both sides based on the statements and evidence.[13]

The decision is rendered within eight days.

The idea is to keep costs down and expand access to remedies. Under the payment information on the website, each side only pays after both sides agree to use FairClaims for arbitration online. If a party pays after both sides agree to arbitrate and the other side doesn't pay for the process in time, FairClaims will give the party who paid a refund if the arbitration doesn't move forward.[14] If both sides agree, one side can pay the fee for both parties. Some employers may agree to this to avoid the time and costs of litigation, or class actions.

FairClaims is one example of an ODR platform created with A2J in mind. To that end, it includes everything from intake forms to case modules to mediation to arbitration (where necessary) to settlement (where possible). Similar to ejudicate, it is a simple process with low costs for the users. Still, any new platform comes with challenges for the developers. It is not easy to be a startup in the arbitration space, where traditional providers have reigned for many years.

These are just a few examples of OArb in the U.S. Of course, AAA, JAMS, and CPR are also using virtual hearings and online case management, as noted earlier. Furthermore, many other companies are starting every day in the OArb area in the U.S. Moreover, OArb is growing internationally by leaps and bounds. Following are examples outside of the U.S.

E. DELOS

Delos is another example of an ADR/ODR company. Hafez Virjee, who is the president and co-founder of Delos Dispute Resolution, spoke as part of the webcast. The name Delos comes from the island of Delos, which was historically a place used as a neutral forum for dispute resolution.[15] Virjee created Delos after practicing law in France, and learning from his clients that traditional high-fee arbitration providers did not work well for smaller-dollar arbitration. The traditional in-person arbitration process is not worth the cost in most lower-dollar cases. Additionally, Virjee examined every step of an arbitration procedure to consider whether it could be done more efficiently, while also ensuring that the goals and interests of users aligned with interests in efficiency. He explained that in forming Delos, he applied a holistic perspective. This included consideration of the needs of users and the arbitral community.

With this mindset, Virjee also was sure to consider what individuals and the arbitral community already understand and are comfortable using. For example, everyone tends to be comfortable with email, cloud storage, and Zoom or Teams. Accordingly, it is sensical to use these tools in which the parties have already invested. One can easily bring together these existing components without taking the risk of designing something new, which will be costly, have limitations and flaws, and require people to have an extra learning curve. Instead, Virjee advocates for leveraging existing investments in different technology products.

Efficiency is very important for Delos. For this reason, the Delos system informs arbitrators up front how long they will have to submit their draft awards. This means that when they are looking at the calendar, they are not only looking at how much time each side wants for discovery and when they should plan a hearing. They also plan for the award itself and ensure that awards are provided on time. Arbitrators also must consider at the start the time that may be needed to address party disputes in the process, or the additional time required for in-person meetings in some cases.

Delos has, since its creation, retrofitted their process for technology and allowance for OArb. In June 2020, Delos conducted a survey and asked people to tell them how they had engaged with remote hearings, to share their level of comfort with OArb, and to share their views on remote hearings moving forward. They found that, generally, remote hearings are part of the toolbox individuals enjoy, even going into the future. Still, the desire for in-person evidentiary hearings grows in cases where the stakes are greater or there is more complexity. Even so, many parties still want to use technology like Zoom for case management and pre-hearing conferences. Some worry that it is more difficult to assess credibility over Zoom. However, Delos is yet another example of OArb that is more than only the use of Zoom. Indeed, Delos is continually expanding its technological offerings.

F. OARB EXAMPLES IN LATIN AMERICA

ODR and OArb are growing not just in the U.S. It is growing globally, as exemplified by the preceding CREK example from India (although CREK is included with U.S. examples because it is now functioning as part of ODR.com). Furthermore, Latin America has seen a surge in interest in ODR and OArb. Santiago Dussan, a professor at the Pontificia Universidad Javeriana in Cali, Colombia, spoke, and we discussed the growth of OArb in Colombia. Professor Dussan explained how arbitration is more efficient, less expensive, and more helpful than the courts, especially for consumer claims in Colombia. The effectiveness of OArb in Colombia rests on enforcement in the national courts. The country has since passed a new law that allows for international arbitration, including OArb procedures.

Still, it is best to avoid the courts or the need for court enforcement when committed to arbitration. Parties may seek arbitration to avoid the courts, but when you face a recalcitrant award debtor, you need to go to the national courts for enforcement, the very thing you were trying to avoid. A better approach with OArb is to foster reputational and other nonjudicial means for encouraging award enforcement. For example, non-legal sanctions can be used that are based primarily on reputation. One of the lead examples of reputational sanctions is trust marks.

There is not yet a central hub or main platform for cross-border consumer OArb within South America, but there is hope for further developments. The institution of ODR is still very new in South America, but there is a great deal of conversation around OArb to assist the courts in Colombia. Indeed, this same topic was top of mind in my interview with Nicolás Lozada Pimiento, who is a partner of the firm Rincón Cuéllar & Asociados and a professor of arbitration, trade, and business law at the universities Externado de Colombia, Javeriana, Sabana, and Santo Tomás.[16] After receiving a master's degree in Singapore, he worked for a British law firm where he became interested in international commercial arbitration and international investment arbitration.

Professor Lozada Pimiento returned to Colombia in 2011 and joined the Ministry of Justice. At the time, he coordinated work on drafting a new arbitration law in Colombia. He also became interested in working on implementing ODR and OArb in Colombia. The Ministry was very open to implementing OArb, and worked on making virtual hearings, electronic briefings, and electronic evidence available in each part of the arbitration procedure. In 2012, an arbitration statute was issued, which provided that every step of arbitration may be conducted online. The Ministry implemented the statute through a decree, which included provisions for virtual arbitration. Lozada Pimiento worked in the government for two more years and became the delegate for UNCITRAL Working Group 3, which sought to create an international cross-border ODR system for resolving small claims. He has been a very vocal advocate for OArb and sees a bright future for ODR and OArb in Latin America.

Latin America is also home to one of the most progressive OArb systems: Kleros. Kleros was created by an Argentinian developer and uses blockchain-tokenized voting within a crowdsourced system. Kleros is discussed in further detail in Chapter 11. Furthermore, Brazil has strong ODR systems that include OArb, while Chile and Mexico also have implemented digital justice on various platforms. Mercado Libre, the Latin American equivalent to eBay, manages hundreds of thousands of disputes using essentially OArb following eBay's example. Some leaders are hopeful that soon there will be a multinational ODR system for cross-border transactions, and momentum toward state-backed OArb and ODR systems.

The platforms discussed are not simply Zoom arbitration. Again, the movement is toward sanctioned platforms. Lozada Pimiento opined that the ideal ODR system would have four main components: (1) easy access (access to the internet is still an issue in Latin America, so improvements are necessary in this area); (2) very affordable or even free, and most likely implemented through a public system or an affordable private system; (3) fast and efficient; and (4) available in Spanish or Portuguese, along with English, if available throughout Latin America.

Change is difficult, but it is possible to move toward more OArb, and this could be especially good for international claims due to enforcement under the New York Convention. There may also be a need for streamlined continental legal regulation in order to assure allowance for OArb. For example, Lozada Pimiento was involved in the creation of an OArb system for resolving secured transactions issues. The process did not have hearings. It was a fast-tracked asynchronous system in which parties simply submit their documents electronically. The process could be completed as quickly as two months. As seen with FairClaims and other OArb mechanisms for smaller dollar claims, it is sometimes better to skip hearings and focus on documents for fast-tracked dispute resolution.

G. ODR AFRICA NETWORK

ODR and OArb are also growing in various forms in Africa. On this issue, Morenike Obi-Farinde, the founder of the ODR Africa Network and managing partner of the Adigun Ogunseitan & Co. law firm in Lagos, Nigeria, spoke.[17] Obi-Farinde pursued alternative dispute resolution early in her legal career as an alternative to the civil justice system, where the backlog was insurmountable in Africa. She quickly became interested in ODR in 2006 and began exploring how technology could improve speed and efficiency in dispute resolution. She attended numerous forums and brought back that knowledge to Nigeria and more broadly to Africa. Obi-Farinde believed that Nigeria could experience great benefits from applying technology to dispute resolution, even with the challenges of access to the internet and good bandwidth.

Africa is similar to the U.S., in that many people see online mediation and online arbitration as almost synonymous with Zoom. ODR Africa is trying to educate and train people to understand that ODR and OArb include much more than using videoconferencing. The challenge is helping leaders see the worth of various technologies. Many learned that technology opened the only avenues for resolving disputes during the Covid-19 pandemic. The Lagos High Court was mostly locked down from March to July 2020, but it could have proceeded with the business if it had embraced and built the necessary infrastructure at the start of the pandemic. The Citizens State Mediation Center does significant work, especially in the area of landlord/tenant disputes, but it was shut down until October 2020. ODR could have been beneficial to keep it running.

Cultural norms also create challenges for OArb and ODR. For example, Obi-Farinde explained how Nigerian culture values in-person contact, and there is less reliance on computers and computer-mediated communication in Nigeria. Accordingly, a text-based OArb platform may not be the most effective for the Nigerian people. However, Nigerians are very accustomed to mobile phones, and mobile-friendly processes may gain traction. Nigeria has been able to move into the digital age because of mobile phones. Furthermore, there is a movement toward various types of ODR and OArb due to the pandemic shutdown.

H. DIGITAL SERVICES ACT

Another new frontier for ODR and OArb is opening due to the Digital Services Act (DSA). In the sixth podcast episode of *The Arbitration Conversation* (after it moved from a webcast on YouTube to a podcast), I discussed the Meta Oversight Board, a dispute resolution body set up by Meta to resolve disputes about Facebook and Instagram content, with Professor Pietro Ortolani.[18] This interview explored the nature of the Board, its procedure, and its prospects. Against that background, the conversation then touched upon the future of content-related dispute resolution, and the role that arbitral institutions will play in Europe in the wake of the DSA.

Professor Ortolani discussed the new Meta Oversight Board as a form of OArb, or at least a form of ODR to some extent. It also implements interesting aspects of procedural law from the EU and elsewhere, creating a new creature of dispute resolution. It opens the door to a new type of ODR for resolving content disputes, which are increasingly important. These are disputes about the veracity or appropriateness of digital content on large platforms, like Facebook and Instagram in this instance. For example, the de-platforming of Donald Trump from Facebook and the Meta Oversight Board's ruling garnered worldwide attention. Still, Professor Ortolani noted how cases involving "little guys" also have received attention from the Meta Oversight Board, especially when the matter could have implications for the Terms of Service at Meta.

Relatedly, I discussed what type of process may work for platform regulation a year before speaking with Professor Ortolani in Episode 62 of *The Arbitration Conversation* in my interview with Professor Rory Van Loo.[19] Professor Van Loo provided insights related to his article proposing a process for determining when and whether posts or parties are eliminated from platforms such as Amazon, Facebook, Twitter (now called X), and so on. He proposed that regulations are necessary, drawing a comparison to credit reporting companies. Additionally, he noted the Meta Oversight Board as an example process and suggested that using online hearings would make sense to cut costs related to content moderation.

Moreover, these new tribunals and ODR mechanisms will become increasingly important now that the DSA has become law in Europe.[20] Professor Pieter Wolters also spoke on this topic. Wolters is an associate professor in the interdisciplinary hub for digitalization and society at Radboud University in the Netherlands. He provided a DSA recap and noted how it gives digital platforms new responsibilities. Examples of companies covered by the DSA include Facebook, Instagram, Amazon, X, and others, and the law applies when there is illegal content posted on these websites. Nonetheless, these websites will not be liable unless they fail to take the required actions under the new law.

In particular, large portals must follow notice and action procedures when they are alerted of illegal content on their websites. This is meant to be an easy process for flagging illegal content, with safeguards to protect freedom of expression. The law does not support the automatic removal of content. Instead, it requires platforms to create internal complaint processing systems for dealing with claims of illegal content. These processes should use ODR of some type, such as online mediation or arbitration.

The DSA is expected to have broad impact, considering that any platform that deals in Europe will have to comply with the law. Similar to the General Data Protection Regulation (GDPR), it is likely that the DSA will have impacts far beyond Europe. Furthermore, its requirement of ODR for notice and action issues creates a new and robust market for ODR.

In sum, ODR and OArb go well beyond the use of Zoom and other video technologies in dispute resolution. There has been an expansion of technologies in dispute resolution worldwide, and it is likely to continue, as technology continually becomes more robust and ever-changing.

NOTES

1 *See Top Breakthrough Technologies of 2023*, MIT Tech. Rev. (Jan. 9, 2023), www.technologyreview.com/2023/01/09/1066394/10-breakthrough-technologies-2023 (see also the previous annual reviews back to 2001).
2 Richard Susskind, Tomorrow's Lawyers: An Introduction to Your Future (2013).
3 Amy J. Schmitz & Colin Rule, The New Handshake: Online Dispute Resolution and the Future of Consumer Protection (2017). *See also* Amy J. Schmitz, *Building on OArb Attributes in Pursuit of Justice*, *in* Arbitration in the Digital Age: The Brave New World of Arbitration, 182–208 (2018).
4 Ethan Katsh & Colin Rule, *What We Know and Need to Know About Online Dispute Resolution*, 67 S.C. L. Rev. 329–30 (2016). *See also* Ethan Katsh & Orna Rabinovich-Einy, Digital Justice: Technology and the Internet of Disputes 1–25 (2017).
5 Amy J. Schmitz & Janet Martinez, *ODR Providers Operating in the U.S.*, *in* ODR and Innovation in the United States, Online Dispute Resolution: Theory and Practice: A Treatise on Technology and Dispute Resolution (Mohamed S. Abdel Wahab, Ethan Katsh & Daniel Rainey eds., 2020), https://papers.ssrn.com/sol3/papers.cfm?abstract_id=3599511.
6 *See id.*
7 Chittu Nagarajan & Amy Schmitz, *Arbitration Conversation No. 50: Chittu Nagarajan, Founder and CEO of CREKODR.com*, YouTube (Nov. 2, 2020), www.youtube.com/watch?v=AUX2PLuyjaQ.
8 Graham Ross & Amy Schmitz, *Arbitration Conversation No. 52: Graham Ross, Head of International Marketing at Smartsettle.com*, YouTube (Nov. 12, 2020), https://www.youtube.com/watch?v=Rd4eiCU9Qdk&t=3s.
9 Richard Ormond, Jake Stango & Amy Schmitz, *Arbitration Conversation No. 64: Richard Ormond and Jake Stango of Ejudicate.com*, YouTube (Jan. 23, 2021), www.youtube.com/watch?v=fJLBF-2yqY8.
10 Brief, Ejudicate, www.thinkbrief.com/ (last visited Jan. 31, 2023).
11 *Id.*
12 Stephen Kane & Amy Schmitz, *Arbitration Conversation No. 67: Stephen Kane, Founder and CEO of FairClaims.com*, YouTube (Feb. 5, 2021), https://www.youtube.com/watch?v=WFzybp-BoSM.
13 FairClaims, How It Works, www.fairclaims.com/how-it-works (last visited July 19, 2023).
14 *Id.*
15 Hafez Virjee & Amy Schmitz, *Arbitration Conversation No. 48: Hafez Virjee, President and Co-Founder of Delos Dispute Resolution*, YouTube (Oct. 26, 2020), www.youtube.com/watch?v=rNU4WBNU6Oo.
16 Nicolás Lozada Pimiento & Amy Schmitz, *Arbitration Conversation No. 33: Prof. Nicolás Lozada Pimiento from Universidad Externado de Colombia*, YouTube (Aug. 24, 2020), www.youtube.com/watch?v=h2Bd3GljIyY.
17 Morenike Obi-Farinde & Amy Schmitz, *Arbitration Conversation No. 44: Morenike Obi-Farinde, Founder, ODRAfrica Network*, YouTube (Oct. 8, 2020), www.youtube.com/watch?v=ZGsgqRwKN9w.
18 Pietro Ortolani & Amy Schmitz, *Arbitration Conversation No. 6: Facebook's Oversight Board, and the Future of Arbitration Under Europe's Digital Services Act*, PodBean (June 28, 2022), https://arbitrate.podbean.com/e/episode-6-facebook-s-oversight-board-and-the-future-of-arbitration-under-europe-s-digital-services-act/.

19 Rory Van Loo & Amy Schmitz, *Arbitration Conversation No. 62: Prof. Rory Van Loo of the Boston University School of Law*, YouTube (Jan. 23, 2021), https://www.youtube.com/watch?v=ZE1i_wL_s94.

20 Pieter Wolters & Amy Schmitz, *Arbitration Conversation No. 11: The Digital Services Act in Europe (Part Two)*, PodBean (Oct. 14, 2022), https://arbitrate.podbean.com/e/episode-11-the-digital-services-act-in-europe-part-two/.

Chapter 11

AI, Data Analytics, and Blockchain

This chapter adds to the prior discussions, delving further into interviews that focused on "the future" of arbitration. For example, data analytics and AI are now entering arbitration practice and policy. Additionally, blockchain arbitration is already in use, and this chapter explains what this is and shares insights from conversations about Kleros, Jur, and other blockchain arbitration mechanisms. Additionally, in my discussions with leaders of CyberArb and ODR.com, we noted how AI and data analytics can be built into arbitration platforms, and we talked about privacy and cybersecurity concerns. This is the future, and the future is now for technology in arbitration.

A. CREATIVE RECONSTRUCTION

In a frank discussion of the future of ADR and ODR with my friend and ODR leader Colin Rule,[1] CEO of Arbitrate.com, Mediate.com, and ODR.com, and a mastermind behind eBay's original ODR system, we discussed how the Covid-19 pandemic created a moment in history, where dispute resolution is at the core. It highlighted how technology is transforming the world, including the world of arbitration.

With technology, we can build a new justice system through the internet. However, we have to engage in creative deconstruction and reconstruction, and take the time to brainstorm ideas to generate a cycle of creation. For example, for every 100 ideas that we generate, 99 will fail, but one may be genius. It is a cycle of creation perfect for dispute resolution and a field built on problem-solving. We should consider mediation, arbitration, negotiation, neutral evaluation, and more as tools in our problem-solving toolbox and not be afraid to consider the full spectrum of these tools in concert. Moreover, technology adds another layer of creativity and promise to reimagine access to remedies, and justice.

The value of technology in arbitration is not merely something that technologists advance to justify their jobs. Arbitrators are also interested in how technology tools can be leveraged to change the way technology-related disputes are resolved. On related topics, Myriam Seers, an international arbitrator and lawyer, and chair of the ICC Canada Arbitration Committee, spoke.[2] We discussed how technology can change the way disputes are resolved, and how there is often no reason to expend the resources for in-person dispute resolution. Technology makes arbitration more affordable for many, including small- and medium-sized businesses. We are still determining what the future has in store, but it is clear that technology will continue to change the way we resolve disputes and practice law. Technology tools should be used to expand A2J internationally, and there is a need for out-of-the-box thinking in arbitration.

At the same time, legal evolution is not easy. Professor Bill Henderson from Indiana University Maurer School of Law spoke on this topic.[3] Professor Henderson is a giant in legal innovation, and conducts research focused on empirical analysis of the legal profession. He has been listed among the 100 most influential lawyers in America and provided important insights into our discussion. Some bottlenecks to innovation and change include the lack of experimentation and legal sandboxes, often due to strict regulations on the practice of law. Generational issues also create hurdles for change; sometimes managers must cycle out for new ideas to take hold.

As noted in the prior chapter, it is difficult to get arbitrators to see that OArb can be so much more than using Teams or Zoom. Diffusion Theory suggests we can speed up innovation through multidisciplinary movements and organizational disruption. Change also requires money, as creating new programs usually comes with startup costs. Having leaders who are invested in change also helps bring about change, as we saw with the Civil Resolution Tribunal (CRT) and its dedicated leaders in British Columbia, Canada. The CRT uses its own code and is made for people to use without a lawyer. Using human-centered technology that is mobile-friendly is also important for technology to expand A2J. At the same time, ADA compliance is necessary, and lawyers must be flexible and open to change.[4]

B. DEEPER DIVE INTO AI AND DATA ANALYTICS

Professor Angie Raymond has explained that there is a great deal of overstatement and confusion regarding artificial intelligence (AI).[5] AI has become a phrase that garners disagreement regarding its meaning. Some state that AI includes everything using technology, even calculators, while others think that AI only includes machine learning and beyond. Regardless of definitions, there is untapped potential for AI in dispute resolution and arbitration. AI is growing in acceptance, and data analytics have been employed to make decisions in many realms. AI is entering the courtroom and disrupting the law.[6] It is helping organize cases files, conduct discovery, and complete legal research.[7] It is possible that AI or data analytics may assist fair and efficient dispute resolution in some areas of law, and seems especially apt for simple small dollar e-commerce cases where parties may appreciate the use of predictive analysis and quick resolutions. At the same time, machine learning and sophisticated algorithms will likely become "smarter" with training and infusion of more data over time.

Indeed, AI is top of mind in law, and every conversation seems focused on AI these days. The pace of change is incredible in this space! The key is to understand the promise and pitfalls of AI and focus on the *responsible use* of AI in arbitration. My tagline about AI in arbitration: "*It is not all good or all bad, it is how you use it!*"

To provide insights directly from AI about AI, I asked ChatGPT "What are the opportunities and challenges for AI in arbitration?" Here is what it said:

> AI presents various opportunities and challenges in the field of arbitration. Here are some of the key aspects:
>
> Opportunities:
>
> 1. **Efficient Case Management:** AI can assist in managing arbitration cases by automating administrative tasks such as document management, scheduling, and tracking deadlines. This allows arbitrators to focus more on substantive issues and expedites the overall arbitration process.
> 2. **Data Analysis and Prediction:** AI tools can analyze large volumes of case data and identify patterns, precedents, and legal arguments. This assists arbitrators in making well-informed decisions and predicting case outcomes based on historical data.
> 3. **Document Review and Discovery:** AI-powered technologies, such as natural language processing (NLP) and machine learning, can aid in the review and categorization of documents, reducing the time and effort required for discovery and facilitating a more comprehensive analysis of evidence.
> 4. **Decision Support:** AI systems can provide arbitrators with relevant legal information, statutes, regulations, and precedents, thereby supporting decision-making and ensuring consistency in rulings.
> 5. **Language Translation:** AI-based language translation tools can help overcome language barriers in international arbitration, enabling efficient communication and understanding between parties from different linguistic backgrounds.
>
> Challenges:
>
> 1. **Bias and Fairness:** AI algorithms are prone to biases based on the data they are trained on, potentially leading to unfair outcomes. Ensuring that AI tools used in arbitration are unbiased and promote fairness is a significant challenge.

2. **Interpretation and Context:** AI systems may struggle with interpreting complex legal concepts, nuanced arguments, and the contextual understanding required in arbitration. The reliance on AI for decision-making needs to strike a balance between automation and human judgment.
3. **Privacy and Confidentiality:** Arbitration involves sensitive information, and the use of AI technologies introduces concerns regarding data privacy and confidentiality. Adequate measures must be in place to safeguard the privacy and security of data used in AI-based arbitration processes.
4. **Ethical Considerations:** AI raises ethical questions, such as accountability, transparency, and the ethical responsibility of decisions made by machines. Addressing these ethical considerations is crucial to ensure the integrity and legitimacy of AI-driven arbitration.
5. **Technical Limitations:** AI technologies are continuously evolving, and their effectiveness in complex legal tasks may still have limitations. Development and implementation challenges need to be addressed to ensure the reliability and accuracy of AI systems in the arbitration context.

> It is important to approach the integration of AI in arbitration thoughtfully, recognizing the potential benefits while carefully managing the associated challenges to maintain fairness, transparency, and the integrity of the arbitration process.[8]

This is a pretty good start! However, the opportunities are more nuanced, as are the challenges. Machine learning and Large Language Models (LLMs like GPT) are only as good as the data upon which they are trained or based, and often more data is needed to improve accuracy and comprehensive analysis. For example, any prediction based on only published cases fails to consider private arbitration awards and private settlements—how most disputes are resolved. Published cases are not the norm.

Also, there is a danger of "*anchoring bias*" in that a human who is provided a prediction based on "the data" may be anchored on that outcome and fail to use independent judgment, which is particularly important when the prediction is false or biased. AI can be problematic for legal determinations and potentially worsen the risk of bias in decision-making.[9] There is evidence that people tend to defer to statistical data instead of using the data to help form an independent judgment.[10] Accordingly, we may hope that a human will remain "in the loop" and only use analytics to assist their decision accuracy, but there is fear that humans will "rubber stamp" AI or algorithmic decisions.

There is concern that using AI to provide "bot" predictions to judges or arbitrators could mean bots decide cases. This is made worse when AI algorithms rely on data that reflects human prejudice or is incomplete or otherwise faulty.[11] This "garbage in, garbage out" problem occurs when AI "learns" from biased information. Some also worry that machine learning may take on a life of its own, rendering it harder to identify the factors leading to a particular outcome as computing becomes more robust and advanced.[12]

Still, AI can be very useful for arbitration and arbitrators, and there is no reason to outlaw its use. Instead, it is important to proceed cautiously, understanding the limitations and risks of the AI you use. This is similar to a builder who would not use a hammer when a job requires a screwdriver. AI is good at some tasks but unsuited for others. For example, AI may be used to expand A2J and help self-represented litigants frame their arguments for an arbitration, but generative AI like GPT is not good at citing recent legal cases.[13]

Of course, the day may come when predictive analytics and AI can render quick *and fair* resolutions. AI and data analytics may have a place in predicting how best to resolve particular disputes, especially in simple low-dollar and low-conflict cases. Some parties may prefer such quick data-driven decisions over a more expensive and time-consuming human-arbitrated process in some cases. Even so, AI and machine learning are currently not sufficiently advanced to provide "bot" resolutions with sufficient accuracy and acceptance as of 2023 when this book is being written. This may change in the future for specific cases, but as of the writing of this book, we are not quite there and should proceed with caution.

Professor Nicolas Vermeys, at the Université de Montréal, in Montreal, Canada, spoke on AI in dispute resolution. Professor Vermeys is the director of the Centre de recherche en droit public (CRDP), and the associate director of the Cyberjustice Laboratory in Montréal. When it comes to AI and the law, Professor Vermeys is truly a leader. Not only is he a member of the Quebec Bar, but he is also a certified information system security professional (CISSP) as recognized by the International Information System Security Certification Consortium (ISC2).

In our discussion, we addressed AI in arbitration and the ways AI can assist with dispute resolution.[14] Professor Vermeys explained how Canada's Civil Resolution Tribunal (CRT) is more of an expert system, in that it leads individuals through a series of questions to help guide them and provides options for the next steps in seeking resolution of small claims disputes. This type of expert system is a form of AI under some definitions and is often referred to as a "solution explorer" or "guided pathway." Under this type of system, a litigant logs in, answers a question, and AI guides them to the next question based on the answer, and so on. This is the form of AI currently used and referenced in most dispute resolution processes. However, this is not machine learning and is based on more of a fixed rule-based system.

The next iteration is to have a bot arbitrator decide using AI. Professor Vermeys has referred to this as Artificial Intelligence Dispute Resolution

(AIDR). As Professor Raymond noted in her interview, discussed earlier, we are still not at a stage where this is happening in legal cases. Courts are not unleashing bot judges, at least not in the U.S. Also, "bot" arbitrators are not deciding cases enforceable under the FAA and New York Convention as of 2023, at least.

That does not mean that AI and machine learning could not be helpful for some tasks in arbitration. The media and commentators are perhaps a bit too quick to rule out all use of AI and data-based decision-making as all tainted with bias. True, there are some scary examples of data analytics gone wrong. Certainly, there have been legitimate concerns raised by some programs used for determining bail or jail, or even sentencing. ProPublica famously uncovered bias in risk assessments used to determine the likelihood of recidivism.[15] AI built on biased data will produce biased results. Garbage in, garbage out.

That does not mean that all data analytics and AI lack value. People have built-in biases, and their life experiences affect their decisions. Studies indicate how various factors impact human decision-making, including what they ate for breakfast, fights with family, hidden biases, and more. With AIDR, having an algorithm means some of those biases are reduced or eliminated, and we may believe that "the data" is at least more transparent than subconscious bias. Additionally, humans create algorithms, which may mean that human biases could lurk behind the algorithms. Perhaps a balanced combination of human + machine could eventually produce even better resolutions than all-human or all-machine?

There are yet more issues that arise in determining the effectiveness of an algorithm. Researchers need to obtain massive amounts of data, and properly structure that data to train an algorithm to create a program. Furthermore, arbitration is supposed to be a private process. Accordingly, it would be challenging, if even possible, to gather sufficient data regarding arbitration proceedings and outcomes to use data from arbitration for predictive analytics. Even if you could find a sufficient and representative sample of public arbitration awards, how do researchers know whether the decisions were "good" or "bad"? Legal determinations are also more complex due to the nuance of information, facts, and other nuances related to arbitration awards.

It may be that the better use of AI in arbitration is to simply provide information. For example, training a "chat bot" to guide individuals involved in dispute resolution could be helpful. Professor Vermeys described what they are working on at Cyberjustice Laboratory, ODRAI. This is especially exciting for expanding A2J. The idea is not to provide statistics on how a case is likely to come out, or how they have come out in prior litigation. Instead, ODRAI would involve providing better tools for individuals in a dispute resolution process. This could include general information about how prior cases with XYZ facts have been decided. The information would be more nuanced and aimed to assist, and not take over, the decision-making for the parties. Parties crave information to assess their positions and those of the other side. Unfortunately, most people cannot afford to hire attorneys and they are already looking to Google and Chat-GPT for help—so the creation of public, vetted, sanctioned, and safe legal wizard technologies would be an improvement over rogue use of tools that are not up to speed for legal analysis.

Arbitrators may also use AI to help them make informed decisions. This is not a "bot" decision. The AI is not deciding for the arbitrator. Instead, an arbitrator could look at the data provided to understand more about themselves as decision-makers, hence exploring the "human plus machine" aspect. For example, looking at data analytics may help arbitrators learn about their own biases. AI also may help arbitrators assess law quickly and fill in gaps in their understanding, still checking all cites and any legal determinations.

Olof Heggemann, Founder of Eperoto.com, was interviewed as an expert with experience from the Swedish public court system, and in banking and law firms. Eperoto is a tool for valuing legal cases using decision science.[16] The tool was inspired by psychology and academics worldwide who have focused on how parties assess risk in deciding whether to bring a case to court. Often parties do not take the time to adequately assess risk, including intangible costs, in deciding to sue—although these are pivotal questions.

Heggemann explained that the Eperto platform is not based on machine learning, but instead uses decision theory and decision analysis, and connection to psychology. It is often hard to comprehend how likely something is to happen due to our psychological nuances. Good lawyers must have a level head in assessing litigation risk, including data analytics. Sound risk analysis is more efficient and helps parties drill down to determine their bottom line. This coincides with other interviews, such as the interview of Professor Lande, highlighting the importance of a problem-solving perspective in dispute resolution.

Using data analytics to assist risk assessment is also in line with interviews regarding the value of AI and data analytics. AI might be a tool to help us, as humans, assess massive amounts of data—often central to litigation risk. Cost-benefit analysis and level-headed consideration of a case is paramount for effective lawyering. Attorneys are asked to serve as counselors for their clients, providing sound advice regarding a given case. AI can help in this endeavor.

There are challenges and hurdles in creating new technological tools in dispute resolution. As we heard from Mr. Kane with FairClaims, there are certainly risks in any startup business. Additionally, it is difficult to remain focused as new ideas emerge. There is always a very broad horizon of things and directions you can move in when you first start a business, but it is essential to remain focused on a goal and look for opportunities to learn and grow.

C. CYBERSECURITY AND PRIVACY

A key issue in OArb is cybersecurity and privacy. Unfortunately, many attorneys and parties do not fully understand or consider the importance of cybersecurity when sending information and participating in online processes. It was for this reason that Wendy Gonzales founded CyberArb, which is an NGO focused on promoting cybersecurity and having a concrete plan to safeguard the safety of data in the "new normal" of OArb.[17] It was fascinating to interview Gonzales, who is passionate about helping individuals and companies with cybersecurity matters. CyberArb provides practical guidance and steps to use daily to protect cybersecurity. This includes online checklists, a blog, and workshops.

It is important to consider every level of privacy and security in OArb. Cybersecurity is a set of measures, and all those measures need to be applied at all levels to maintain integrity. Gonzales explains that it is like a house, and you need to protect everything, not only the main door, or that one portion of the garden; every level in the house should be protected. First, make sure that you are using a secure network. It is too easy to "let your guard down" and use public networks, but they are not safe and could be very dangerous. Additionally, there may be some cases where blockchain could be used to further the safety of information. Moreover, there are ways to use AI for cybersecurity.

Relatedly, Sophie Nappert, an independent practice arbitrator based in London, spoke. Before becoming a full-time arbitrator, she pursued a career as an advocate and was head of International Arbitration at a global law firm. Arbitrator Nappert pioneered scholarship on technology in arbitration that is cited as a reference on the topic, and, in 2021, she co-founded ArbTech, a worldwide, online community forum fostering cross-disciplinary dialogue on technology, dispute resolution, and the future of justice. Nappert is also a mentor for the CyberArb initiative.

The discussions with Nappert focused on the intersection between arbitration and technology and the increasing importance of cybersecurity, data protection, and cryptography tools such as blockchains in the process of conducting arbitrations online.[18] Nappert highlighted the need for practical information regarding cybersecurity in arbitration, as noted earlier, and access to training and education like that provided by CyberArb. There is a special need for smaller organizations with different cybersecurity resources that smaller organizations can access, as most do not have on-staff cybersecurity counsel. Moreover, arbitrators need to understand the importance of protecting privacy and data going forward in order to have a vibrant arbitration practice. As an ethical arbitrator, you must pay attention to cybersecurity. In cases with state entities, for example, it's surprising people quite high up in government departments may, use their private email addresses to hear about a case. As an arbitrator, when you spot this at the beginning, you must address this issue and use secure platforms for exchanging documents.

The importance of cybersecurity and privacy was also top of mind in speaking with Gary Benton, an internationally recognized arbitrator and mediator with expertise in international business, private investment, technology, IP, and emerging growth matters. Mr. Benton is the founder and currently serves as the chairman of the Silicon Valley Arbitration and Mediation Center (SVAMC) in Palo Alto, California.[19] Mr. Benton explained how he became involved in technology arbitration and has been working to educate people about the benefits of arbitration for technology-related claims. This includes large group presentations, as well as one-on-one meetings with firms. He explained how companies in Silicon Valley have been very comfortable with litigation but need to understand the benefits of ADR and arbitration. Additionally, he noted how technology companies are looking for more specialized expertise, which is available in arbitration and mediation.

At the same time, cybersecurity and cryptocurrency disputes are becoming more common—including blockchain and smart contracts. In these cases, it is essential to have an expert arbitrator who understands the technical issues, can speak the language, and knows how important it is to protect the privacy and cybersecurity of the process. Mr. Benton also provided predictions about the future of arbitration. This includes:

- Blockchain and everything that derives from it;
- Biotechnology and genetic engineering;
- Artificial intelligence; and
- Quantum computing.

These areas all open up new arbitral opportunities, including opportunities for younger and newer arbitrators. Disputes will not go away in the digital age. Instead, new technologies create more and different disputes. Additionally, technology disputes are not necessarily high value. There are also lower dollar claims, creating yet more opportunities for younger individuals who would like to gain arbitration experience.

D. BLOCKCHAIN ARBITRATION

On the topic of blockchain and smart contracts, I interviewed Oladeji M. Tiamiyu, who at the time was a Clinical Fellow at the Harvard Negotiation and Mediation Clinical Program (HNMCP). Before joining HNMCP, Oladeji was an Online Dispute Resolution Fellow with the Resolution Systems Institute in Chicago, Illinois, where he helped develop a pilot ODR program for family law disputes. Professor Tiamiyu has also worked with Gambia's Truth and Reconciliation Commission and Constitutional Review Commission. He has experience as a teacher on Reunion Island off the coast of Madagascar and as a community organizer with Organizing for America in Ohio. Oladeji has been a member of teaching teams for Harvard Law School's Negotiation Workshop, an executive-level program at the Harvard Negotiation Institute, and with the Harvard Graduate School of Education.[20]

Professor Tiamiyu explained blockchain as a simple way to store data in a digital ledger. We discussed how this transparent ledger and blockchain-based enforcement is a means for creating trust. Still, there will be disputes. As noted throughout the book, technology creates new and different types of disputes. This opens opportunities for arbitration and ODR. Smart contracts will have bugs and errors in code, and there will be uncertainty; uncertainty leads to confusion, and confusion leads to disputes.

Accordingly, there must be a way to resolve these new blockchain-related disputes. In this new world, "fitting the forum to the fuss" takes on a whole new life as we seek to "fit the technology to the fuss." Professor Tiamiyu advocates in the interview for optionality—a "one size fits all" approach will not work for blockchain dispute resolution. There must be different types of ODR to fit various disputes and parties. One system will not be acceptable to all parties and all disputes. Party satisfaction in dispute resolution is often tied to choice; individuals tend to be more satisfied in a process that they agreed to use and for which they feel a sense of ownership.

With this in mind, we have seen an expansion of the available arbitration types. This book talks a great deal about OArb, which often involves a virtual hearing. Indeed, OArb with an expert arbitrator may be quite well suited for blockchain-related disputes. However, tokenized arbitration goes further in using technology to help end disputes. In contrast to simple OArb, tokenized dispute resolution allows anonymous users to vote on who they think should "win" a dispute using digital tokens. Selected voters have the power in crowdsourced dispute resolution, in which the voters' majority opinion ends the dispute.[21]

For example, Kleros is a crowdsourced online arbitration "court" built on the Ethereum public blockchain for the resolution of blockchain related disputes.[22] Kleros aims to be "[a] fast, inexpensive, transparent, reliable and decentralized" ODR system built on game theory and crowdsourced justice.[23] Kleros enlists "jurors" from around the world based on the number of "Pinakion" tokens (cryptocurrency) jurors deposit to show their interest in resolving a given dispute.[24] Parties to a dispute present their cases to the jurors based on the documents, using an online platform. The jurors then use their tokens to vote.[25]

After the vote is closed, the party with the most juror support wins. Additionally, jurors benefit from selecting the party with the most votes by taking the tokens of jurors who sided with the "losing" party.[26] Jurors also earn compensation from the arbitration fees that the parties pay to use the Kleros court.[27] Kleros has done various research experiments and works to combat fraud and collusion among jurors. For example, jurors are penalized for communicating with each other.[28] Furthermore, a fraudster would have to buy 51 percent of the staked work tokens to "buy" the jury.[29] At the same time, Kleros can force the system to stop fraud if necessary because it controls the tokens.[30]

Ideas around decentralized justice and tokenized arbitration continue to evolve, but it has seen some success. For example, in September 2020, a disagreement arising from a rental estate leasing agreement in Mexico led to the use of the Kleros Protocol to guide the arbitral decision. The parties in the case stipulated in their agreement that if a disagreement arose, it would be referred to an arbitrator who was to use the Kleros system as the basis of their award. Accordingly, the arbitrator in the case compiled all the evidence and digital materials from both parties and submitted it to Kleros, which submitted it to three Kleros jurors. Based on the jurors' unanimous ruling for the landlord, the arbitrator rendered an arbitral award ordering payment of rent. The landlord then took the award to a Mexican court, and got it judicially confirmed. This was a significant step in recognizing a blockchain platform as a legitimate form of arbitration.[31] It was notable that the arbitrator still rendered the award, and it was not directly the Kleros "award" without arbitrator action.

E. METAVERSE

The metaverse is no single "place" at this point. It is more of a concept: a 3D digital world where individuals use virtual avatars to interact with other users to "make friends, rear virtual pets, design virtual fashion items, buy virtual real estate, attend events, create and sell digital art—and earn money to boot."[32] Some examples include virtual reality platforms: Decentraland, The Sandbox, and Meta, where users can interact in complex and immersive ways. Accordingly, individuals can create avatars and meet, discuss, make purchases, and even open law firms in the metaverse. At least one major law firm has opened an office in the metaverse, and it would not be surprising to see arbitrations conducted through avatars in the metaverse (if that is not already happening, especially by the time of this book's publication).

Regarding arbitration in the metaverse, Paul Cohen spoke as part of the new audio-only *Arbitration Conversation* series.[33] Mr. Cohen is a leading international arbitrator and practitioner concerning energy, technology, and finance. He became interested in technology after seeing an HD videoconference for the first time. Furthermore, he talked about the vision for metaverse arbitration, using a holographic recreation of the real world. Still, he noted how avatars may be too difficult to take seriously in an arbitration, if all parties and the arbitrators were to appear as glorified cartoons. Nonetheless, this may become "normal" due to the speed of change with technologies. Mr. Cohen also opined that using the metaverse for arbitration could be an equalizer, although, currently, it is cost prohibitive for most disputes. Still, metaverse arbitration seems especially promising for disputes arising in the metaverse as it allows parties to resolve their disputes in the same "location" where the dispute arose.

Metaverse arbitration is in the conception stages, and more musings by commentators than actual arbitration proceedings with binding authority as of this book's writing. The conception raises numerous questions about how the structure of arbitration can be adapted to a metaverse environment.[34] If law firms can set up shop in the metaverse, it seems that arbitrations could occur in the metaverse, but what rules will apply? Also, what restrictions will be in place to verify humanity, especially if parties can stay anonymous and operate only through avatars? How can the law grapple with anonymity, especially as AI-created avatars and deepfakes emerge?

Arbitrators could potentially arbitrate as avatars in the metaverse and remain anonymous in the process, but how would parties then be able to assess partiality? Or perhaps metaverse arbitrators would appear as avatars but be required to prove their identity and humanity, which could enhance enforcement. Otherwise, there may be fear that the arbitrators are fraudsters or even bots. If everyone is anonymous, there would be no bias concerns since an arbitrator would not know who the parties are, so the arbitrator would have no reason to be biased for or against a party. How can one harbor bias for a party if they have no idea who the party is? On the other hand, would the parties be truly anonymous after putting forth evidence? An arbitrator would immediately know if a close associate was presenting a case based on the evidence presented, and even the language used in submissions. Accordingly, it seems wise that arbitrators must disclose and prove their identity to preserve integrity and address perceptions of bias.

Other questions relate to arbitration law itself, asking whether a metaverse arbitration would pass legal muster under the FAA and New York Convention. Arbitration, by its definition must include a neutral third party. This, again, raises questions if the arbitrator remains anonymous. Additionally, how would other provisions, such as finality and limited review, apply when the process is in the metaverse? It is unclear how courts would receive any application to compel arbitration in the metaverse, let alone enforce the resulting arbitration award. What law would apply if the "seat" is in the metaverse? Would sufficient "writing" exist for an award to be confirmed? Many questions remain, but parties may be able to address these issues in an arbitration agreement to use the metaverse for the hearing. With the pace of technological changes, one cannot say whether metaverse will become an accepted reality backed by law.

F. SUMMARY

In sum, the pace of change is great when it comes to technology in arbitration. Technology is a powerful tool in dispute resolution that keeps getting more robust, and perhaps scarier in some ways. Many concerns have emerged with respect to AI, and there is need to address bias in AI as well as unethical and unsafe systems. There may be a time in the not-too-distant future when parties and arbitrators must prove that they are human if using OArb. Deepfakes and ever-evolving generative AI provide unique risks for arbitration. Policymakers, practitioners, and educators must work to protect the integrity of arbitration and champion the responsible use of AI. The same is true for blockchain and metaverse. Again, technology is not all good or all bad—it is how you use it.

NOTES

1 Colin Rule & Amy Schmitz, *Arbitration Conversation No. 30: Colin Rule, CEO, Mediate.com/Arbitrate.com*, YouTube (Aug. 21, 2020), https://www.youtube.com/watch?v=HhAfIWDtDdY.

2 Myriam Seers & Amy Schmitz, *Arbitration Conversation No. 54: Canadian Arbitrator Myriam M. Seers, Senior Associate at Torys LLP*, YouTube (Nov. 20, 2021), https://www.youtube.com/watch?v=U1ar_0gcRGs.

3 Bill Henderson & Amy Schmitz, *Arbitration Conversation No. 10: Prof. Bill Henderson, Indiana University Maurer School of Law*, PodBean (Sept. 29, 2022), https://arbitrate.podbean.com/e/episode-9-prof-bill-henderson-indiana-university-maurer-school-of-law/.

4 Prof. Henderson has a website and wonderful resources related to the Institute of the Future of Law Practice (IFLIP) at www.legalevolution.org/.

5 Angie Raymond & Amy Schmitz, *Arbitration Conversation No. 75: Prof. Angie Raymond, Kelley School of Business, Indiana University*, YouTube (Mar. 24, 2021), www.youtube.com/watch?v=MT40W3oWyYk.

6 Matt O'Brien & Dake Kang, *AI in the Court: When Algorithms Rule on Jail Time*, Phys. Org (Jan. 31, 2018), https://phys.org/news/2018-01-ai-court-algorithms.html.

7 Alex Chohlas-Wood, *Understanding Risk Assessment Instruments in Criminal Justice*, Brookings (June 19, 2020), https://www.brookings.edu/articles/understanding-risk-assessment-instruments-in-criminal-justice/; *Artificial Intelligence and the Courts: Materials for Judges: Artificial Intelligence, Legal Research, and Judicial Analytics*, Am. Ass'n Advancement Sci. (Sept. 2022), https://www.aaas.org/sites/default/files/2022-09/Paper%203_AI%20Legal%20Research%20and%20Judicial%20Analytics_NIST_FINAL_1.pdf?adobe_mc=MCORGID%3D242B6472541199F70A4C98A6%2540AdobeOrg%7CTS%3D1701032564.

8 ChatGPT 3.5.

9 Stephen Buranyi, *Rise of the Racist Robots—How AI Is Learning All Our Worst Impulses*, The Guardian (Aug. 8, 2017), www.theguardian.com/inequality/2017/aug/08/rise-of-the-racist-robots-how-ai-is-learning-all-our-worst-impulses.

10 *Id.*

11 *Id.*

12 *Id.*

13 *See* Amy J. Schmitz & John Zeleznikow, *Intelligent Legal Tech to Empower Self-Represented Litigants*, 23 Colum. Sci. & Tech. L. Rev. 142–91 (2021), https://journals.library.columbia.edu/index.php/stlr/article/view/9391. Some may also be interested in Amy Schmitz & Elwood L. Thomas, *Data Analytics and AI in the Courts: Advancing, or Hindering, Justice?*, YouTube (Oct. 12, 2021), www.youtube.com/watch?v=M23WX-OMaww.

14 Nicolas Vermeys & Amy Schmitz, *Arbitration Conversation No. 40: Prof. Nicolas Vermeys of the University of Montreal Law School*, YouTube (Sept. 9, 2020), https://www.youtube.com/watch?v=M01wtPuoExA.

15 Julia Angwin, Jeff Larson, Surya Mattu & Lauren Kirchner, *Machine Bias*, ProPublica (May 23, 2016), www.propublica.org/article/machine-bias-risk-assessments-in-criminal-sentencing.
16 Olof Heggemann & Amy Schmitz, *Arbitration Conversation No. 95: Olof Heggemann, Founder, Eperoto*, YouTube (Oct. 13, 2021), www.youtube.com/watch?v=hYZjQXA2NpQ.
17 Wendy Gonzales & Amy Schmitz, *Arbitration Conversation No. 60: Wendy Gonzales, Founder of Cyberarb*, YouTube (Jan. 15, 2021), https://www.youtube.com/watch?v=rhvFfYotKDE.
18 Sophie Nappert & Amy Schmitz, *Arbitration Conversation No. 66: Independent Arbitrator Sophie Nappert*, YouTube (Jan. 29, 2021), https://www.youtube.com/watch?v=2Gs0ETYVQMwnappert.
19 Gary Benton & Amy Schmitz, *Arbitration Conversation No. 98: Arbitrator Gary Benton*, YouTube (Nov. 19, 2021), www.youtube.com/watch?v=kq0fINsn3jk.
20 Oladeji Tiamiyu & Amy Schmitz, *Arbitration Conversation No. 85: Oladeji Tiamiyu, Clinical Fellow, HNMCP at Harvard Law School*, YouTube (June 23, 2021), www.youtube.com/watch?v=FS7HYrJzw9c.
21 Yueh-Ping (Alex) Yang, *The Crowd's Wisdom in Smart Contract Dispute Resolution: Is Crowdsourced Dispute Resolution Arbitration?*, 15(2) Contemp. Asia Arb. J. 175 (2022).
22 Clément Lesaege, Federico Ast & William George, *Kleros* (Sept. 2019), https://kleros.io/assets/whitepaper.pdf.
23 *Id.*
24 *Id.* at 4.
25 *Id.* at 7.
26 *Id.* at 8. Under its proposed governance, Kleros will create subcourts and update and adapt the program as necessary.
27 *Id.* at 7.
28 *Id.*
29 *Id.*
30 *Id. See also* Clément Lesaege & William George, *Kleros and Augur—Keeping People Honest on the Blockchain through Game Theory*, Medium (Feb. 11, 2018), https://medium.com/kleros/kleros-and-augur-keeping-people-honest-on-ethereum-through-game-theory-56210457649c (explaining why the Kleros system is more just than other crowdsourced dispute resolution in the founders' estimation).
31 *See* Mauricio Virues Carrera, Accommodating Kleros as a Decentralized Dispute Resolution Tool for Civil Justice Systems: Theoretical Model and Case Application (June 8, 2022).
32 Mark Purdy, *How the Metaverse Could Change Work*, Harv. Bus. Rev. (Apr. 5, 2022), https://hbr.org/2022/04/how-the-metaverse-could-change-work.
33 Paul Cohen & Amy Schmitz, *Arbitration Conversation No. 7: Envisioning Arbitration in the Metaverse*, PodBean (Aug. 9, 2022), https://arbitrate.podbean.com/e/episode-7-envisioning-arbitration-in-the-metaverse/.
34 *See* Jalal El Ahdab & Claire Bentley, *Paris Arbitration Week Recap: Blockchain, NFTs and the Metaverse*, Kluwer Arb. Blog (May 14, 2022), http://arbitrationblog.kluwerarbitration.com/2022/05/14/paris-arbitration-week-recap-blockchain-nfts-and-the-metaverse/.

Chapter 12
New Ethical Obligations

The move to OArb raises new ethical obligations. Interviewees talked about the duty of technological competence under the American Bar Association's (ABA's) Model Rules of Professional Conduct, as well as heightened attention to privacy in OArb. This chapter discusses ethical issues that should be considered in order to be "technologically competent" in using technology in arbitration. It also discusses the various "protocols" and guidance that many institutions have promulgated with respect to ODR, OArb, and virtual hearings. What do these protocols mean for counsel and arbitrators? Do "protocols" and guardrails set new ethical standards, or are these just friendly suggestions? What about cybersecurity and digital trust when it comes to OArb? The use of technology raises new ethical obligations for arbitration, which many interviews emphasized.

A. ETHICAL GUIDANCE AND STANDARDS

The ABA Dispute Resolution Section ODR Task Force formed in May 2019, and focused on finding ways to promote ethical ODR, including OArb. The ABA Section on Dispute Resolution appointed David Larson, Alan Wiener, and me as its co-chairs, and authorized us to appoint Task Force members. The members of the Task Force are listed in footnote 2 of the official "Guidance," which is available on the ABA Dispute Resolution Section website and in the *Ohio State Journal on Dispute Resolution*.[1] This group included some of the most prominent ODR innovators, technology developers, practitioners, court ADR staff, and legal services advocates, including leaders and fellows of the National Center for Technology and Dispute Resolution (NCTDR) and the International Council for Online Dispute Resolution (ICODR).

The Guidance was substantially built upon the 2017 ICODR Online Dispute Resolution Standards.[2] Indeed, the ICODR standards were updated in 2022 and provide an important lens for viewing the duty of technological competence in dispute resolution. Additionally, the ABA ODR Guidance provides additional considerations for ethical use of technology in dispute resolution.[3] Some of the key considerations for OArb flow from these standards and guidance, as well as various protocols for OArb that have been developed, especially in the wake of the pandemic shutdown when arbitration quickly moved online. Nonetheless, the discussion herein is different in that it is focused on OArb, and not ODR generally, which was the focus of the standards and guidance. The OArb protocols that various bodies and authors developed, however, are focused on OArb and there is a chart of many protocols in Appendix A of this book.

B. ACCESSIBLE

Online hearings are not a panacea and only appropriate for some parties. Arbitrators should consider accessibility and be careful in ordering online hearings. One arbitrator explained that they would only order an online arbitration hearing over a party's objection if there was a delay due to the wait for an in-person hearing and there would be prejudice to one of the parties if further delay occurred.[4] For example, if an employee in a labor dispute was discharged, left unemployed, and the employer was dragging their feet in proceeding with OArb to determine back pay and reinstatement during the pandemic shutdown, it would be quite reasonable for an arbitrator to force the online hearing so that the employee could access remedies. Justice delays would be justice denied in some cases.

Still, there are real concerns about accessibility when it comes to online hearings. As noted in prior chapters, arbitrators should consider the parties' capacity to present their cases online. Rick Bales, a professor and a labor arbitrator, explained how some union employees may not have access to a laptop but may find Zoom via their mobile devices quite convenient and accessible. Professor Bales surmised in his interview that most parties usually prefer hearings in person, but online hearings are here to stay due to the cost and time savings. Many parties and arbitrators now state that they prefer online over in-person hearings.[5]

That said, interviews highlighted best practices and tips for OArb. Concerning security and witness coaching, Professor Bales suggested that counsel should explain that no unauthorized documents or people would be allowed in the room from which a witness is testifying. Steps should also be taken to stop witnesses and parties from recording the Zoom hearings unless it is an official recording requested by the parties and their counsel.

Notably, emphasizing accessibility and equal access, Professor Bales also recommended that parties and witnesses practice with Zoom or whatever hearing platform they plan to use to ensure it is accessible for all involved. Arbitrators should do a "test run" with counsel and parties and answer any questions that the parties have before proceeding with OArb. Wise arbitrators will also explain to the participants that "glitches" happen and should set forth a "backup" plan for when technical problems arise. For example, it is prudent for participants to exchange mobile numbers and means for pivoting to a teleconference if necessary.[6] Arbitrators have an ethical duty to ensure a full and fair opportunity to be heard, which extends to ensuring accessible online hearings.

C. ACCOUNTABLE AND SUBJECT TO AUDIT

The referenced ABA ODR Guidance goes into further depth with respect to what it means for a system to be accountable and subject to audit for fairness and legality. This includes many aspects of the system. For example, any system, including OArb, must comply with applicable statutes, rules, or other laws that might apply. This will differ depending on jurisdictions, suggesting that platform developers would be prudent to create systems compliant with the most stringent ethical standards. Furthermore, designers should aim for consistency, and continually monitor for system and process quality. In addition, system providers should be careful with data, including how that data is managed and used for monitoring, learning, and evaluation.

Data and its interaction with arbitration was one of the topics discussed when interviewing Doctor and Professor Anjanette (Angie) Raymond, with the Department of Business Law and Ethics at the Kelley School of Business, Indiana University, and an adjunct associate professor of law at Maurer Law School (Indiana).[7] Professor Raymond emphasized the importance of data ethics, and even how we talk about data in arbitration.

For starters, we must be careful in what we call "arbitration" and how we define "AI." Some automated decision-making should not even qualify as "arbitration" because there is no real third-party decision applying clear and transparent rules when it comes to machine learning in which the algorithm may be continually changing. Professor Raymond suggested we should be precise in what we consider "fair" or "just" in using technology in dispute resolution. Again, machine learning generally depends on historical data. This may be problematic if we allow historical data to drive justice determinations that require new ideas and nuanced application of rules and norms.

Some technology experts argue that judicial data, for example, is not the type of data that was contemplated for use in machine learning because the law evolves. Indeed, biases are often baked into past data. For this reason, any arbitration system using AI should be subject to audits to check for biases.

Arbitration is also distinct from other dispute resolution processes because it is generally a final and binding process enforceable under the FAA and New York Convention. This means we must be cautious in using data to drive arbitration awards. Talk of "bot resolutions" is often overstated, as current law may not support enforcement of purely computer-driven arbitration awards. Furthermore, there are legal issues around technologies essentially infringing on the practice of law. For example, LegalZoom ran into some issues with allegations around the unauthorized practice of law. Again, systems must be accountable and lawful.

There is no question that we will see more and more use of AI and data analytics in assisting arbitral decision-making. AI is already helping parties determine case value and likely outcomes as a catalyst for reaching a settlement.[8] It is even feasible that an e-court program could use AI to determine results based on an analysis of similar cases. Predictive systems are not new. Actuarial scientists have long used predictive systems and algorithms to determine probabilities in the insurance industry, but AI and machine learning add a whole new dimension to the predictions. Systems can learn and change over time. This can be good or bad, as systems may stray in the direction of bias underlying the training data, or the algorithm, or both. Competent systems should provide the same results based on the same data. Accordingly, to be accountable, systems must be subject to audit to test whether same data provides same outcomes. Additionally, individuals may game a system by strategically changing their behavior or entering false inputs, and coding errors and coders' biases also may lead to skewed results.[9] More on impartiality will be noted later in this chapter.

On the other hand, AI and well-built algorithms may sometimes help individuals make more objective determinations.[10] They also may produce determinations without the delay involved with traditional arbitration. For example, an arbitrator may be able to look to data regarding damage assessments in a contracts case, instead of listening to days of expert testimony in a typical battle of the experts. As noted earlier in the book, an AI-powered valuation program could provide an arbitrator with a damage assessment to help her arrive at a fair award with less time and cost. Similarly, a consumer in a small claims arbitration may benefit from a case value prediction in reaching a resolution with a seller. In these ways, AI and algorithms may lead to faster and more accurate determinations or mutual resolutions.[11]

AI may also play a part in legal discovery. In *Winfield v. City of New York*, the court looked at the use of predictive coding to sort and gather documents relevant to a discovery request.[12] In *Winfield*, plaintiffs charged that the City's use of algorithms to influence document requests led to the underrepresentation of relevant documents in this case.[13] The argument was that this resulted in skewed document review, and thus skewed results. The court disagreed, and affirmed that predictive coding was a viable means of achieving reasonable and proportional document production at a lower cost.[14]

Nonetheless, it is essential that any use of AI remains accountable, such that researchers, government, and societal watchdogs have access to the data sets and rules used by the algorithms. Policymakers may also consider using open-source software to improve transparency, and seeking public input to improve its use in dispute resolution processes.[15] Accountability is essential. Furthermore, AI cannot replicate essential human capabilities for promoting human values, especially in dispute resolution processes in which empathy is necessary.[16] Legal futurists who predict that "robot lawyers" will eventually perform all legal work may view the rule of law as providing a "clear prescription" that can be plugged into algorithms to produce legally correct determinations.[17] However, accountability requires deeper considerations and a realization that it is nearly or completely (in some cases) impossible to reduce knowledge and judgment to a series of algorithms a machine could apply.[18]

Rather than replace humans with "bots," humans should seek to use technology to improve their performance.[19] As discussed earlier, AI can augment human intelligence and serve as a tool to aid decision-makers in analyzing information, while mitigating bias and other human failings.[20] Technology could even help expand A2J. For example, a chatbot may help individuals navigate legal terminology. Still, this use of technology must be accountable and subject to audit.

D. TRANSPARENT

Related to accountability and audits is the question of transparency. An OArb system, or practitioner using any technology in arbitration, should be transparent in this use of technology in arbitration. This is especially true with respect to incorporation of AI technologies in legal processes, with clear communication provided to all parties involved, especially where AI is used in decision-making.

Transparency goes beyond disclosure around the use of AI in a decision-making process. Algorithmic transparency is also essential. This means that AI systems must used in arbitration must use algorithms that are, discernible to relevant stakeholders, including judges, lawyers, arbitrators, and parties to a process. Regular independent audits should be conducted to evaluate the fairness, accuracy, and adherence to legal standards of AI systems—but this is only possible if the system is sufficiently transparent. External experts should provide these impartial assessments. Adequate training and awareness programs also should be provided to legal professionals, enabling them to grasp the intricacies of AI technologies and their potential biases. Moreover, AI systems should abide by stringent data privacy and security measures, as will be discussed later.

The tension between privacy and transparency is significant and complicated. Transparency is not easy, as dispute resolution processes also are private, and often cloaked in confidentiality. With transparency in mind, Professor Catherine A. Rogers, a scholar of international arbitration and professional ethics, who has held several academic appointments in the U.S, E.U. and U.K, spoke on this topic. Professor Rogers co-chaired the ICCA-Queen Mary Task Force on Third-Party Funding in International Arbitration and is the founder of Arbitrator Intelligence, a global information aggregator and legal tech startup that aims at improving transparency, fairness, and accountability in arbitrator selection.[21]

Professor Rogers created Arbitrator Intelligence to expand and refine the information that is provided about arbitration. The project went from an academic research endeavor to a legal tech startup. The project collects information and arbitration awards through an online platform that does not capture confidential or private information. The platform uses crowdsourcing to allow for anonymous and confidential exchange of information. Additionally, the platform provides nuanced analytics to help practitioners prepare for arbitration hearings. Furthermore, the platform is international and includes "ambassadors" from around the world who assist with the work from various angles. This volunteer team creates a dialogue that is continually helping to promote the work.

The team at Arbitrator Intelligence is learning a great deal from the data, and this type of transparency. The data evidence discernable differences among arbitrators and regional differences in arbitration practice. There are also significant differences in the time it takes some arbitrators to move a case from filing to award. They are also hoping to provide greater detail about process changes, for example, asking whether bifurcation helps or hinders the efficiency of a process. The project is ongoing, and this type of transparency around arbitration could be helpful for expanding the pool of arbitrators and making the process more accessible.

Another interview highlighting transparency in arbitration was part of the latest iteration of *The Arbitration Conversation* in the new form, moving from webisodes with video to longer conversations in a purely audio format. Again, as noted in the Introduction, the series moved to a podcast after reaching 100 webisodes. In the fifth episode of the newly configured podcast, I interviewed Debi Slate, the COO and co-founder of Dispute Resolution Data (DRD), the first global database pertaining to international commercial arbitration and mediation dispositions.[22] Ms. Slate was the founding director of the South Carolina Council for Mediation and a national vice president for Online Services with the AAA before co-founding DRD.

DRD was created with the understanding that data has always been core for understanding a process. More data and more transparency illuminate the field of arbitration. DRD grew from partnerships with international commercial arbitration bodies and institutions from around the world. Subscribers include law firms, law schools, and any other clients that may be able to use the data to understand procedures and trends. Having the data also can assist strategy development.

The data DRD collects is not simply the awards and outcomes, but is also the process data. Every point in the process is gathered, which informs process improvement and assists with training practices as well.[23] For example, the data has informed understanding of when parties usually settle during a process: the data has indicated that settlement has usually occurred after the preliminary hearing but before the final evidentiary hearing. However, the data from DRD indicates that construction cases are more likely than other types of cases to go to an evidentiary hearing.

The "trick" in promoting transparency while protecting privacy and confidentiality is collecting and aggregating data in an anonymized way. DRD does not collect the "whos": who the parties are, who the arbitrators are, and so on. Furhermore, DRD does not collect any other private or confidential information. Moreover, the data is aggregated so that it is not identifiable. Data is provided by region and case types for analysis and use.[24]

The topic of transparency in international arbitration was also central in my *Arbitration Conversation* with Janet Walker, an independent arbitrator with chambers at Arbitration Place in Toronto, the International Arbitration Centre in London, and the Sydney Arbitration Chambers in Australia.[25] Janet Walker has also been a professor and has a long history in the practice and research around arbitration. Transparency is vital in international arbitration, despite a need for privacy, where public issues are at stake and accountability is needed. Public accountability can be crucial in cases involving issues related to health and safety, for example. Furthermore, process transparency helps promote the legitimacy of international arbitration.

Still, the amount of data available can be overwhelming in today's digital world. Years ago, there was little to no data on international arbitration. Moreover, it was essentially the same individuals who were continually appointed as arbitrators, and it appeared that the same people were running the show in international arbitration. There is still a lack of new voices in international arbitration, and it is a tough area to break into as a new lawyer.

Nonetheless, companies like DRD, Arbitrator Intelligence, and many websites are providing greater information about arbitration. It is easy to "Google" anyone and everything, and a great deal of data analytics is provided on many legal research sites. At the same time, we are in the information era in which many law firms and arbitral institutions will boast their successes, suggesting that researchers should understand that a great deal of the information is promotional and possibly skewed (such as particular legal tool companies boasting satisfaction rates).[26]

The difficult part is determining what is reliable information that properly adds to the transparency around arbitration processes. The key is to sift through the noise to find and consider the most reliable and helpful information. Detailed research findings from independent sources can be more helpful than promotional materials, but there are often concerns about how that data is interpreted. With generative AI and the advent of ChatGPT and other such tools, there is even more information than ever, although it is unclear whether it is reliable or accurate. It may be that access to reasoned awards would be more helpful because awards provide information about thought processes, but that may again open a can of interpretive and privacy worms. Moreover, a certain dynamic develops during an arbitration process that cannot be captured by "data" in a case.[27]

The availability of data, and need for transparency raise new ethical questions. For example, should arbitral platforms be required to provide more information? What about asymmetries in access to information that could augment power imbalances? A type of data colonialism is developing, with the "haves" gaining further power through access to data.

That said, transparency and data analysis is important for process change. Data can assist with system design and changes that will improve an arbitration process. For example, international dialogue and comparative research regarding online courts is helping to inform system design.[28] Many countries are beginning to integrate technology into their administrative justice processes and moving certain dispute resolution processes online. Each new online program provides a laboratory for investigation from which others can learn. Furthermore, it is essential that policymakers consider core transparency and due process requirements to audit systems and ensure that any use of technology remains legal and accountable. Indeed, it is essential to build OArb systems for contexts in consideration of due process standards.[29]

Audits, accountability, and transparency go together. Transparency means not only that individuals have full information about a process at the outset or information to assist them in preparing their cases. It also means that administrators should publish reports on the system and provide these reports to auditors with power and expertise to assess whether the use of technology is prejudicial in any way, or otherwise failing to further fairness. For example, an arbitration provider should gather data to analyze party cost savings pre- and post-implementation of a new technology. Providers should also gather data on how many individuals are using and benefiting from a new system, when they are accessing the system, and whether they are able to access the system using a mobile device. Examining the time it takes to complete a process or otherwise obtain a remedy is also important.

Again, data and transparency can assist improvements. This means that providers are also wise to gather quantitative and qualitative information. This qualitative research could include survey and interview data regarding satisfaction, perception, and user experience. This should include not only e-surveys but also focus groups of system users who can offer more precise feedback and ideas for improvements. Mixed methods research can add to the depth and breadth of information to catalyze process improvements.

E. IMPARTIAL AND FAIR

"Fairness" and impartiality are discussed throughout this book. Certainly, issues related to fairness and power imbalances come up in consumer and employment arbitration, discussed earlier, and there are continual debates around arbitration and A2J. Related ethical questions came up in my interview of Professor Kristen Blankley.[30] Professor Blankley teaches alternative dispute resolution, advocacy in mediation, mediation, family mediation, and arbitration at the Nebraska College of Law. Her work largely focuses on the crossroads of alternative dispute resolution and ethics, and she is a co-chair of the ABA Section of the Dispute Resolution Committee on Ethics.

Professor Blankley discussed ideas around a regulatory framework for arbitration. The FAA was enacted in 1925, and there is no evidence that Congress was considering employment, consumer, and other "one-shot-player" arbitrations. Nonetheless, there may be room for agency regulation to ensure the fairness of arbitration. Specifically, Professor Blankley suggested that agencies may be able to craft regulations about arbitration—and we may see more action in this direction. For example, we may see the Department of Education be given power to regulate arbitration within its sphere.[31] There have often been discussions around fairness and impartiality, and how the Consumer Financial Protection Bureau might regulate arbitration in consumer financial products cases as well.

Marsha Ternus spoke on the topic of arbitration in education.[32] Arbitrator Ternus was appointed to the Iowa Supreme Court in 1993 and selected as chief justice in 2006. She was the first woman to serve as chief justice of Iowa's highest court but has since left the bench and is now an avid arbitrator. We talked about her work arbitrating student conduct proceedings, although Title IX cases are slightly different in that, for example, no attorneys are usually present. Fairness and impartiality are essential in these proceedings, as is true in all arbitration. Furthermore, former Justice Ternus discussed her work as an "ad hoc" arbitrator, as she is often asked to arbitrate without the oversight or involvement of an administrator (AAA, JAMS, etc.). In these situations, arbitrators have an even higher level of ethical vigilance because no administrator can act as a middle institution if issues arise. Again, impartiality and fairness remain key.

Impartiality and fairness are always important in any arbitration, and imperative to protect the integrity of the award and system overall. Still, these issues rise even higher in areas where corruption may occur. Fernando Sanquírico Pittevil, a partner at Lega Abogados in Venezuela, spoke on the topic of corruption in arbitration.[33] Fernando is also a professor of civil law in Universidad Central de Venezuela, Universidad Católica Andrés Bello, and Universidad Monteávila. Professor Sanquírico Pittevil is also a member of the list of arbitrators in both the Arbitration Centre of the Caracas Chamber and the Business Centre for Conciliation and Arbitration. He was also a member of the board of directors of the Venezuelan Arbitration Association from 2019 to 2021. We discussed whether issues of corruption may be subject to arbitration, and an award on these issues is enforceable. This raises interesting public policy issues.

The community of arbitration is continually thinking about fairness and protecting the integrity of arbitration. Furthermore, there is special concern with the insurgence of AI in arbitration and how regulations may impact AI in any legal application. For example, the proposed U.S. Algorithmic Accountability Act of 2022 (AAA) and the EU Artificial Intelligence Act (EU AI Act) are two legislative movements aimed at addressing the implications of innovative technologies, particularly AI.[34] The parameters of the EU AI Act are still being worked out, and now there are new developments in the U.S. in the wake of the Executive Order on Safe, Secure, and Trustworthy Artificial Intelligence.[35]

The EU AI Act is meant to be a comprehensive and horizontal legislation targeting AI systems in general, based on the EU's fundamental rights framework. It seeks to govern the development and use of AI systems, introducing a "technology-neutral" definition of AI and classifying AI systems into different risk-based categories. The EU aims to ensure that AI is trustworthy and safe for citizens while unlocking its benefits. It prohibits the use of AI systems that pose "unacceptable risk" to individuals and seeks to mitigate connected risks for European citizens. The EU AI Act classifies AI systems into risk-based categories, and focuses on user rights and developing an "ecosystem of trust." The AI Act places primary responsibility on Member States to enforce the act.

On the other hand, the proposed AAA in the U.S. focuses on large technology companies and requires them to conduct impact assessments for automated decision systems (ADS) and augmented critical decision processes (ACDP) that significantly impact consumers' lives. The bill defines ADS broadly and excludes intermediary technologies that do not influence decision-making. The FTC would oversee this regulation, and companies falling under its jurisdiction must submit annual summary reports for ongoing impact assessments of their deployed ADS and ACDP. At the same time, the White House released news in July of 2023 regarding voluntary commitments from top AI companies Amazon, Anthropic, Google, Inflection, Meta, Microsoft, and OpenAI for various safety measures:[36]

- Internal and external security testing of AI systems before release;
- Share information across the industry and with governments, civil society, and academia on managing AI risks;
- Invest in cybersecurity and insider threat safeguards to protect proprietary and unreleased model weights;
- Facilitate third-party discovery and reporting of vulnerabilities;
- Create robust technical mechanisms to ensure that users know when content is AI generated, such as a watermarking system;
- Abide by public reporting of AI systems' capabilities, limitations, and areas of appropriate and inappropriate use;

- Prioritize research on societal risks that AI systems can pose, including on avoiding harmful bias and discrimination, and protecting privacy; and
- Develop and deploy advanced AI systems to help address society's greatest challenges.

The new Executive Order in the U.S. goes further. It outlines key actions across different domains, aiming to balance the opportunities and challenges posed by AI. In terms of AI safety and security, the order compels AI developers to share safety test results with the U.S. government. Additionally, it calls on the National Institute of Standards and Technology to establish rigorous standards, tools, and tests with a focus on national security risks. An AI Safety and Security Board is set to be created to apply these standards to critical infrastructure sectors.[37]

With respect to privacy, the order calls on Congress to pass bipartisan data privacy legislation, advocating for privacy-preserving techniques involving AI. It also emphasizes the need to strengthen privacy-preserving research and technologies. To address issues of equity and civil rights arising from AI, the order suggests providing guidance to prevent discriminatory use of AI algorithms in housing, justice, and healthcare. It calls for measures to counter algorithmic discrimination through training and coordination between the Department of Justice and civil rights offices. It also calls for responsible AI use in healthcare and creating resources to support educators deploying AI-enabled educational tools. The order also addresses workforce issues, international leadership, and research cooperatives around best practices with respect to AI.

In summary, while the EU has been more proactive in advancing general AI regulations using a more holistic approach to regulate AI systems across industries based on a risk-based framework, the U.S. has been more limited and reserved in advancing regulations. It has spent more time on gathering feedback and seeking to garner industry agreement with respect to regulations. Additionally, the U.S. has focused on large companies' impact assessments concerning decision-making processes and critical decision-making using AI, although the new Executive Order underscores the necessity of responsible AI governance, privacy protection, equity, and international collaboration, recognizing the diverse impact of AI across various sectors.

While the law continues to evolve, these conversations and proposals are important in guarding ethics for all use of AI in the law, including use in arbitration. We have seen diplomatic efforts in AI governance grow, reflecting the global significance of AI regulation. There is need for greater collaboration among public and private actors to regulate the fairness of AI in dispute resolution, especially arbitration—where there is fear that efficiency-focused systems will prevail over fairness. Open public consultation and feedback mechanisms can further foster responsible AI practices, incorporating societal values into the implementation process. The establishment of comprehensive guidelines and standards by regulatory bodies and professional organizations will set clear ethical expectations for the use of AI in arbitration and court proceedings. This will help all in the community as we move forward in the brave new world of OArb, augmented by AI and other technologies.

Again, OArb includes any use of technology in arbitration—which calls on consideration of the benefits and risks of using technology in any process. This is part of the duty of technological competence for lawyers, and should be part of the duty for any arbitrator or arbitral body. Considerations of accessibility, accountability, transparency, and fairness must remain paramount. While this chapter talked a great deal about the ethical issues related to use of AI, these duties are likewise important with respect to any use of technology—including virtual hearings and online communications. Again, Appendix B provides more insights into best practices for virtual hearings, per the various protocols that have been developed in recent years.

NOTES

1 American Bar Association Section on Dispute Resolution Guidance for Online Dispute Resolution (ODR), 38 Ohio State J. on Disp. Resol. 241 (2023).

2 ICODR Standards, https://icodr.org/standards/ (2017, updated in 2022). The standards emanate from the NCTDR, Ethical Principles for Online Dispute Resolution, https://odr.info/ethics-and-odr/#_ftn2. *See also* Leah Wing, *Ethical Principles for Online Dispute Resolution: A GPS Device for the Field*, 3 int'l j. online disp. resol. 12–29, 11–15 (2016).

3 David Larson, Amy Schmitz & Alan Weiner, *ABA ODR Guidance Has Been Adopted*, 38 Ohio State J. on Disp. Resol. 235 (2023).

4 Rick Bales & Amy Schmitz, *Arbitration Conversation No. 27: Prof. Rick Bales of Ohio Northern School of Law*, YouTube (Aug. 13, 2020), https://www.youtube.com/watch?v=-lmqqMQqA6Y.

5 *Id.*

6 *Id.*

7 Anganette Raymond & Amy Schmitz, *Arbitration Conversation No. 75: Prof. Angie Raymond, Kelley School of Business, Indiana University*, YouTube (Mar, 24, 2021), https://www.youtube.com/watch?v=MT40W3oWyYk.

8 Bernard Marr, *How AI and Machine Learning Are Transforming Law Firms and the Legal Sector*, Forbes (May 23, 2018), www.forbes.com/sites/bernardmarr/2018/05/23/how-ai-and-machine-learning-are-transforming-law-firms-and-the-legal-sector/#3d6ef0b032c3.

9 *See* Richard C. Kraus, *Artificial Intelligence Invades Appellate Practice: The Here, The Near, and The Oh My Dear*, A.B.A. (Feb. 5, 2019), https://www.americanbar.org/groups/judicial/publications/appellate_issues/2019/winter/artificial-intelligence-invades-appellate-practice-the-here-the-near-and-the-oh-my-dear/.

10 Pamela S. Katz, *Expert Robot: Using Artificial Intelligence to Assist Judges in Admitting Scientific Expert Testimony*, 24 Alb. L.J. Sci. & Tech. 1, 41 (2014).

11 *Id.*

12 Winfield v. City of New York, No. 15-cv-05236 (LTS) (KHP), 2017 WL 5664852, at *10–11 (S.D.N.Y. Nov. 27, 2017).

13 *Id.* at *5.

14 *Id.* at *11–12 (so holding but allowing plaintiffs to review a random sample of non-relevant documents to determine whether relevant documents which should have been produced were improperly omitted).

15 Arthur Rizer & Caleb Watney, *Artificial Intelligence Can Make Our Jail System More Efficient, Equitable and Just*, SSRN 34–39 (Feb. 18, 2018), https://papers.ssrn.com/sol3/papers.cfm?abstract_id=3129576.

16 *See* Frank Pasquale, *A Rule of Persons, Not Machines: The Limits of Legal Automation*, 87 Geo. Wash. L. Rev. 1, 29–30 (2019).

17 *Id.* at 44.

18 *Id.* at 48.

19 *Id.* at 47.

20 *See* Robin Tible, Note de lecture: Yannick Meneceur, "Quel avenir pour la justice prédictive? -Enjeux et limites des algorithmes d'anticipation des décisions de justice" [Reading note: Yannick Meneceur: "What future for predictive justice? Challenges and limits of anticipation algorithms of court decisions"] La Semaine Juredique Edition Générale no. 7 (Feb. 12, 2018), www.cyberjustice.ca/en/publications/note-de-lecture-quel-avenir-pour-la-justice-predictive-enjeux-et-limites-des-algorithmes-danticipation-des-decisions-de-justice/.

21 Catherine Rogers & Amy Schmitz, *Arbitration Conversation No. 70: Catherine Rogers, Founder, Arbitrator Intelligence*, YouTube (Mar. 2, 2021), https://www.youtube.com/watch?v=4uibMKDC4hM.

22 Debi Slate & Amy Schmitz, *Arbitration Conversation No. 5: Finding Insights in Data about International Commercial Arbitration*, arbitrate.com & Podbean (Apr. 13, 2022), https://arbitrate.podbean.com/e/episode-5-finding-insights-in-data-about-international-commercial-arbitration/.

23 *Id.*

24 *Id.*

25 Janet Walker & Amy Schmitz, *Arbitration Conversation No. 53: Janet Walker*, YouTube (Nov. 16, 2020), https://www.youtube.com/watch?v=vb-dxrW098w.

26 *Id.*

27 *Id.*

28 *See The Digitalisation of Tribunals: What We Know and What We Need to Know*, Pub. L. Project 27–35 (Apr. 5, 2018), https://publiclawproject.org.uk/content/uploads/2018/04/The-Digitalisation-of-Tribunals-for-website.pdf.

29 *See* Raymond & Schmitz, *supra* note 7.

30 Kristen Blankley & Amy Schmitz, *Arbitration Conversation No. 89: Prof. Kristen Blankley of the Nebraska College of Law*, YouTube (July 27, 2021), https://www.youtube.com/watch?v=ZjLyIjaJHi8.

31 *Id.*

32 Marsha Ternus & Amy Schmitz, *Arbitration Conversation No. 61: Former Chief Justice of the Iowa Supreme Court Justice Marsha Ternus*, YouTube (Jan. 22, 2021), https://www.youtube.com/watch?v=mhs_MbG8fxU.

33 Fernando Sanquírico Pittevil & Amy Schmitz, *Arbitration Conversation No. 79: Fernando Sanquírico Pittevil, Parter at Lega Abogados*, YouTube (May 13, 2021), www.youtube.com/watch?v=zjkvsnAkceQ.

34 Noha Lea Halim & Urs Gasser, *Vectors of AI Governance—Juxtaposing the U.S. Algorithmic Accountability Act of 2022 with The EU Artificial Intelligence Act* (May 9, 2023), https://ssrn.com/abstract=4476167 or http://dx.doi.org/10.2139/ssrn.4476167.

35 Press Release, The White House, FACT SHEET: President Biden Issues Executive Order on Safe, Secure, and Trustworthy Artificial Intelligence (Oct. 30, 2023), https://www.whitehouse.gov/briefing-room/statements-releases/2023/10/30/fact-sheet-president-biden-issues-executive-order-on-safe-secure-and-trustworthy-artificial-intelligence/.

36 Press Release, The White House, FACT SHEET: Biden-Harris Administration Secures Voluntary Commitments from Leading Artificial Intelligence Companies to Manage the Risks Posed by AI (July 21, 2023), www.whitehouse.gov/briefing-room/statements-releases/2023/07/21/fact-sheet-biden-harris-administration-secures-voluntary-commitments-from-leading-artificial-intelligence-companies-to-manage-the-risks-posed-by-ai/.

37 Press Release, *supra* note 35.

Conclusion

The Arbitration Conversation started as a fun and creative idea to expand knowledge and understanding regarding arbitration. Arbitration is a private process, and often information is unavailable due to additional confidentiality requirements in the applicable rules or arbitration agreements. Shining a light on arbitration and opening the door for fresh voices was also essential to the project.[1] It is vital to capture a record of arbitration and learn how it works, and should work, from diverse voices from around the world in the field of arbitration. Furthermore, as I discussed with Colin Rule in Episode 30, we were eager to gather information about the role of technology in arbitration and dispute resolution.[2]

At the same time, the idea of an arbitration podcast took hold because we were all experiencing Covid-19 shutdowns and were stuck at home. Educators were grasping for online content to enliven their classes—me included! Moreover, talking to arbitration experts and gaining essential insights regarding arbitration law and practice sounded like good, clean, fun.

The more than 100 interviews that are part of *The Arbitration Conversation* (100 on YouTube and already an additional 19 audio podcasts, with more on the way on all venues for podcasts) raise interesting lessons learned and shed light on practice, policy, and law around arbitration. Furthermore, the interviews provided unique insights into the flexibility of arbitration. Courts shut down and struggled to move online during the beginning days of the Covid-19 pandemic shutdown, while arbitration moved online relatively quickly. The arbitral institutions already had the capacity to move online, and nimble arbitrators learned how to masterfully commandeer virtual hearings.

As noted earlier in the book, OArb is flexible and includes using technology and digital tools beyond Zoom, Teams, and other online hearing mechanisms. For example, OArb may use a wide range of asynchronous and synchronous communication tools that allow parties to save time, cost, and stress of traveling to and attending in-person processes. Such OArb systems may even provide more accurate and complete redress for consumers than class actions, which have sometimes been criticized for providing insufficient and inequitably distributed relief.

At the same time, we see a new digital divide: of course, there is already differential access to the internet, but there is also differential access to the best technological tools. For example, having an excellent computer, two large screens, a great camera, and the best lighting is more effective than relying on a mobile device in a virtual hearing. Furthermore, the advent of new AI tools has created an imbalance of power to the extent that those with more resources have more access and understanding of new technologies. Furthermore, there is an imbalance in the ability to pay for subscription technology services that are generally much more accurate and advanced than free open-access technologies.

On the other hand, technology may lower the cost of access to arbitration and help expand A2J. AI is getting fancier and more powerful in ODR and OArb. The idea of a robot arbitrator does not seem as far-fetched as it once appeared. An AI arbitrator may be able to resolve a dispute in minutes at meager costs instead of requiring one to pay high administration costs and pay $300 plus per hour for an arbitrator who takes a great deal of time to sift through legal briefs and reams of supporting documentation. Also, some argue that an AI decision may even be less biased than a human decision. Of course, we need more data, and serious concerns regarding biases built into AI systems exist.

Still, it is essential to recognize the value of humans in dispute resolution. As some interviewees expressed in *The Arbitration Conversation*, it is unlikely that "robots" or AI will replace arbitrators, especially in more complex matters. Ethical rules and conflict checks are integral for arbitrators and the integrity of arbitration processes. Human sensibilities, empathy, and the opportunity to "vent" in person still have immense value. Technology is not a replacement for third-party neutrals like arbitrators and mediators. Instead, technology is the "fourth party." As Colin Rule and Ethan Katsh have long explained, the disputants are party one and party two, the arbitrator is party three, and technology (in all its forms) is party four. This conceptualization emphasizes the collaboration between human neutrals and technology because there are some tasks the third party can do better and some tasks the fourth party can do better. The primary question instead becomes how to optimize the partnership to achieve our shared objective, which is finding a fair resolution and helping the parties solve their problems in a way best suited to their interests and goals.

There is a long way to go in expanding and improving our use of technology as the fourth party in arbitration. For example, humans can partner with modular assistance from natural language processing, predictive analytics, document analysis, agreement technologies, and so on. Additionally, generative AI will continue to improve as a tool for helping parties to frame their arguments. The improvements in technological tools in even the last five years are stunning, and AI may eventually be fit for resolving specific disputes.

As Colin Rule and I included in a short article in the ABA *Dispute Resolution Magazine:*

> What do these improvements in machine learning mean for the future practice of arbitration? Several opportunities jump to mind.
>
> 1. Predictive analytics: Machine learning algorithms can analyze data from past disputes to identify patterns and predict the likelihood of future disputes. This can help mediators, arbitrators, and other dispute resolution professionals anticipate and prevent disputes before they arise.
> 2. Decision support: Machine learning algorithms can help dispute resolution professionals make more informed decisions by providing them with insights and recommendations based on data analysis. For example, an algorithm could analyze data from past disputes to identify common factors that led to successful resolutions and suggest strategies for resolving similar disputes in the future.
> 3. Automated dispute resolution: Machine learning algorithms can be used to automate certain aspects of the dispute resolution process, such as document analysis and contract interpretation. This can help to speed up the process and reduce the workload for dispute resolution professionals.
> 4. Enhanced collaboration: Machine learning algorithms can facilitate collaboration between dispute resolution professionals by providing them with real-time data and analytics that can help them make more informed decisions.
>
> Overall, the use of machine learning in dispute resolution has the potential to improve the efficiency and effectiveness of the process, helping to resolve disputes more quickly and accurately.
>
> Now, consider that we didn't write the points above. Starting with "Predictive analytic" and ending with "resolve disputes more quickly and accurately," a new algorithm called ChatGPT3 wrote that passage. We asked the algorithm to respond to the question, "how will machine learning change the practice of dispute resolution?" The response easily passes the Turing Test.[3]

Of course, GPT is no longer new, and is joined by many generative AI systems. Even the comparison of current Zoom arbitration hearings to the old video technologies we used ten years ago is stunning. Consider that our cell phones are more powerful than the most powerful computers 20 years ago. Indeed, what we can imagine now will be old news in five years!

Accordingly, one can never say "never" it seems. If *The Arbitration Conversation* taught me one thing, it taught me to never say never. I would never have imagined moving all my classes from in person to online on a weekend (literally). I never would have imagined doing a webcast, let alone 100 video interviews. I would never have imagined the accelerated move from in-person arbitration to OArb during the pandemic shutdown. I would never have imagined having the opportunity to talk with so many interesting and intelligent arbitration experts, and having the gift of making so many friends along the way in hosting *The Arbitration Conversation*.

In summary, arbitration and OArb continue to provide important means for resolving disputes and solving problems. With its historical roots as a private and flexible conflict resolution tool, arbitration is uniquely equipped to expand and mature in the digital age. The rules of civil procedure do not hamstring arbitration, and arbitral institutions have already demonstrated resilience and ability to pivot during the Covid-19 shutdown.

Used correctly, digital tools will expand the reach of arbitration into dispute types and geographies that traditional in-person arbitration could not serve. OArb also could be used to help fuel expansion in access to remedies worldwide, with more fairness and justice for more people in certain contexts and for certain people who are more comfortable operating online than in person. Many questions still need to be answered, and we must remain cognizant of the risks of any technology in arbitration. Policymakers and practitioners should work together to build and refine OArb and AI mechanisms to devise the optimal fourth-party partner that can best assist arbitrators in helping parties achieve fair resolutions at lower costs.

Nonetheless, optionality remains essential, as noted throughout the book. There will always be a need for in-person processes, and the human touch cannot be fully replicated by machines and robots. Human empathy is a cornerstone in dispute prevention and resolution. Human connection is foundational to our mental health. *The Arbitration Conversation* certainly confirmed that for me. I am forever thankful to each and every person who agreed to participate in *The Arbitration Conversation*! It was like a lifeline for my teaching and mental health during the Covid-19 shutdown, and it continues to be a highlight in my day when I get to talk with yet another arbitration expert.

Thanks to all who participated to date and will participate as we continue the journey of *The Arbitration Conversation*.

NOTES

1 Colin Rule & Amy Schmitz, *Arbitration Conversation No. 30: Colin Rule, CEO, Mediate.com/Arbitrate.com*, YouTube (Aug. 21, 2020), www.youtube.com/watch?v=HhAfIWDtDdY.

2 *Id.*

3 Amy Schmitz & Colin Rule, *OArb Enters the Age of Artificial Intelligence*, 29(2) Disp. Resol. Mag. 36, 36–39 (2023).

Appendix A

OArb Protocol Digest[1]

Tech Comfort & Accessibility	• Arbitrator or a designated third party should provide technical support to troubleshoot the virtual proceeding.[1, 2, 3, 5, 10, 11, 15, 18, 19] • Conduct a preliminary check of compatibility of platforms.[1, 3, 5, 10, 11, 13, 14, 15, 18] • Have a designated messaging system, backup platform, or other plans if parties lose connection.[2, 5, 8, 9, 15, 18] • Terminate any proceeding if technology is not working or is prejudicial to a party or the case in any way.[3, 5, 11] • Parties shall have the necessary equipment conditions and technical capabilities for online arbitration (emails, other communication tools, video court hearings, printers to print exhibits, etc.).[8, 11, 16] • Have a designated location, such as the arbitration service platform, to upload and import online electronic data.[16] • Arbitrators and counsel should possess basic technology competence and should ensure all parties are familiar with platform technology beforehand.[1, 2, 3, 5, 7, 12, 18] • Have mock or practice sessions using the platform beforehand.[1, 2, 5, 6, 17] • Recommend using devices with large monitor size; or ideally have dual monitors for managing video and documents.[6, 18, 21, 22] • Use platforms that are free and reliable to use.[10, 12, 13, 14, 17]
Physical & Language Accessibility	• If parties realize it is necessary to hold meetings in person, reschedule without delay.[1] • Consider need for interpreters or virtual transcription.[1, 2] • Machine learning AI can provide automatically generated translations of documents; consider accuracy concerns and licensing issues.[1, 14]

	• Maybe use multiple audio feeds for simultaneous interpretation or use sequential interpretation, but parties shall decide if interpretation shall be consecutive or simultaneous.[2, 15, 18] • Consecutive interpretation is often preferred and sometimes required.[5, 11, 14] • Consider potentially different time zones for different parties.[1, 3, 18] • Have the arbitrator, case manager, or panel member send the invitations for attendees via email to join and limit attendance to attendees only.[8] • Allow interpreters to be with witness while they are giving testimony.[11] • Discuss beforehand whether parties and neutrals or tribunal members can be in the same location.[5, 13] • Find a quiet location without background noise.[6] • Try to join counsel teams and/or party representative to sit together in one venue in a "cluster."[1, 2, 5, 11]
Cybersecurity	• Determine "cyber-protocol" for data privacy regulations. This includes suggested clauses.[1, 3] • Cybersecurity measures should be reasonable to the circumstance of the matter; factors to consider are the case subject matter, identity of case participants, the size and value of the dispute, and consequences of a breach.[1, 2, 15, 17, 23] • At minimum, security requires a robust protection for confidentiality and data security. Arbitrators should enforce measures to protect confidentiality of documents and information.[5, 18, 23] • Password protect meetings and share passwords separately for added security.[3, 6] • Attendees should not share the hearing link or password.[8] • Participants should consider encrypting all data in transit.[1, 2] • Participants should not be allowed to record any part of the proceedings for their own use; only authorized recordings should be allowed, and only the authorized parties and counsel shall be given access to the live video or audio feed.[5, 8, 9, 17, 18] • Use unique meeting IDs for each virtual hearing instead of personal meeting IDs.[6, 7, 10] • Parties should agree on a list of participants and limit attendance to those on the list provided to the tribunal in advance.[2, 15, 17, 21] • Disable the private chat feature.[7] • Limit access to breakout rooms to allocated participants.[13] • Procedure should comply with any cybersecurity laws of the jurisdiction.[10, 15, 16] • Any variable security settings should be set to the most secure security option available.[1, 11, 12]

	• Licensed document sharing platforms have greater security than free programs.[1] • Parties should familiarize themselves with Zoom security vulnerabilities.[3] • Participants should not use public Wi-Fi; only use secure internet networks.[3, 5, 7, 9] • Utilize the waiting room feature on platforms to monitor attendance.[7, 10] • ICCA-NYC-Bar-CPR provides its own in-depth framework on cybersecurity concerns and hazards.[20] • Consider additional safety factors such as two-factor authentication.[21]
Online Etiquette	• Identify each individual present in each room at the start of the hearing.[1, 5, 6, 8] • The arbitrator should be the meeting host.[2] • Disable popups, close down any other applications or tabs besides the hearing.[2, 6] • Allow for general chat functions for non-time-sensitive questions, and disable private chat functions.[2, 3, 6, 7] • Enable screen-sharing.[5] • Avoid speaking when others speak to avoid interruption.[1] • Don't have any more than two people in camera.[2] • Consider muting and turning off all cameras besides the tribunal and active speakers; some procedures might require all participants to be visible at all times.[2, 12, 13, 21] • Remain muted when not speaking.[3, 7, 8] • Do not use virtual backgrounds.[3, 5] • Do not disconnect from the hearing during recess.[3, 9] • Encourage the use of headphones with embedded microphones.[5] • Discourage the use of smartphones.[5] • Use a high-quality camera and background with no backlighting.[6, 7, 10, 18] • Have webcam at eye level; sit so head, shoulders, and hand gestures are visible.[10] • If somebody disconnects, suspend the session until they rejoin.[17] • Arrive early, approximately ten minutes, to troubleshoot and prepare for the hearing.[17]
Testimonial Evidence	• Consult on witness examination: consider order, connection, virtual sequestration, and how to avoid potential hidden channels of communication.[1, 2, 8, 9, 15] • Witness should show that they are not relying on using other materials or persons and may be asked to provide a 360° view of the room to show that they have an empty desk or table.[1, 2, 3, 8, 9, 11, 14, 15, 21] • If there is another person present in the room, they must be identified.[8, 9, 15, 19]

	• Witness should be visible and the center of the camera; don't use a virtual background.[2, 3, 5, 8, 9, 11, 14] • Consider a virtual witness oath and whether the jurisdiction allows it.[2, 5, 18] • Don't talk about subject matter of testimony while in progress.[5] • Witnesses may testify by telephone only in exceptional circumstances.[5, 18] • Sequester witness in breakout rooms until scheduled to testify.[9] • Testimonial evidence can be recorded with voice recognition technology to create court trial records.[16]
Documentary Evidence	• There are a variety of different document sharing platforms and services that the parties should agree upon using beforehand.[1, 2, 5, 7, 8, 10, 11, 15, 18, 21] • Agree beforehand which documents will be uploaded to the platform and made available to witnesses/experts during their examination.[19] • Identify whether counsel will use multiple screens for sharing.[1, 2, 5, 6, 7, 11, 18] • There should be simultaneous access to documents on a screensharing platform.[13, 15, 17, 18] • Consider the case's factual and legal complexity and whether using technology for documents would be too cumbersome or unreasonably increase time/costs for a party.[1, 14] • Consider using e-briefs (briefs with embedded hyperlinks to exhibits) and having searchable text formats for documents.[1] • If possible, give hard copies to witnesses beforehand and should also be made available electronically.[2, 5, 8, 9, 11, 13, 18] • Ensure documents are forwarded to neutrals before session.[10] • Parties should have full and fair access to any exhibits to be examined before and during proceedings by submitting evidence to the service platform.[5, 8, 9, 11, 16, 18] • Documents should be paginated and made available without annotations.[11, 15] • Have witnesses open sealed packages containing exhibits on camera.[2, 14, 18] • Pre-mark when documents should be submitted electronically.[3] • Parties should be able to trace the origin of documents and should see the path to outcome when artificial intelligence is employed.[17]
When to Proceed Virtually	• If parties object to virtual hearings, consider if award will be enforceable and provide a rationale.[1, 15, 18] • Have the parties agree to not challenge on the basis of the hearing being virtual.[2, 5, 15, 18]

	• Rules that say parties should be heard in person don't preclude virtual "in-person" hearings.[1] • Consider when site visits or inspections can be done via video.[1, 21] • Consider whether substantial written submissions have already been exchanged.[1] • Consider whether technology would provide greater security for sensitive data.[1] • Default: procedural meetings and case management are virtual; hearings on the merits are in person and virtual hearings require consent.[4] • A hybrid manner may be appropriate if participants are located together but separate from other parties.[5] • The arbitrator/panel finds that conducting the hearing online is a reasonable alternative due to stay-at-home orders or travel limitations.[8] • Consider that the state where the proceeding is may affect the law; be sure to confirm in writing where the virtual hearing "is located."[9] • Make the request to use videoconferencing before the hearing.[11, 15] • Consider jurisdictional guidelines for when remote hearings are allowed.[13]
Other Procedural Efficiency Measures	• Have additional case management conferences to modify the procedural timetable if needed.[1] • Use partial awards and document-only hearings when possible.[1] • Ensure there is a written record of the technical and organizational measures that will apply to the case.[1] • Tribunal should consider how to allocate costs of using technology.[1] • Consider formal legal requirements in relevant jurisdictions before relying on electronic signatures.[1] • Conduct a test session at least 48 hours prior to the scheduled start of the proceedings.[5] • Log into the platform at least ten minutes early to the hearing.[5] • Join the hearing using full names.[7] • Provide a list of platform features that should be enabled and why they might be useful.[7] • Discuss the costs between parties for videoconferencing and other additional costs.[8, 9, 18] • Have all notepads, beverages, and essential items nearby so that you don't have to leave the room once proceedings begin.[10] • The parties may also request, according to specific circumstances, to change part of the online arbitration procedure.[16] • Consider ethical obligations that come along with arbitrating over video.[17] • Utilizing presentation technology can help with efficiency.[22]

	• Arbitrators may direct consolidation or joinder of two or more cases taking into account relevant circumstances including serving the interests of justice and efficiency.[23] • Arbitrators have the ability to determine the method of proceedings.[23]

Table of Authorities

1 *ICC Guidance Note on Possible Measures Aimed at Mitigating the Effects of the COVID-19 Pandemic*, Int'l Ct. of Arb. (Apr. 9, 2020), https://iccwbo.org/news-publications/arbitration-adr-rules-and-tools/icc-guidance-note-on-possible-measures-aimed-at-mitigating-the-effects-of-the-covid-19-pandemic/; *Leveraging Technology for Fair, Effective and Efficient International Arbitration Proceedings*, Int'l Chamber of Com. (Feb. 2022), https://iccwbo.org/wp-content/uploads/sites/3/2022/02/icc-arbitration-and-adr-commission-report-on-leveraging-technology-for-fair-effective-and-efficient-international-arbitration-proceedings.pdf.

2 *Hogan Lovells Protocol for the Use of Technology in International Arbitration Hearings*, Hogan Lovells (Feb. 2021), www.hoganlovells.com/~/media/hogan-lovells/pdf/2021-pdfs/2021_02_11_06429_hl_protocol.pdf.

3 Stephanie Cohen, *Draft Zoom Hearing Procedural Order*, Transnat'l Disp. Mgmt. (Apr. 14, 2020), www.transnational-dispute-management.com/journal-advance-publication-article.asp?key=1815.

4 Alison Ross, *What If Parties Don't Agree on a Virtual Hearing? A Pandemic Pathway*, Glob. Arb. Rev. (May 6, 2020), https://globalarbitrationreview.com/what-if-parties-dont-agree-virtual-hearing-pandemic-pathway.

5 *CPR's Annotated Model Procedural Order for Remote Video Arbitration Proceedings*, Int'l Inst. For Conflict Prevention & Resol. (Aug. 26, 2021), https://static.cpradr.org/docs/Annotated%20Model%20Procedural%20order%20for%20Remote%20Video%20Arbitration%20Proceedings%20August%202021.pdf.

6 *AAA-ICDR Virtual Hearing Guide for Arbitrators and Parties* (2021), Am. Arb. Ass'n, https://go.adr.org/rs/294-SFS-516/images/AAA268_AAA%20Virtual%20Hearing%20Guide%20for%20Arbitrators%20and%20Parties.pdf.

7 *AAA-ICDR Virtual Hearing Guide for Arbitrators and Parties Utilizing Zoom* (2021), Am. Arb. Ass'n, https://go.adr.org/rs/294-SFS-516/images/AAA269_AAA%20Virtual%20Hearing%20Guide%20for%20Arbitrators%20and%20Parties%20Utilizing%20Zoom.pdf.

8 *Order and Procedures for a Virtual Hearing via Videoconference*, Am. Arb. Ass'n, https://adr.org/sites/default/files/document_repository/AAA270_AAA-ICDR_Model_Order_and_Procedures_for_a_Virtual_Hearing_via_Videoconference.pdf (last visited Sept. 15, 2022).

9 P. Jean Baker, *During the Pandemic, Virtual Arbitration Offers a Promising Alternative—Provided You Know What You Are Doing*, 74(4) Disp. Resol. J. 157, 157–64 (2020).

10 *JAMS Videoconference Guide*, JAMS (Feb. 2023), www.jamsadr.com/files/uploads/documents/jams-videoconference-guide.pdf; *Virtual ADR & Security—FAQ*, JAMS, www.jamsadr.com/faq-virtual-adr (last visited Sept. 15, 2023); *JAMS ADR Insights*, JAMS, www.jamsadr.com/pdf-viewer.aspx?pdf=/files/Uploads/Documents/JAMS-Virtual-ADR-Tips.pdf (last visited Nov. 12, 2023).

11 Kevin Kim, Yu-Jin Tay, Ing Loong Yang & Seung Min Lee, *Seoul Protocol on Video Conferencing in International Arbitration*, www.lockelord.com/-/media/seoul-protocol-on-video-conference-in-internationa.pdf (last visited Sept. 15, 2023).

12 Evan Hoffman, *CIIAN's Best Practices for Online Dispute Resolution*, CIIAN (Oct. 2018), www.researchgate.net/publication/328251225_CIIAN's_Best_Practices_for_Online_Dispute_Resolution.

13 Kateryna Honcharenko & Mercy McBrayer, *Guidance Note on Remote Dispute Resolution Proceedings*, Chartered Inst. of Arbs. (2020), https://www.ciarb.org/media/8967/remote-hearings-guidance-note.pdf.

14 Brianna Kostecka & Jessica Sabbath, *Best Practices for Conducting Arbitration Hearings Remotely*, King & Spalding (Apr. 17, 2020), www.jdsupra.com/legalnews/best-practices-for-conducting-56006/.

15 *Protocol on Virtual Hearings in Africa 2020*, Africa Arb. Acad. (Apr. 2020), https://africaarbitrationacademy.org/protocol-virtual- hearings/.

16 *SCIA Online Arbitration Rules*, Shenzhen Ct. of Int'l Arb. (Feb. 21, 2022), www.scia.com.cn/index.php/Home/index/rule/id/814.html.

17 *ICODR Video Arbitration Guidelines*, Int'l Council for Online Disp. Resol. (Apr. 2020), https://icodr.org/guides/videoarb.pdf; *ODR Standards*, Int'l Council for Online Disp. Resol., https://icodr.org/standards (last visited June 3, 2022).

18 *The Efficacy of Virtual Arbitration Proceedings amidst Covid-19 and a Checklist of Best Practices*, Fasken (Apr. 8, 2020), www.fasken.com/en/knowledge/2020/04/8-covid-19-virtual-arbitration-proceedings-best-practices/.

19 *Hearings in Times of Covid-19: Delos Checklist on Holding Arbitration and Mediation Hearings in Times of Covid-19*, Delos (Mar. 20, 2020), https://delosdr.org/checklist-on-holding-hearings-in-times-of-covid-19/.

20 *Protocol on Cybersecurity in International Arbitration*, ICCA–NYC Bar–CPR (2022), https://cdn.arbitration-icca.org/s3fs-public/document/media_document/ICCA-reports-no-6-icca-nyc-bar-cpr-protocol-cybersecurity-international-arbitration-2022-edition.pdf.

21 James Hosking & Marcel Engholm Cardoso, *Practical Considerations for Holding a Remote Arbitration Hearing*, 13(2) NYSBA New York Disp. Resol. Law. 14–17 (Summer 2020), https://nysba.org/app/uploads/2020/08/FINAL_DisputeResolutionLawyer_Summer-2020.pdf.

22 Kap-You (Kevin) Kim et al., *Advocacy in Virtual Hearings*, Glob. Arb. Rev. (Aug. 18, 2023), https://globalarbitrationreview.com/guide/the-guide-advocacy/sixth-edition/article/advocacy-in-virtual-hearings.

23 *Commercial Arbitration Rules and Mediation Procedures including Procedures for Large, Complex Commercial Disputes*, Am. Arb. Ass'n (Sept. 1, 2022), https://go.adr.org/rs/294-SFS-516/images/Commercial_Rules_Web.pdf.

NOTE

1 Special thank you to Cooper Karras for assistance in placing the information into this chart.

Appendix B
The Arbitration Conversation

<https://arbitrate.com/the-arbitration-conversation/>

You can find these on YouTube and at https://arbitrate.com/the-arbitration-conversation/. After the first 100 webisodes, the series moved to an audio-only podcast. These are longer conversations at https://arbitrate.podbean.com/ and anywhere you get your podcasts (Apple, Spotify, Amazon, Podbean, etc.). Eighteen are currently posted, and more are on the way. Note that this list also appears in substantial part on Arbitrate.com and in the online teaching materials for Tom Stipanowich and Amy J. Schmitz, ARBITRATION: PRACTICE, POLICY AND LAW, 1ST ED. (Aspen 2022).

- Episode 1: Svetlana Gitman, American Arbitration Association—Discussing AAA's move online in the pandemic; how the AAA is assisting the move of their arbitrators in conducting online arbitrations in the wake of Covid.
- Episode 2: Prof. Dave Larson, Mitchell Hamline School of Law—Discussion of accessibility for differently abled individuals to arbitration processes, especially when they are online.
- Episode 3: Prof. Bob Bailey, University of Missouri School of Law—Discussion of *The New Prime v. Oliveira* SC case, and how it applies to employment arbitration.
- Episode 4: Prof. Ben Davis, University of Toledo College of Law—Diversity in arbitration, and providing opportunities for arbitrators of color.
- Episode 5: Prof. Tom Stipanowich, Pepperdine Caruso School of Law—Mixed mode and dispute resolution using mixed methods, including arbitration.
- Episode 6: Prof. Mohamed Abdel Wahab of the Cairo University Faculty of Law—Arbitration in Cairo and developments abroad.

*Materials listed in this Appendix have previously been available on SSRN, Arbitrate.com

- Episode 7: Prof. Sarah Cole of the Moritz College of Law at OSU—Discussion of diversity in arbitration.
- Episode 8: Prof. Richard Frankel of Drexel University Thomas R. Kline School of Law—Employment and labor arbitration issues.
- Episode 9: Charles E. Harris II, Partner, Mayer Brown—Important issues related to drafting arbitration agreements, including pros and cons of carve-outs.
- Episode 10: Prof. David Horton, UC Davis School of Law—Employment arbitration issues and Prof. Horton's latest article re "infinite arbitration clauses," which ultimately won the AALS Section Award.
- Episode 11: Theo Cheng on Intellectual Property Arbitration—IP (intellectual property) arbitration and the special issues such cases raise.
- Episode 12: Arbitrator Katherine Haennicke from AAA—Consumer arbitration and special issues related to arbitrating pro se cases.
- Episode 13: Prof. S.I. Strong of the University of Sydney—Trust arbitration and new laws in New Zealand related to arbitration.
- Episode 14: Prof. Maureen Weston from Pepperdine Law School—Sports arbitration, including arbitration related to the Olympics and "doping" cases.
- Episode 15: Prof. Chris Drahozal of KU Law—Discussion of the *Henry Schein, Inc. v. Archer and White Sales, Inc.*, cases I and II: one that already has been decided by the U.S. Supreme Court and another that is pending the decision after oral arguments.
- Episode 16: Prof. Michael Z. Green of Texas A&M School of Law—Prof. Green's latest articles, with a focus on diversity in arbitration.
- Episode 17: Arbitrator Bill McGrath of Davis McGrath in Chicago—Motion practice in arbitration.
- Episode 18: The "Blues Lawyer" Aric Garza on consumer arbitration—Discussion of consumer arbitration and how to promote fairness in consumer cases.
- Episode 19: Prof. Anthony Daimsis of the University of Ottawa—The *Uber* case in Canada (unconscionability applied to the arbitration clause at issue under Canadian law).
- Episode 20: Prof. Catharine Titi of the University of Paris—ICSID and investment arbitration.
- Episode 21: Prof. Jill I. Gross of Pace Law School—FINRA arbitration and Prof. Gross's work regarding securities arbitration.
- Episode 22: Prof. Carrie Shang of Cal State Polytechnic University, Pomona—Arbitration issues emanating from Hong Kong and China, including recent relational issues.

- Episode 23: Dr. Nudrat Piracha, Member of the ICSID Ad Hoc Committee—ICSID and her leadership as the first Pakistani woman to earn her SJD.
- Episode 24: Hilary Mofsowitz, South African Labor and Employment Arbitrator—Discussion of labor arbitration in South Africa and description of the process.
- Episode 25: Arbitrator Nicholas Gowen, Partner at Burke, Warren, MacKay & Serritella—Practical insights on how arbitration fits in a larger problem-solving strategy.
- Episode 26: Arbitrator Clifford Shapiro, Partner at Barnes & Thornburg, Chicago—Construction arbitration and special issues related to multiparty processes.
- Episode 27: Prof. Rick Bales of Ohio Northern School of Law—Labor arbitration in the age of Covid and how labor arbitration moved online in the wake of the pandemic.
- Episode 28: International Arbitrator and Mediator Wolf Von Kumburg—Investment treaty arbitration and other international forms of arbitration.
- Episode 29: Jonathan Eades, Senior Legal Counsel, BC Attorney General—Insights regarding a new Canadian Arbitration Law.
- Episode 30: Colin Rule, CEO of Arbitrate.com and Mediate.com—Insights for the future of RIS, including the strategy for Mediate.com and Arbitrate.com moving into 2021 and beyond.
- Episode 31: Prof. John Lande, University of Missouri School of Law—Considerations of risk management, and how arbitration fits into an overall conflict management plan.
- Episode 32: Prof. Santiago Dussan of Pontificia Universidad Javeriana, Cali—Online dispute resolution in Latin America, and advances in application of technology to arbitration.
- Episode 33: Prof. Nicolás Lozada Pimiento from Universidad Externado de Colombia—UNCITRAL Working Group III revisited and Online Dispute Resolution in Colombia, as well as the rest of Latin America.
- Episode 34: Prof. Brian Farkas, Cardozo Law School—Politics in arbitration and how to discuss politics in the context of an arbitration class; the Trump administration's perspective on arbitration.
- Episode 35: Prof. Joshua Karton, Queens University Law School—Discussion of the new Canadian Journal of Commercial Arbitration and his new sociolegal study of arbitration on an international scale, seeking to understand the profession of commercial arbitration.
- Episode 36: Mirèze Philippe Special Counsel ICC International Court of Arbitration—Discussion of her role in creating and leading ArbitralWomen and diversity in arbitration.

- Episode 37: Sports Arbitrator Clifford J. Hendel—International sports arbitration, including arbitration of FIFA and basketball cases in Europe.
- Episode 38: Arbitrator Jo Delaney of Baker McKenzie—A discussion of how she got into arbitration and became a leader in this space; a discussion of her work with ICSID, construction, and other international cases; a discussion of arbitration law and some high-profile cases in Australia.
- Episode 39: Arbitrator and Professor Moti Mironi—Arbitration in Israel, and the latest developments related to law and practice in Israel.
- Episode 40: Prof. Nicolas Vermeys of the University of Montreal Law School—Explanation of "AI" and discussion of AI in arbitration along with ways it can assist with dispute resolution.
- Episode 41: George Friedman, Editor-in-Chief of Securities Arbitration Alert—Discussion of securities arbitration and how arbitration proceeds in FINRA, especially in the wake of the Covid-19 pandemic.
- Episode 42: Prof. Victoria Sahani of Arizona State University—Director of the Faculty Inclusion Research for System Transformation Initiative, or FIRST Initiative, a university-wide initiative supported by the ASU president's office looking at the history of race and inclusion among faculty at the university. Discussion of what makes investment treaty arbitration different than regular international commercial arbitration, and why it is important to focus on investment treaty arbitration at this particular moment. Discussion of reforms in investment treaty arbitration that are likely to be implemented in the near future.
- Episode 43: Prof. Andrea Bjorklund of McGill University Faculty of Law—Discussion of investor-state arbitration and Working Group III of UNCITRAL, which is considering potential reforms to investor-state dispute settlement; consideration of specific issues discussed in WG III, and its mandate to consider procedural reform issues as well as the biggest hurdles to progress at WG III.
- Episode 44: Morenike Obi-Farinde, Founder, ODR Africa Network—Online arbitration in Africa and the latest developments in ODR Africa.
- Episode 45: Prof. Steven Ware, Kansas University School of Law—Discussion of Prof. Ware's new book on arbitration, including current case law on evolving topics, such as delegation clauses, contracts formed by clicking links on cell phones, and substitutes for the class actions limited by *Concepcion*; discussion of arbitration issues from pop culture such as a Justin Bieber tweet, and contemporary disputes involving Uber's app, Donald Trump's confidentiality agreement, and Jay-Z's impact on arbitrator diversity.

- Episode 46: Arbitrator, Mediator, and Trainer DeAndra Roaché of Cynergis ADR—Discussion of arbitration in the railroad industry and how railroad arbitration proceeds.
- Episode 47: Ludvig Hambraeus of the Chartered Institute of Arbitrators—Discussion of CIArb, and his role as policy executive as well as consideration of how CIArb adapted to the impact of the Covid-19 pandemic and CIArb's priorities going into 2021.
- Episode 48: Hafez Virjee, President and Co-Founder of Delos Dispute Resolution—Discussion of online arbitration and his work as an online arbitrator with Delos; discussion of his journey in founding Delos as a stand-alone dispute resolution entity.
- Episode 49: Michael Waibel, Professor of International Law, University of Vienna—Investment-treaty arbitration and the latest developments from his perspective in Europe.
- Episode 50: Chittu Nagarajan, Founder and CEO of CREKODR.com —Development of CREK as an ODR and online arbitration platform, and how arbitration fits within the ODR spectrum.
- Episode 51: Tanya Venter, Director of Tokiso Dispute Resolution in South Africa—Discussion of arbitration in South Africa, focusing on how South Africa deals with discrimination cases in the workplace, considering the history of apartheid; discussion of how racism and other forms of discrimination are commonly found and resolved in the workplace.
- Episode 52: Graham Ross, Head of International Marketing at Smartsettle.com—Discussion of Smartsettle, and how it works as a form of online arbitration; discussion of other online means for supporting and facilitating arbitration using algorithms.
- Episode 53: Janet Walker, Canadian Professor and Arbitrator—Discussion of transparency in international commercial arbitration, and Prof. Walker's recent work in the area, including considerations of what information we need and how it could be helpful to increase transparency in certain ways.
- Episode 54: Myriam M. Seers, Senior Associate, Torys LLP—Discussion of how technology tools can be leveraged to change the way disputes are resolved; discussion as well around the types of disputes that arise in the technology space, and what needs to change in order to make dispute resolution tools accessible for smaller technology disputes.
- Episode 55: Jan Martinez, Director, Gould ADR Program, Stanford Law School—Discussion of dispute system design and how arbitration fits into design considerations.
- Episode 56: Deborah Hylton, Fellow of the Chartered Institute of Arbitrators—Discussion of arbitrators as problem-solvers and how full spectrum ADR and mediation can work in tandem with

party-driven arbitration to urge counsel to work within a problem-solving framework.

- Episode 57: Julie G. Hopkins, Independent Arbitrator from Calgary, Canada—Discussion of her paper with Daniel Urbas titled "Virtual Practice Makes Virtually Perfect—Practical Considerations for Virtual Hearings Identified through Simulations with Experienced Counsel and Arbitrators," including lessons learned from leading arbitration/advocacy professionals from across North America.
- Episode 58: Prof. Rachel J. Goedken, Director, Werner Institute, Creighton Law—Discussion of how to get into labor arbitration and a discussion of how labor arbitration works.
- Episode 59: Mediator, Arbitrator, and Special Master Karl Bayer—Discussion of virtual hearings and important tips and considerations for those moving their arbitration practice online.
- Episode 60: Wendy Gonzales, Founder of Cyberarb—Discussion regarding the creation of "CyberArb" as means for promoting cybersecurity in arbitration as well as the importance of cybersecurity and having a concrete plan to safeguard the safety of data in the "new normal" of online arbitration.
- Episode 61: Former Chief Justice of the Iowa Supreme Court Justice Marsha Ternus—Discussion regarding student conduct procedures and how they are similar to arbitration as well as how "ad hoc" arbitration differs from administered arbitration.
- Episode 62: Prof. Rory Van Loo of the Boston University School of Law—Discussion of his recent article proposing a process for determining when and whether posts or parties are eliminated from platforms such as Amazon, Facebook, Twitter, and so on.
- Episode 63: Prof. Pamela Bookman of the Fordham University School of Law—Discussion of arbitral courts, courts that mimic arbitration's traditional features but that, unlike arbitration, bind third parties, develop law, and wield the power of the state.
- Episode 64: Richard Ormond and Jake Stango of ejudicate.com—Discussion with the founders of ejudicate.com, a new ODR startup that focuses on B2B online arbitration (OArb) describing their process, their reasons for founding the company, and how text-based arbitration can be both fair and efficient.
- Episode 65: Prof. Michael Pitton of the University of Iowa College of Law—Discussion about conducting in-person arbitrations safely by following the CDC Guidelines and the U.S. Supreme Court Protocol during the age of Covid, and conducting arbitrations in a university setting.
- Episode 66: Independent Arbitrator Sophie Nappert—Discussion about the intersection between arbitration and technology and the increasing importance of cybersecurity, data protection, and

cryptography tools such as blockchain in the process of conducting arbitrations online.

- Episode 67: Stephen Kane, Founder and CEO of FairClaims.com—Conversation with Stephen Kane, an ODR and OArb provider working with sharing economy and B2B marketplaces, insurance companies, construction companies, self-insured Fortune 500s, the Better Business Bureau, and others to resolve disputes quickly and effectively.
- Episode 68: Prof. Imre Szalai of Loyola University New Orleans—In this episode of the Arbitration Conversation, Amy interviews Prof. Imre Szalai, a nationally known scholar regarding the Federal Arbitration Act, on delegation clauses in arbitration law, as well as his research regarding the enactment and development of modern arbitration laws. This includes discussion about his book *Outsourcing Justice: The Rise of Modern Arbitration Laws in America*.
- Episode 69: Stephen Anway, Partner and Co-Chair of IDR at Squire Patton Boggs—In this episode of the Arbitration Conversation, Amy interviews Arbitrator Stephen Anway, global co-chair of Squire Patton Boggs' International Dispute Resolution (IDR) Practice. The discussion focuses on international investment arbitration and the latest issues Mr. Anway has seen in practice.
- Episode 70: Catherine Rogers, Founder, Arbitrator Intelligence—In this episode of the Arbitration Conversation, Amy interviews Catherine A. Rogers, a scholar of international arbitration and founder of Arbitrator Intelligence. The discussion focuses on Arbitrator Intelligence and its journey as a legal tech startup company that is seeking to add transparency in arbitration and arbitrator selection.
- Episode 71: Ashley Rafael, General Counsel, Midway Moving & Storage, Inc.—In this episode of the Arbitration Conversation, Amy interviews Ashley Rafael, an arbitrator for the American Arbitration Association, serving on its Commercial, UM/UI, and Consumer Panels. She is also an adjunct professor of law at the University of Illinois at Chicago Law School. She provides great insights for students looking to enter the field, and talks about the arbitration work from an in-house counsel perspective.
- Episode 72: Paul Barker, International Arbitrator and Fellow, Stanford Law School—In this episode of the Arbitration Conversation, Amy interviews Paul Barker, a barrister at Doughty Street Chambers specializing in international arbitration, investor-state dispute settlement (ISDS), international law, climate finance, and sustainable investing. Paul has been recognized as a leading junior barrister for international arbitration (Who's Who Legal: UK Bar). He is also ranked as one of the leading international arbitration lawyers

globally under the age of 45. He talks about the latest issues in investor-state arbitration, and where he sees movement for changes in the field as a younger practitioner.

- Episode 73: Rana Sajjad Ahmad, Founder of CIICA Arbitration Center, Pakistan—In this episode of the Arbitration Conversation, Amy interviews Rana Sajjad Ahmad, founder and president of the Center for International Investment and Commercial Arbitration (CIICA) in Pakistan, as well as a fellow of The Chartered Institute of Arbitrators and partner at the Rana Ijaz & Partners law firm. This is a conversation about arbitration in Pakistan, especially with respect to international investment arbitration.
- Episode 74: Peter Merrill, CEO of Construction Dispute Resolution Services—In this episode of the Arbitration Conversation, Amy interviews Peter Merrill, a leading provider of arbitration and mediation services in the construction industry, based in Santa Fe, New Mexico. This conversation focuses on construction arbitration—an area where they both practiced. Discussion includes ideas about promoting fairness and efficiency in construction arbitration.
- Episode 75: Prof. Angie Raymond, Kelley School of Business, Indiana University—In this episode of the Arbitration Conversation, Amy interviews Anjanette (Angie) Raymond, an associate professor in the Department of Business Law and Ethics, at the Kelley School of Business, Indiana University, and an adjunct associate professor of law at Maurer Law School (Indiana). She is currently a visiting fellow in international commercial law at the Centre for Commercial Law Studies, Queen Mary, University of London, as well as a professor in the International Business Law Program at the University of Navarra, Spain, and lectures on international arbitration at the World Intellectual Property Organization. The conversation sheds light on AI—what it means and how it may be deployed in conjunction with arbitration.
- Episode 76: Prof. Steven Shapiro, American University Washington College of Law—In this episode of the Arbitration Conversation, Amy interviews Prof. Steven Shapiro, the founder and director of the Hospitality & Tourism Law Program, and a senior affiliate in the Program on Law & Government, including his work in teaching construction law. The conversation focuses on teaching arbitration and ideas for student engagement.
- Episode 77: Lawyer David Tenner, a Colorado Arbitrator and Special Master—In this episode of the Arbitration Conversation, Amy interviews David Tenner, an arbitrator, a special master to area courts, and a trained mediator. He is a member of the commercial panel of the American Arbitration Association. He is a fellow of the Academy of Court-Appointed Masters, and in 2015 he was

appointed to the Academy's board of directors. He currently serves as ACAM's secretary. The conversation focuses on the recent ABA statement promoting commercial arbitration.

- Episode 78: Arbitrator Edna Sussman, of SussmanADR.com—In this episode of the Arbitration Conversation, Amy interviews Edna Sussman, who serves full-time as an arbitrator and mediator and has been appointed as the Distinguished ADR Practitioner in Residence by the Fordham University School of Law. She started her career as an associate and litigation partner at the international law firm of White & Case. Over the past 15 years she has served as an arbitrator in well over 300 arbitrations and as a mediator in well over 200 mediations in both domestic and international complex commercial disputes. The conversation focuses on practical insights for arbitrators looking to balance fairness and efficiency.
- Episode 79: Fernando Sanquírico Pittevil, Associate, InterJuris Abogados S.C.—In this episode of the Arbitration Conversation, Amy interviews Fernando Sanquírico Pittevil. Fernando is professor of civil law in Universidad Central de Venezuela, Universidad Católica Andrés Bello, and Universidad Monteávila. In his academic career, he has been invited to teach the international arbitration subject in the Procedural Law LLM at Universidad Central de Venezuela. He is currently the director of the Research and Studies Centre for Dispute Resolution of the Universidad Monteávila. He is also the academic coordinator of the Advanced Studies Programme on Arbitration in the Universidad Monteavila. Mr. Sanquirico Pittevil is also a member of the list of arbitrators in both the Arbitration Centre of the Caracas Chamber and the Business Centre for Conciliation and Arbitration. Fernando is a member of the board of directors of the Venezuelan Arbitration Association for the period 2019–2021.
- Episode 80: Adriana Vaamonde, Exec. Director, Centro de Arbitraje Cámara de Caracas—In this episode of the Arbitration Conversation, Amy interviews Adriana Vaamonde, a legal advisor in international commercial arbitration, arbitrator and secretary of Arbitral Tribunals, university professor of national and international commercial arbitration, lawyer of the Universidad Monteávila (UMA), specialist in corporate law at the Universidad Metropolitana (UNIMET), and master in foreign trade at UC3M. She is also former executive director of the Arbitration Center of the Caracas Chamber of Commerce and member of the Academic Council of the CIERC and of its editorial council of the magazine *Principia* as well as member of the board of directors of the AVA, of the CEA-40, and of the LIAYP.
- Episode 81: Erin Archerd, Assoc. Prof. of Law, University of Detroit Mercy School of Law—In this episode of the Arbitration

Conversation, Amy interviews Erin Archerd. Erin joined the Detroit Mercy Law faculty in Fall 2015. Prior to becoming a professor, she was an associate in the San Francisco office of Covington & Burling LLP, where she focused on corporate transactions, primarily in the information technology and biotechnology sectors, as well as preparing an amicus brief for the Supreme Court on language education policy. The conversation focuses on Early Neutral Evaluation, and how it may be used to assist dispute resolution.

- Episode 82: Prof. Ronald Brand, University of Pittsburgh School of Law—In this episode of the Arbitration Conversation, Amy interviews Ronald Brand, the Chancellor Mark A. Nordenberg University Professor and John E. Murray Faculty Scholar at the University of Pittsburgh School of Law. Ron was the driving force behind the creation of the University of Pittsburgh's Center for International Legal Education (CILE) and its Master of Laws Program for Foreign Law Graduates. The conversation focuses on the Viz Moot competition and its value in teaching arbitration.
- Episode 83: Gary Born, Chair, International Arbitration Practice Group, WilmerHale—In this episode of the Arbitration Conversation, Amy interviews Gary Born. Mr. Born is widely regarded as the world's preeminent authority on international commercial arbitration and international litigation. He has been ranked for more than 20 years as one of the world's leading international arbitration advocates and the leading arbitration practitioner in London. The conversation focuses on the Hague choice of court convention and reasons why states should not adopt it.
- Episode 84: Hiro Aragaki, Professor of Law at Loyola Law School—In this episode of the Arbitration Conversation, Amy interviews Prof. Hiro Aragaki. Prof. Aragaki's work has appeared in the University of Pennsylvania Law Review, the UCLA Law Review, and the Yale Law Journal Online, among others. His most recent work, Equal Opportunity for Arbitration, was selected for presentation in the Civil Litigation & Dispute Resolution category at the Stanford/Yale Junior Faculty Forum. The discussion focuses on the contractual and procedural elements of arbitration, and how theory matters in practice.
- Episode 85: Oladeji Tiamiyu, Clinical Fellow, HNMCP at Harvard Law School—In this episode of the Arbitration Conversation, Amy interviews Oladeji M. Tiamiyu. Prior to joining HNMCP, Oladeji was an Online Dispute Resolution Fellow with the Resolution Systems Institute in Chicago, Illinois, where he helped in developing a pilot online dispute resolution program for family law disputes. Oladeji has also worked with the Truth and Reconciliation Commission and Constitutional Review Commission in The Gambia.

He has experience as a teacher in Reunion Island off the coast of Madagascar and as a community organizer with Organizing for America in Ohio. Oladeji has been a member of teaching teams for Harvard Law School's Negotiation Workshop, an executive-level program at the Harvard Negotiation Institute, and with the Harvard Graduate School of Education. He is a member of the Illinois Bar, holds a BA in political science, magna cum laude, from the University of Toledo, and a JD from Harvard Law School. The conversation focuses on Online Dispute Resolution (ODR) and blockchain arbitration in particular.

- Episode 86: Travis Lenkner, Managing Partner of Keller Lenkner LLC—In this episode of the Arbitration Conversation, Amy interviews Travis Lenkner, Managing Partner of Keller Lenkner LLC. Travis has previous experience as a litigator at an AmLaw 25 law firm, a legal entrepreneur and investment manager, in-house counsel at a Fortune 50 company, and a law clerk at the Supreme Court of the U.S. He is listed on Lawdragon's 500 Leading Lawyers in America and the National Trial Lawyers' Top 100. He is also a member of the board of advisors of the Institute of Judicial Administration at New York University School of Law. Travis also served as a senior counsel at The Boeing Company, where he represented the company in litigation matters and advised senior executives on significant regulatory issues. This conversation focuses on mass arbitration filings against Amazon and others, and how this has caused a shift in corporate arbitration policy in some cases—a hot issue and interesting discussion.
- Episode 87: Prof. Leonardo Oliveira, Lecturer, Royal Holloway, University of London—In this episode of the Arbitration Conversation, Amy interviews Prof. Leonardo Valladares Pacheco de Oliveira. Leonardo qualified as a lawyer in Brazil in 2002. Having graduated and passed the Brazilian Bar exam, he worked as a legal assistant at the Rio de Janeiro State Control System Secretariat in the sphere of the Rio de Janeiro State Government. Leonardo is now a lecturer in law at Royal Holloway, University of London. The conversation focuses on how arbitration intersects with A2J, and ideas for arbitration to be a vehicle in expanding A2J.
- Episode 88: Prof. Steven Shapiro and Prof. Shaheeza Lalani—In this episode of the Arbitration Conversation, Amy interviews Prof. Steven Shapiro and Prof. Shaheeza Lalani. Prof. Shapiro has been an arbitrator since 1999. He has been a construction law professor at the American University Washington College of Law, author of professional books on design and construction, and invited presenter at national and international conferences. Prof. Lalani is executive director at the University of Lausanne. Previously she was director

of the doctoral program and senior researcher at the World Trade Institute, and senior legal counsel at the Swiss Chambers' Arbitration Institution. She was also legal counsel at the Swiss Institute of Comparative Law, and assistant legal officer at The Hague Conference on Private International Law. The conversation focuses on the upcoming Lausanne Arbitration Conference. See https://shapiroarbitration.com/lausan.

- Episode 89: Prof. Kristen Blankley of the Nebraska College of Law—In this episode of the Arbitration Conversation, Amy interviews Professor Kristen Blankley, who teaches alternative dispute resolution, advocacy in mediation, mediation, family mediation, and arbitration at the Nebraska College of Law. Her research has largely focused on the crossroads of alternative dispute resolution and ethics and on contemporary issues in arbitration law. Professor Blankley currently sits as a co-chair of the American Bar Association Section of Dispute Resolution Subcommittee on Ethics.
- Episode 90: Arbitrator Richard D. Faulkner—In this episode of the Arbitration Conversation, Amy interviews Arbitrator Richard D. Faulkner, fellow of the Chartered Institute of Arbitrators and holder of a diploma in international commercial arbitration. Richard is one of the foremost arbitration experts in the country, having arbitrated over 300 commercial, construction, employment, professional credentialing, insurance coverage, reinsurance, international, non-competition, trade secret, loan default, commercial lease, maritime, securities, personal injury, and internet "domain name" disputes. This conversation focuses on international arbitration.
- Episode 91: Chimdimma Onyedebelu, Operations Manager, International Mediation Institute—In this episode of the Arbitration Conversation, Amy interviews Chimdimma Onyedebelu, a certified arbitrator and mediator, and consultant for various stakeholders in dispute management. She is a member of the International Council for Online Dispute Resolution (ICODR), Online Dispute Resolution (ODR) Africa Network, Institute of Chartered Mediators and Conciliators (ICMC), Chartered Institute of Arbitrators (UK), ICMC Young Mediators Forum, Chartered Institute of Arbitrators Young Members Group, Young International Arbitrators Group, London Court of International Arbitration, DIAC 40—Young Practitioners Group, Dubai International Arbitration Centre, Young Mediators Initiative, International Mediation Institute (IMI), Association of Young Arbitrators (AYA), Nigerian Bar Association (NBA), Pan African Lawyers Union (PALU), International Federation of Women Lawyers (FIDA), and Nigerian Society of International Law (NSIL). Chimdimma was a former student in Amy's class and

the two discuss ideas for young lawyers to get involved in arbitration in Africa.

- Episode 92: Arbitrator Lisa Munro, Partner at Lerners LLP—In this episode of the Arbitration Conversation, Amy interviews Arbitrator Lisa Munro. She brings to this role more than 25 years of experience as counsel in commercial/business litigation and both international and domestic commercial arbitration. She is a fellow of the Chartered Institute of Arbitrators (FCIArb) and has obtained the ADR Institute of Canada's Qualified Arbitrator (Q.Arb) designation. She is also a roster arbitrator with Arbitration Place, the Toronto Commercial Arbitration Society, and the Vancouver International Arbitration Centre (VanIAC). Lisa is the editor of *Arbitration Matters*, featuring summaries of key decisions on arbitration issues as they are released by courts across the country. The website now features over 500 of these case notes and has been read by hundreds of Canada's leading arbitration professionals. A digest of the most recent notes is sent to subscribers on a regular basis. The discussion focuses on this new development and arbitration in Canada.
- Episode 93: Prof. Guillermo Jose Garcia Sanchez, Texas A&M School of Law—In this episode of the Arbitration Conversation, Amy interviews Prof. Guillermo Jose Garcia Sanchez. Guillermo teaches courses on arbitration and international petroleum transactions, and he's been an affiliate scholar at the Center for U.S. and Mexican Law, University of Houston Law Center and the Center for Energy and Natural Resources, ITAM University Mexico since 2014. He also was an associate at Curtis, Mallet-Prevost, Colt and Mosle, LLP, where he practiced international investment arbitration with a focus on cases related to the hydrocarbons industry in Latin America, and he served as a legal advisor on international law and the law of the sea at the Ministry of Foreign Affairs of Mexico.
- Episode 94: Arthur Pearlstein, Director of Arbitration, FMCS—In this episode of the Arbitration Conversation, Amy interviews Arthur Pearlstein, director of arbitration and of the Office of Shared Neutrals at the Federal Mediation and Conciliation Service (FMCS). He has previously served FMCS as a mediator, as general counsel of the agency, and as head of the ADR and International Program. In addition, he has worked extensively in the area of dispute systems design in the workplace. Arthur was professor of law and inaugural director of the Werner Institute for Negotiation and Dispute Resolution at Creighton University in Omaha. The conversation gives an overview of FMCS and what it does within the arbitration world.
- Episode 95: Olof Heggemann, Founder, Eperoto—In this episode of the Arbitration Conversation, Amy interviews Olof Heggemann,

founder of Eperoto.com. Olof has a professional background in the Swedish public court system and experience from working in both banking and law firms. Eperoto is a tool for valuing legal cases using decision science. Tech in arbitration is the focus of the conversation.

- Episode 96: Allen Waxman, President & CEO of CPR—In this episode of the Arbitration Conversation, Amy interviews Allen Waxman. Prior to joining CPR, Mr. Waxman served as general counsel of Pfizer, at Eisai Inc—the North American affiliate of the Japanese-based pharmaceutical company, Eisai Co., Ltd.—where he also led the Market Access business unit, and at Roivant Sciences, a startup building biotech and healthcare technology companies. He also practiced law as a partner at Williams & Connolly, in Washington, D.C. The conversation focuses on the workings of CPR and new developments.
- Episode 97: Lela Love, Director, Kukin Program for Conflict Resolution, Cardozo Law—In this episode of the Arbitration Conversation, Amy interviews Lela Porter Love, a professor of law and director of the Kukin Program for Conflict Resolution at Benjamin N. Cardozo School of Law (NYC) and founder (in 1985) of Cardozo's Mediation Clinic—one of the first clinical programs to train law students to serve as mediators. The focus is on teaching arbitration versus mediation and ends with a joke! This was fun!
- Episode 98: Arbitrator Gary Benton—In this episode of the Arbitration Conversation, Amy interviews Gary Benton, an internationally recognized arbitrator and mediator with expertise in international business, private investment, technology, IP, and emerging growth matters. His practice is focused on technology development, distribution, licensing, infringement (trade secret, copyright, and patent), and cybersecurity disputes. He has handled hundreds of cases around the world and serves on the panels of the leading international arbitral institutions in the U.S., Europe, and Asia. Mr. Benton is the founder and currently serves as the chairman of the Silicon Valley Arbitration and Mediation Center (SVAMC) in Palo Alto, California. He was previously a partner with the leading international law firms Pillsbury Winthrop Shaw Pittman LLP and Coudert Brothers LLP in San Francisco and Palo Alto. As well, he served as chief legal officer for a cloud and mobile cybersecurity company supporting U.S. national security interests. He is a chartered arbitrator and fellow of the Chartered Institute of Arbitrators (CIArb), a fellow and board member of the College of Commercial Arbitrators (CCA), an academy member of the National Academy of Distinguished Neutrals (NADN) and a member of the Institute for Transnational Arbitration (ITA) advisory board and the International

Council for Commercial Arbitration (ICCA). He is a founder and Executive Committee member of the California International Arbitration Council (CIAC) and a member of other U.S. and international arbitral associations. Great conversation about international arbitration.

- Episode 99: Chris Poole, CEO of JAMS—In this episode of the Arbitration Conversation, Amy interviews Chris Poole, chief executive officer of JAMS, the largest provider of alternative dispute resolution (ADR) services worldwide. Poole joined JAMS in 2007 and since that time has led the organization through an unprecedented period of growth, which also helped elevate the ADR industry as a whole. In his role as president and CEO, Poole works closely with senior management and the highly trained panelists who own the company. Prior to joining JAMS, Poole was CEO at Thomson Elite, part of The Thomson Corporation. Poole was COO of Elite Information Systems from 1995 to 1998, chair and CEO of Elite Information Group from 1999 to 2003, and president and CEO of Thomson Elite from 2003 to 2006. Before joining Elite, Poole was executive director of Latham & Watkins LLP in Los Angeles. Poole was the recipient of the 2002 Ernst & Young Entrepreneur of the Year Award. He earned his BA in economics from Harvard University in 1979 and his MBA in computers and marketing from the Anderson Graduate School of Management at UCLA in 1984. This conversation focuses on JAMS and new developments.
- Episode 100: Congressman Robert C. "Bobby" Scott of Virginia—In this episode of the Arbitration Conversation, Amy interviews Congressman Robert C. "Bobby" Scott, who has represented Virginia's third congressional district in the U.S. House of Representatives since 1993. Prior to his service in Congress, he served in the Virginia House of Delegates from 1978 to 1983 and in the Senate of Virginia from 1983 to 1993. Chairman Scott and Amy discuss new legislation regarding arbitration that Chairman Scott reintroduced in 2021!

About the Author

Amy J. Schmitz is an arbitrator, mediator, and dispute resolution specialist based in Ohio where she is a professor at The Ohio State University Moritz College of Law and Program on Dispute Resolution as the John Deaver Drinko-Baker & Hostetler Endowed Chair in Law. She is a co-director of the Translational Data Analytics Institute's Responsible Data Science Research Community of Practice and is also working with the Program on Data Governance and the Divided Community Project—all at The Ohio State University. Before teaching at Ohio State, Professor Schmitz taught at the University of Missouri School of Law and Center for the Study of Dispute Resolution as the Elwood L. Thomas Missouri Endowed Professor of Law, starting in 2016. Previously, she was a professor at the University of Colorado School of Law for more than 16 years. Prior to teaching, Schmitz practiced law with large law firms in Seattle and Minneapolis, with a specialty in arbitration. Prior to practice, she served as a law clerk for the U.S. Court of Appeals for the Eighth Circuit.

Schmitz teaches courses in arbitration, contracts, lawyering and problem-solving, online dispute resolution (ODR), AI, data analytics and the law, international arbitration, social media and conflict, and consumer law. She has been heavily involved in arbitration and ODR teaching and research for a long time and is a fellow of the National Center for Technology and Dispute Resolution and was the co-chair of the ABA Technology Committee and the ODR Task Force of the Dispute Resolution Section.

Schmitz has delivered presentations on various topics throughout the world and is regularly interviewed and quoted on arbitration and contract law in the media—this includes The New York Times, Washington Post, Forbes, Bloomberg, Economist, NPR, Wallethub, Kiplinger's, Bottom Line, Consumer Reports, Money Mag., NBC, ABC, and many others. Some of her awards include the Loyd E. Roberts Memorial Prize in the Administration of Justice (2021); the American Association of Law Schools Section Award for Technology, Law and Legal Education; the Conflict Prevention and Resolution Professional Best Short Article Award (Feb. 2020) and Outstanding Book Award (2023); Shook Hardy Bacon Best Publication Award

(2017); four-time winner of the Sandgrund Award for Best Consumer Law Work; and the Calhoun Award for Outstanding Public Service at the University of Colorado.

Schmitz also hosts *The Arbitration Conversation*, a highly regarded podcast that has reached more than 100 webisodes, and more than 2018 audio podcasts, with more on the way. She also is a researcher with the ACT Project exploring AI and dispute resolution at the Cyberjustice Lab in Montreal. She has published more than 75 articles in law journals and books, is a co-author of a leading casebook, *Resolving Disputes: Theory, Practice and Law* (Aspen 2021); the new book with Tom Stipanowich, *Arbitration: Practice, Policy and Law* (Aspen 2022); and a book with C. Rule, *The New Handshake: Online Dispute Resolution and the Future of Consumer Protection*.

Schmitz also is a Fulbright Specialist, has been elected into the American Law Institute, and won Honorable Mention at the American Legal Technology Awards as an individual who has "demonstrated success throughout their career in making a positive difference in the world as it relates to legal innovation." The author would like to dedicate this book to her sisters who have been a beacon for teaching, learning and great conversations.

Index